Migration Governance Across Regions

Migration policies are rarely effective. Examples of unintended and undesirable outcomes abound. In Latin America, very little is known about the impact and long-term sustainability of state policies toward emigrants. Following a worldwide trend, Ecuador, Uruguay, Mexico, Argentina, and Brazil have developed new institutions and discourses to strengthen links; assist, protect, and enfranchise migrants; and capture their resources. As an adaptation of governmental techniques to global realities, these policies redefine the contours of polities, nations, and citizenship, giving place to a new form of transnational governance.

Building on field research done in these five countries and two receiving countries in the last decade, Ana Margheritis explains the timing, motivations, characteristics, and implications of emigration policies implemented by each country and discusses the emergence of a distinctive regional consensus around a postneoliberal approach to national development and citizenship construction. Margheritis argues that these outreach efforts resemble courting practices. Courting is a deliberate expression of the ambivalent, still incipient, and open-ended relationship between states and diasporas that is not exempt from conflict, detours, and setbacks. For various reasons, state–diaspora relations are not unfolding into stable and fruitful partnerships yet. Thus, she makes "diaspora engagement" problematic and investigates to what extent courting might become engagement in each case.

Studying emigration policies of five Latin American countries and migrant responses in Southern Europe sheds light on the political dynamics and governance mechanisms that transnational migration is generating across regions. It illuminates possible venues for managing multiple engagements of migrants with societies at both ends of their migration journeys and unveils the opportunities for states and nonstate actors to cooperatively manage migration flows.

Ana Margheritis is Reader in International Relations at the University of Southampton. Her areas of expertise include transnational migration, comparative regional integration, foreign policy, inter-American relations, and Latin American political economy.

Conceptualising Comparative Politics:
Polities, Peoples, and Markets
Edited by Anthony Spanakos
(Montclair State University)
and
Francisco Panizza
(London School of Economics)

Conceptualising Comparative Politics seeks to bring a distinctive approach to comparative politics by rediscovering the discipline's rich conceptual tradition and interdisciplinary foundations. It aims to fill out the conceptual framework on which the rest of the subfield draws but to which books only sporadically contribute and to complement theoretical and conceptual analysis by applying it to deeply explored case studies. The series publishes books that make serious inquiry into fundamental concepts in comparative politics (crisis, legitimacy, credibility, representation, institutions, civil society, reconciliation) through theoretically engaging and empirically deep analysis.

1. **Moments of Truth**
   The Politics of Financial Crises in Comparative Perspective
   Edited by Francisco Panizza and George Philip

2. **From Religious Empires to Secular States**
   State Secularization in Turkey, Iran and Russia
   Birol Başkan

3. **The Politics of Governance**
   Actors and Articulations in Africa and Beyond
   Lucy Koechlin and Till Förster

4. **Conceptualizing Comparative Politics**
   Edited by Anthony Petros Spanakos and Francisco Panizza

5. **Migration Governance Across Regions**
   State–Diaspora Relations in the Latin American–Southern Europe Corridor
   Ana Margheritis

Migration Governance Across Regions

State–Diaspora Relations in the Latin American–Southern Europe Corridor

Ana Margheritis

Routledge
Taylor & Francis Group
New York London

First published 2016
by Routledge
711 Third Avenue, New York, NY 10017, USA

and by Routledge
2 Park Square, Milton Park, Abingdon, Oxon, OX14 4RN

First issued in paperback 2017

*Routledge is an imprint of the Taylor & Francis Group,
an informa business*

Library of Congress Cataloging-in-Publication Data
Names: Margheritis, Ana, author.
Title: Migration governance across regions : state-diaspora relations
    in the Latin American-Southern Europe corridor / Ana Margheritis.
Description: New York, NY : Routledge is an imprint of the
    Taylor & Francis Group, an Informa Business, [2016] | Series:
    Conceptualising comparative politics: polities, peoples, and
    markets ; 5 | Includes bibliographical references and index.
Identifiers: LCCN 2015027890| ISBN 9781138909649 (hbk) |
    ISBN 9781315693897 (ebk)
Subjects: LCSH: Latin America—Emigration and immigration—
    Government policy. | Transnationalism—Political aspects—Latin
    America. | Latin Americans—Europe, Southern.
Classification: LCC JV7398 .M327 2016 | DDC 325/.28—dc23
LC record available at http://lccn.loc.gov/2015027890

ISBN 13: 978-1-138-30746-9 (pbk)
ISBN 13: 978-1-138-90964-9 (hbk)

Typeset in Sabon
by Apex CoVantage, LLC

Contents

Series editors' foreword

Aristotle's study of the various polities of his time and his (or his school's) collection of the various actual constitutions represent some of the earliest research in comparative politics. Despite thorough analysis of the politics in the various polities, he gave little attention to the politics between them. This might be particularly odd as he was as Stagirite, came to study in, and later famously fled from, Athens. That is, despite his seminal work on citizenship and polities, he did not seem to include his own experiences as a migrant—one who operated in poleis in which he was not and would not be a citizen—nor did he give much consideration to the idea that his native Stagira might have interest in, or obligations to, him while in Athens. While some of his contemporaries were more concerned with what might later be considered 'international relations,' traditionally comparative politics scholarship has not engaged enough with international relations literature and the studies of migration have themselves been strangers to the two sub-disciplines of political science.

If that characterization is fair, Ana Margheritis's *Migration Governance Across Regions* presents a powerful argument that the lines between the two subfields need be blurred, particularly in the case of migrants who literally live and must be studied both in-between and squarely in the mainstream of both comparative politics and international relations. This is perhaps the biggest conceptual contribution of the present volume: to make the claim and provide evidence for a study that incorporates key questions of citizenship, governance, the role of the polity (above and beneath the state), and the nation which are fundamental for both comparative politics and international relations, concepts that are at the heart of the politics of migration.

To address these key questions that have received considerable scholarly interest in distinct sub-disciplines, Margheritis selects cases from spaces that where scholars have been more silent. There is no shortage of studies of Latin American migration to the United States but there has been little addressing the reverse migration whereby Latin American citizens migrate to Southern European countries. Her examination of the relations between sending states, emigrants, and receiving states (though the case of Uruguayans, Ecuadoreans, Argentines, and Brazilian) is a rich exploration of new forms of identity formation, institutional inclusion, and governance in an environment in which declaredly post-neoliberal leftist governments in the sending country have tried to re-found their countries political systems and/ or re-assess how political inclusion (including of overseas nationals) ought take place in a democratic context.

Acknowledgments

I am very grateful to the colleagues and institutions that facilitated the field research for this study: Gioconda Herrera at the Program on Sociology of Migrations and Globalization of FLACSO (Facultad Latinoamericana de Ciencias Sociales) in Quito, Ecuador; Ignacio Sánchez-Cuenca at the CEAS (Center for Advanced Studies in Social Sciences), Juan March Institute in Madrid, Spain; Riva Kastoryano and Christian Lequesne at the CERI (Center d'études et de Recherches Internationals), Sciences Po in Paris, France; Maurizio Ambrozini at the Dipartamento di Studi Sociali e Politici of Università Degli Studi di Milano, Italy; Rafael Fernández de Castro at the Department of International Studies of ITAM (Instituto Tecnológico Autónomo de México), Mexico, D.F., Mexico; and Celso Castro at CPDOC (Centro de Pesquisa e Documentação de História Contemporânea do Brasil) within the Getulio Vargas Foundation in Rio de Janeiro, Brazil. I am also grateful to Brian Read, Adrián Zeh, Tomás Castellanos, and Michelle Asunción for their research assistance.

Funding for field research for this study was provided by the University of Florida at Gainesville (US) under the Humanities Scholarship Enhancement Fund, Faculty Enhancement Opportunity Award, Rothman Summer Fellowship, Faculty Research Award, Course Enhancement Award, and New Course Development Award. Colleagues Carmen Diana Deere and Philip Williams at the UF Center for Latin American Studies graciously shared their expertise and enriched my work.

The University of Southampton (UK) also contributed with research funds and time flexibility to complete field research and writing. The Politics and International Relations Unit and the Centre for Citizenship, Globalization and Governance provided assistantship and travel support. The Social and Human Sciences School awarded me the Strategic Research Development Fund to conduct further research in Brazil and Argentina. In particular, Jane Falkingham, Derek McGhee, and David Owen kindly supported my work.

The manuscript improved considerably thanks to the suggestions of two anonymous reviewers and the editors of the Conceptualizing Comparative Politics Series, Anthony Spanakos and Francisco Panizza. Further thanks goes to editors Natalja Mortensen and Lilian Rand at

Routledge and project manager Tina Cottone at Apex CoVantage, for bringing this book to fruition. My gratitude goes to all of them.

I am also grateful to the editors of the following journals for granting permission to use material previously published. Chapter 3 revisits some material that appeared in my article "Piecemeal Regional Integration in the Post-Neoliberal Era: Negotiating Migration Policies within MERCO-SUR" from the *Review of International Political Economy*, 20(3), June 2013, pp. 541–575. Chapter 4 reworks my article "Todos Somos Migrantes (We Are All Migrants): The Paradoxes of Innovative State-Led Transnationalism in Ecuador," published in *International Political Sociology*, 5(2), June 2011, pp. 198–217. Chapter 5 draws upon my piece "Redrawing the Contours of the Nation-State in Uruguay? The Vicissitudes of Emigration Policy in the 2000s," forthcoming in the 2015 winter issue of the *International Migration Review*. Chapter 6 builds upon my article entitled "State-Led Transnationalism and Migration. Reaching Out to the Argentine Community in Spain," from *Global Networks: A Journal of Transnational Affairs*, 7(1), January 2007, pp. 87–106. Some of the empirical information in Chapter 8 is incorporated in a forthcoming article: "Transnational Associational Life and Political Mobilization of Ecuadorians and Argentines in Spain and Italy: What Role for Sending State Policies?" *Diaspora*, Winter 2015–2016.

Special thanks to colleagues and friends who over the years generously commented and encouraged my work: Tony Pereira, Paul Lewis, Javier Gallardo, Alan Gamlen, Jorge Lanzaro, Michael Collyer, Mario Carranza, Eduardo Domenech, Adela Pellegrino, and Manuel Vásquez. I would also like to recognize my postgraduate students for lively and stimulating discussions in my seminar on Globalization, Governance, and Diasporas at both sides of the Atlantic.

There is one more person who made much more than intellectual contributions: Mark Thurner, my husband, has supported me in times of "sickness and health, of joy and sorrow" beyond what I could possibly ever imagine. He also helped me make sense of my own migration journey. He pushes me to get the best out of every day. As I am writing this, we are preparing to move once again to start a new phase of our wonderful nomadic life together. I am happily learning that home is where *he* hangs his hat.

1 Introduction

States Courting Diasporas

This book is about understanding why and how Latin American states have been courting their diasporas lately. Courting is a deliberate expression of the ambivalent, open-ended relationship between states and diasporas. In its British definition, to court is "to try to please someone because you want them to join you," which is close to the American English definition: "to try to please someone in the hope of receiving that person's support, approval, or affection, or to try to get something that benefits you."[1] When applied to romantic relations, courting may be the first step toward further engagement, often leading to a stable partnership or marriage. In short, courting involves overtures to beloved others, and it holds out the possibility of becoming a committed engagement and, potentially, a permanent relationship.

I argue that the policies under consideration here have involved all these elements: sending states have turned to friendly discourses, cultivation of links, and attempts to capture the support and resources of their citizens residing abroad. The potential to establish broad, stable, and mutually beneficial partnerships is present in such initiatives, though in incipient form. Some of these policies took a long time to develop and be adopted. Some have been implemented only for a few years. Most of them are facing recurrent controversies and setbacks. None of them is exempt of conflict. For various reasons, it is not evident that these incipient state–diaspora relationships will unfold into stable and fruitful partnerships. In nonacademic terms, it might be argued that there has been considerable flirting and some consistent courting, but no serious marriage proposal yet.

This book explores the politics and policymaking processes that underpin such courting. For the reasons stated previously, I do not assume the existence of full-fledged, effective "diaspora engagement policies." Instead, I make that assumption problematic and investigate to what extent courting might become engagement. Thus, the book focuses on the motivations, timing, characteristics, and implications of four Latin American sending states' outreach efforts toward their populations abroad: Uruguay, Ecuador, Argentina, and Brazil. Because Mexico provides a vantage point to engage in comparisons, it is included in the analysis, too. In particular, I look at the engagement mechanisms attempted in South America toward the post-1980s wave of emigration that redirected flows toward Southern Europe. In the last few decades, although some Latin American emigrants followed the traditional path toward the US, an increasing number of them landed in Spain and Italy (even if as a first destination in a series of displacements within Europe), thus creating an intense traffic along the cross-regional corridor.

The main research questions that guided this study refer to why countries of origin are implementing such initiatives, why they are doing this now, through what policy mechanisms they are implementing them, and what the results are. The main goal is to delineate the trajectory each country has taken in this realm and to stimulate comparisons of analytical and policy relevance. I note from the outset that, besides the specific aims, vicissitudes, and results, such initiatives follow a worldwide trend and are part of a broader phenomenon with global repercussions. As an adaptation of governmental techniques to the consequences of increasing international migration, these policies are redefining the contours of polities, nations, and citizenship, thus giving place to novel, innovative forms of transnational governance.

A Note on Terminology and Lenses

Sending states' courting is explored here through the lenses and some of the concerns of international relations, a field that has only slowly and lately taken note of diasporas' agency in global politics. An emphasis on the state side of the relationship and a concern with the redefinition of the territorial basis of state power undoubtedly come from that background. Yet, this work also engages with notions that have been central concepts for other fields, such as belonging, membership to the nation, and citizenship beyond borders. Thus, the book goes beyond disciplinary boundaries and borrows from other disciplines that have taken the lead in studying international migration, and it incorporates valuable insights on policymaking and domestic politics coming from another political science subfield: comparative politics. This not only helps account for apparent tensions and contradictions in state-led transnationalism but also for the similarities and differences across cases. In addition, this work builds upon concepts and analytical contributions that bridge international and migration studies and calls for inter- and intradisciplinary dialogues.

One of those contributions comes from transnational studies, a field that has grown by leaps and bounds over the last two decades. Led by the excellent work of sociologists, anthropologists, and others, a considerable number of studies have accumulated (see general overviews of the field in Levitt and Jaworsky 2007 and Vertovec 2009). Although those studies are still coping with conceptual, methodological, and other problems that were identified more than a decade ago (Portes et al. 1999), transnationalism has gained considerable visibility within the social sciences, with increasing theoretical and empirical research providing valuable insights about the details of transnational life in different domains (political, social, cultural, economic, religious, etc.). The study of migrant transnationalism, as a subset of inquiry, has developed likewise, although there are differences in scholarly concerns and perspectives between the US and Europe (Portes and DeWind 2004). The ways transnationalism and diasporas overlap and intersect have given place to thoughtful interdisciplinary debates and conceptual refinements (for a synthesis, see Faist 2010).

This study is concerned with the political aspects of migrant transnationalism in general and state-led transnationalism in particular. Following Vertovec (2009:13), *migrant transnationalism* is used here as "a broad category referring to a range of practices and institutions linking migrants, people and organizations in their homelands or elsewhere in a diaspora." *State-led transnationalism* is defined as "institutionalized national policies and programs that attempt to expand the scope of national state's political, economic, social, and moral regulation to include emigrants and their descendants outside the national territory" (Goldring 2002:64). Examples of those policies include the creation of institutions to address the needs and demands of emigrants; efforts to monitor and channel the transfer of remittances; incentives for investment, cultural exchanges, and tourism in the home country; support for migrants' cultural activities and organizations; and passing of legislation regarding dual citizenship, political representation, voting rights, and so forth. These measures are usually accompanied by the elaboration of a political discourse that stresses nationhood bonds and recognizes emigrants as part of the nation. Most of the policies explained here have been initiated by the states in question and largely follow a top-down dynamic. Thus, the concept of state-led transnationalism correctly captures the path that courting is taking.

Given that courting diasporas involves extending state authority to govern populations abroad, and this is done in (formal and informal) collaboration with other states and nonstate actors, the process falls within new forms of governance that involve relations at various levels of analysis (e.g., national, regional, bilateral, multilateral, inter- and cross-regional global). As a result, a number of institutions and mechanisms to manage migration flows have been created that link countries and regions and open up opportunities for partnerships. Sending states' attempts to reach out to their diasporas are only one of the forms this process is taking (Betts 2011b). The cases examined here illustrate this trend and provide detailed evidence to support studies that call attention to the broader phenomenon involving both sending and receiving countries across regions. Such is the case of Betts, who argues: "The most important aspect of the emerging global migration governance . . . is taking place in relation to trans-regionalism. Powerful 'receiving' states are striving to find ways to exert direct or indirect extra-territorial control over migration from and among 'sending' states in the developing world. Trans-regional governance is the means by which they are exerting the authority to do this, developing and supporting a complex tapestry of bilateral, regional, and inter-regional mechanisms, both formal and informal, as states, through the regional organizations or through regional organizations such as IOM." Therefore, the author argues that "trans-regional governance can be defined as sets of formal and informal institutions that cut across and connect different geographical regions, constituting or constraining the behavior of states and non-state actors in a given policy field" (Betts 2011a:29).

Regarding these processes, there is some related terminology worth clarifying. Rather than emphasizing the transnational character of the previously mentioned measures (which still carry a reference to territory and borders), some studies have emphasized the links with the diasporas and states' purposeful strategies to capture both material and non-material resources of their citizens abroad by enlisting them in broad overseas networks that may or may not have a territorial basis (including virtual and cyber networks). Therefore, the phenomenon is also referred to in the literature as *diaspora engagement policies* (among others, Ancien et al. 2009; Ho and Lynn-Ee 2011; Larner 2007). To differentiate such measures from related initiatives in the area of migration (namely, immigration policy) and to emphasize that the targeted subjects are those involved in migration outflows (who also tend to be seen as outside of the core body of the nation and likely to remain outside of the national territory), the term *emigration policies* is also used (e.g., Délano 2011). I tend to use the latter term more often because, in most cases, engagement is too incipient and it needs to be problematized. For the same reason, I also use the term *linkage* for those programs (or *políticas de vinculación,* in Spanish) that focus on building ties with the emigrant community.

Qualifying states as "sending" does not imply that states had direct responsibility for displacements that have indeed been voluntary. Such assumption would not be totally accurate since most states are today the scenario of flows arriving and leaving. Migration now has a more temporary and fluid character than in the past, blurring clear-cut categorizations. Here the *sending country* is a simplification for *country of origin,* which has also become part of the jargon of the field. I prefer this over *home state* because transnational practices highlight the ambiguous and precarious character of attachments, the existence of multiple allegiances, and the possibility of cultivating simultaneous engagements in various geographical sites. In that context, defining where home actually is becomes problematic.

Regardless of the analytical focus of the book, this study speaks of a relationship. The social side of such a link is obviously acknowledged and, to some extent, investigated. It takes different forms across the five cases because those who left their countries of origin relate to state institutions both individually and collectively, and they do so through diverse mechanisms. Not all emigrants engage in associational life or mobilize to take part in home politics. Some of them cultivate ties with co-nationals more than others. Some of them are more proactive in becoming integrated in the host society. All migrants make choices when reconstructing their national identities during an often harsh migration journey; as a result, their self-identification as part of a diasporic population with ethnic and other elements in common varies. Most likely, none of the groups studied here would actually meet all criteria to call itself and be called *diaspora* in a strict sense (e.g., Cohen 2008). Aware of the contentious character of the concept of diaspora, I refer simply to *emigrants* most of the time. I still use the expression *state–diaspora relations,* and by that I mean the state–emigrant community as a whole. I use this terminology to reproduce informants' language and in reference to a growing literature on the subject that endorses an expanded, flexible meaning of the term diaspora.[2]

Practical and Academic Relevance

Migration policies are rarely effective. From border controls, to guest worker programs, to immigrant integration measures, there are plenty of examples of the gaps between intended effects and unexpected, undesirable outcomes. The policy of courting the diaspora is not an exception, especially in South American countries that built their national identities around the idea of being countries of immigration, not emigration, and therefore find it difficult to acknowledge and address the outflows as a policy problem. These are also countries with long records of domestic instability and inconsistent policies. Several of the initiatives in question require governments to negotiate simultaneously with receiving states in the context of asymmetric relations of power and with transnational nongovernmental actors. Thus, analyzing sending-state stances and actions sheds light not only on the specificities of such policies and whether they may become effective and sustainable, but also on the political dynamics and new mechanisms of governance that transnational migration is generating across regions. By doing so, this study illuminates possible venues to manage dual (often simultaneous and conflictive) engagements of migrants with societies at both ends of their migration journey. In other words, it unveils the potential engagement opportunities for home and host states in the cooperative management of migration flows and encourages open debate around best international practices.

More concretely, and in terms of real-world impact, this work expands our understanding of transnational sociopolitical processes, addresses pressing issues, and is also timely. Migration-related political discourses and policies are largely constructed on the basis of fears, misleading assumptions, and vaguely defined notions of nation, belonging, and the preservation of national identity. These issues are particularly sensitive ones in Europe and the UK today, although they also resonate worldwide. A better understanding of them is crucial to ground policymaking on the needs and aspirations of increasingly heterogeneous constituencies. In particular, my work speaks to ongoing controversies and encourages open dialogue on contested issues such as the implications of (both sending and receiving) state policies for immigrant integration, the evolution of national identities and political allegiances, and the regulation of migration flows and citizenship regimes.

From an academic point of view, it is particularly relevant for scholars in the field of international relations to look at how the transnational actions of states are redefining the notions of national identity, citizenship, and polity. By courting diasporas, states are transforming the nature of politics and policymaking to address constituencies that reside outside their territories. Ironically, by doing this, states are implicitly undermining the basic principles of sovereignty and non-intervention that, in theory, have defined their political authority and characterized the post-Westphalia international system for centuries. Although in practice the exercise of sovereignty has always gone beyond national borders, the expansion and intensification of transnational politics and policies is gradually affecting the nature of international relations and global mechanisms of governance. State-led transnationalism, then, has repercussions on our understanding of territoriality, sovereignty, citizenship, belonging, and the very notions of both states and nations.

The concrete mechanisms at work are not fully evident, though. Contributions abound but remain fragmented. While there is booming literature on governance, controversies about the term and its real-world implications continue. The politics of governance vary across policy areas. The legitimacy, accountability, and effectiveness of global governance are matters of debate (Karns and Mingst 2009; Weiss 2013; Weiss and Wilkinson 2014; Welch 2013, among others). Migration stands out as a policy area in which, in contrast to most areas of human activity, there is no formal global regime to regulate the movement of people. Multilateral cooperation has proven elusive and has exposed sending and receiving countries' opposite interests. Power asymmetries hinder mutually beneficial agreements. Yet, migration governance has been advancing in overlapping arenas through both formal and informal, binding and nonbinding coordination mechanisms within a multilayered architecture (Kunz et al. 2011).

Within that framework, sending states have received less attention than receiving states, and the politics behind their transnational outreach efforts have been relatively less explored and theorized. Although an increasing number of empirical studies have been published in the last decade, only a few engage in regional comparisons and aim at assessing results and implications (e.g., Ancien et al. 2009; Brand 2006). The work of international institutions has also contributed to identifying best practices and promoting diaspora engagement policies around the world under the assumption that these policies may make significant contributions to development (e.g., Agunias and Newland 2012). Thus, engagement is generally assumed as a positive and relatively uniform trend. Although consensual narratives have contributed to depoliticizing migration issues (Pécoud 2015, among others), their contentious nature persists, and there are several gaps in knowledge. There is, for instance, no conclusive answer regarding the impact of new emigration policies and what difference it makes that some states are more active than others in this policy area. Therefore, investigating those initiatives contributes to filling these gaps in the literature.

In terms of regional coverage, there are some gaps in the literature, too. Within Latin America, Mexico, and a few other Central American and Caribbean countries that are the places of origin of large immigrant communities in the United States (e.g., Dominican Republic, Haiti, Puerto Rico, and El Salvador) tend to be the focus of much of the scholarly work in this area, but less is known about how South American countries deal with their emigrants who do not reside close by. Because the literature is almost oblivious of some of the cases selected here, the sources of similarities and differences remain relatively underresearched and comparisons have not been attempted. Moreover, very little is known about the concrete impact of state outreach efforts of the Southern Cone countries and what factors might make these policies sustainable and effective in the long run. Given state institutional deficiencies and the record of state violence and dramatic economic and political crises, I argue that these cases can shed much light not only on migration patterns and policy challenges, but also on the kind of concrete impact emigration policies might have in the context of a complex and often conflictive relationship between migrants and state institutions over long distances. As the next chapter explains in detail, these cases provide new evidence and suggest theoretical refinements that contribute to moving the discussion of migrant transnationalism forward.

The Argument in Short

South American states have recently joined a global trend with roots in old practices: they have established and/or intensified links with their citizens living abroad. These outreach efforts resemble courting practices.

Courting diasporas is a figurative way of presenting states' attempts to redefine "the art of government" (Burchell et al. 1991); they have formally defined the identity of a new constituency and new areas of state intervention, thus shaping emigrants' existing and potential engagements with the home country.

Although the policies put in motion to do so may not follow a comprehensive and clear design, it is possible to identify common inspirational elements that make these cases distinct and worth exploring. The overarching ideas underpinning courting attempts include: bringing the state back to regulate socioeconomic relations; reviving nationalist development projects; cooperating on the multilateral management of migration flows; upholding human rights considerations; and exploiting the positive links between economic development, migration, and social policies. In postneoliberal times, these ideas translate into a combination of practices: state protection, control, and regulation together with market-oriented principles; expanding universal rights and increasing individuals' obligations; and extending selective, fragmented social assistance within the general contraction of welfare programs. In other words, South American–style diaspora engagement invokes collective identities and shared responsibilities to entice migrants' self-entrepreneurial and self-disciplinary actions.

The distinctive character of this set of ideas and aims has given place to a regional normative consensus on how to manage migration flows, including not only emigration but also other dimensions of transnational displacements. Such a consensus contributes to delineating policy trajectories that differ from those observed in other countries. While most of the literature on emigration policies assumes that sending states have followed a neoliberal rationale, this book explores cases in which a distinct postneoliberal rationale prevails. Thus, the South American policy trajectories herein do not fit exactly with existing typologies, which suggests the need to expand analytical frameworks and comparisons to incorporate the nuances and tensions of postneoliberal forms of governing diasporas.

This study provides evidence of why, why now, and how those policies developed. The policy innovations exhibit some similarities across cases in the small selected sample. They all include a combination of similar policy instruments, namely friendly rhetoric, institutional building, enfranchisement, and linkages programs. There are policy inconsistencies, controversies, and setbacks in all cases, including Mexico, which has the most far-reaching and institutionalized set of programs to liaise with its diaspora in the US. In general, there are serious intentions and courting, but not full and permanent engagement yet.

Differences across cases delineate various approaches to emigration and engagement: a very proactive and innovative one in Ecuador, including intense work at destinations for some years and evolving now toward a more traditional consular approach; a slow, gradual, and relatively consistent path in Uruguay, though still limited by attachment to territorial and traditional notions of citizenship and with an emphasis on return; an assistance-centered perspective in Argentina that, to some extent, works today in inertial mode and has neglected relations and substantive engagement with emigrants; and a low-visibility, technical approach led by consular offices in Brazil, where the state has focused on a reform of the consular service to meet migrant demands and on organizing the diaspora to closely graduate emigrants' access to migration policymaking.

The differences across cases indicate that state motivations were diverse and, in some cases, strategic and conjunctural depending on specific political projects. Crises and high politico-economic instability created windows of opportunity for change. Thus, regardless of the absolute size of the diaspora and the state resources, policymakers acted to seize those opportunities. Instrumental goals (i.e., capturing resources) were closely intertwined with efforts to redefine national narratives and build governing coalitions, thus showing the analytical relevance of domestic politics variables.

As for the timing, these policies were launched once the social repercussions of changes in the migration dynamics (either massive exit or exit of precious human capital) or dramatic episodes (e.g., deportations, accidents due to precarious working conditions) became publicly visible and called for government action. The launching of state initiatives was instrumental to building up the identity of new governing coalitions that flag migration to differentiate themselves from previous governments or opposition parties. Moreover, policy innovations gained momentum as political discourses acquired neopopulist overtones, and governments converged on the sociopolitical agenda mentioned previously and the harmonization of migration norms within regional integration agreements. They did so as part of a critical approach to the legacies of neoliberal policies, building upon social disappointment and promising reparatory measures. Such a move also aims at repositioning South American countries and using regional blocs as a platform to gain leverage on global political debates in which they voice an alternative, moderately contestatory approach not only to migration but also, more broadly, to neoliberal policies. This regional dynamic and its postneoliberal character—of which the existing literature is oblivious—suggest analytical refinements to instrumental explanations and existing typologies. Hence, this study shows that the implications of emigration policies in Latin America are better understood within the synergies that we observe today among processes of regional integration, economic restructuring, international migration, and democratization.

Results have been mixed, too. While some general changes have become institutionalized through national legislation and regional agreements, consistent and effective policy implementation faces challenges.

In particular, bureaucratic practices and intrastate politics keep policies subject to constant comings and goings. Therefore, the fact that emigration policies are part and parcel of a new normative regional consensus makes their reversal unlikely, but the pragmatic and ambivalent nature of the postneoliberal projects and the uncertainty about the future of some governing coalitions have thus far represented a fragile base to ground policies firmly and move from courting to engagement.

From an analytical point of view, the incorporation of both domestic and regional politics suggests a new path for the study of state-led transnationalism: to go beyond the state level of analysis and explore the dynamics below and above the state (i.e., the domestic processes and institutions that shape state involvement and the regional spaces that articulate foreign policies with intra- and extraregional relations). In this respect, this work speaks to a growing literature on new forms of global governance in which states rely on relations (and potential partnerships) with nongovernmental institutions, migrant associations, international organizations, and epistemic communities, as well as other states.

Also, this study suggests that in order to move the discussion on emigration policies further, it might be helpful to (a) problematize engagement and ground it in historical and geographic contexts, going beyond celebratory discourses to assess the real transformative and democratic character of engagement; (b) monitor and analyze the specific long-term effects that today's incipient and hybrid postneoliberal governance techniques might produce; and (c) not take state capacities for granted and, instead, explore the ongoing processes by which the state is transforming itself and its relations with society (i.e., society that resides within its territory and abroad, too). Ironically, it is a focus on state reform that may help international relations and migration studies to decenter the study of migration politics and policies from the traditional nation-state level.

Plan of the Book

Following this introduction, Chapter 2 presents a detailed analytical framework. It builds upon the relevant academic literature to delineate the theoretical framework at length and clarify the contributions of this study. It explains the research strategy pursued, the rationale for case selection, and the methodology. In short, it lays the analytical ground for the empirical parts that follow.

Chapter 3 opens with a background overview of migration dynamics and policies in Latin America, placing emigration within broader regional trends and pointing out differences across subregions (i.e., the Andes; the Southern Cone; Mexico, Central America, and the Caribbean). This chapter shows that the outreach efforts identified here are only one component of a number of policy innovations, and they are better understood in the context of a distinctive normative regional consensus on how to manage transnational migration. Such a consensus impinges upon the content and timing of emigration policies, encouraging policy convergence in South America along postneoliberal ideas and some policy continuity in cases where courting remains on hold. The harmonization of norms has helped South American countries strengthen a rights-based, cooperative approach in all dimensions of migration policy; has become embodied in new national legislation and agreements signed within regional organizations such as Mercado Común del Sur (MERCOSUR) and UNASUR; and is paving the way for more innovation: the construction of regional citizenship. It has also given blocs a discursive (presumably progressive, inclusive, and pluralist) identity that is being voiced in negotiations with the North as an alternative, reformist approach that emphasizes shared responsibility of sending and receiving states and contemplates the interests of all countries. From an analytical point of view, these developments suggest the need for a multilevel analysis that decenters emigration politics and policies from the nation-state level and explores the scope and limits of the synergies among processes of democratization, regional integration, global economic restructuring, and international migration.

Chapters 4 through 7 present the case studies. The order of the case studies does not carry any connotation. The first two cases are small Latin American countries with large communities abroad. Ecuador and Uruguay are representative of nations that occupy a small land area and have relatively few resources and serious population problems (among others, massive emigration in the first decade of the 21st century of around 15–20% of their total population). Chapters 4 and 5 revolve around the policy innovations recently implemented by Ecuador and Uruguay to tackle that problem, with references and comparisons to other cases. In both cases, the findings highlight that the size of the diaspora and the volume of remittances are not necessarily the best predictors of state behavior. Instead, some political variables need to be explored, such as intrastate politics and obsolete bureaucratic practices, specific political projects of the coalitions in government, the leadership role of key political actors, and the impact of geography, long distance, and territory-based notions of citizenship and belonging on transnational practices. Policy is today at a different stage in these two cases. This suggests some factors that might make emigration policies more effective and sustainable in the long run.

Chapters 6 and 7 revolve around two cases that have received little attention in the migration literature in English and contrast with the previous ones: Brazil and Argentina. They occupy vast areas of well-endowed territory in Latin America and are among the most dynamic and developed economies of the region. These two cases have relatively small emigrant communities (around 1–3% of their total population). These nations have also engaged in outreach efforts, although in a more selective and intermittent fashion than the small cases in the previous two chapters. Also,

Argentina has been particularly active at the regional level to advance a new multilateral migration agenda and the harmonization of migration norms. In contrast, Brazil has acquiesced to those initiatives but not led them and has cultivated a low-profile, technical approach to relations with its emigrants. The modality of these two stances begs explanation and leads to further comparisons. In the light of differences in the postneoliberal and neopopulist projects in Brazil and Argentina, these countries also offer an opportunity to revisit and refine some of the assumptions of the literature on the links between diaspora engagement policies and processes of economic and institutional restructuring and democratic consolidation.

Chapter 8 elaborates on policy results, implications, and migrant responses. Whereas the previous chapters delve into the what, why, when, and how questions about sending-state involvement in transnational migration, this chapter focuses on whether policies have achieved intended goals and might contribute to shaping migrant political engagements. It explores and compares migrant responses by looking at policy impact on migrant associational life and political mobilization for two communities (Ecuadorians and Argentines) in two major destinations (Madrid and Milan). The analysis does not focus on the entire set of engagement mechanisms, but rather only on measures directly related to transnational political engagement. It draws on all the other cases for comparisons.

The conclusions of this chapter indicate that states have been relatively effective in tapping into migrants' symbolic and emotional attachments to homeland (more so in the case of Ecuador), but they have obtained meager results in terms of grounding that attachment in strong organizations, persistent transnational political engagement, and partnership links. The modality of policy implementation resulted in a sporadic and "sentimental" political mobilization of both emigrant communities, which still face serious organizational problems and are far from working as strong influential groups at home or as ethnic lobbies in receiving countries. In other words, while courting may encourage the development of transnational spaces and practices and affect both migrants' integration in the host society and their sense of belonging and engagement with the home country, concrete effects on migrants' chances of accumulating human and social capital, acquiring and exercising rights, and becoming organized and empowered to pursue collective goals across long distances are more elusive.

Chapter 9 includes a brief account of the Mexican case, which contributes to broadening comparisons across the region and over time. This is one of the best known cases in the literature on diaspora engagement policies. However, most studies do not include an up-to-date account. Policy developments under the current administration (i.e., since late 2012) have not been the focus of academic publications yet.

This chapter includes the latest information available and is the first step in filling such a gap. Moreover, it has been suggested that Mexico might have worked as a model for other countries to emulate. I did not find conclusive evidence on that point, but I did find that Mexico is lately becoming closer than ever to South American countries in terms of migration discourse and the interplay of domestic and international processes. The cyclical nature of its engagement with its diaspora in the US is part of a historical pattern that South American countries seem to follow. Thus, its incorporation in this book expands not only the comparison but also our understanding of explanatory factors in national and regional contexts.

In Chapter 10, I recapitulate policy lessons and analytical contributions. This chapter also summarizes the main features of the policy trajectories examined and the answers to the research questions that guided this project. The book closes with an analysis of policy-relevant and analytical implications of the findings, as well as suggestions for a future research agenda.

Notes

1 Cambridge Dictionaries Online, http://dictionary.cambridge.org/dictionary/british/court_5?q=courting, accessed May 15, 2014.
2 For old and recent debates around the term diaspora and studies on it, see Brubaker (2006); Tölölyan (2007); Cohen (2008:1–20); Dufoix (2008:4–34).

Works Cited

Agunias, Dovelyn R. and Kathleen Newland. 2012. *Developing a Road Map for Engaging Diasporas in Development: A Handbook for Policymakers and Practitioners in Home and Host Countries*. Washington, DC: International Organization for Migration and Migration Policy Institute.

Ancien, Delphine, Mark Boyle, and Rob Kitchin. 2009, June. "Exploring Diaspora Strategies: An International Comparison." Workshop report. National University of Maynooth, Ireland.

Betts, Alexander. 2011a. "The Global Governance of Migration and the Role of Transregionalism." In *Multilayered Migration Governance: The Promise of Partnership*, ed. by Rahel Kunz, Sandra Lavenex, and Marion Panizzon. London: Routledge. pp. 23–45.

Betts, Alexander. 2011b. *Global Migration Governance*. Oxford, UK: Oxford University Press.

Brand, Laurie A. 2006. *Citizens Abroad: Emigration and the State in the Middle East and North Africa*. Cambridge, UK: Cambridge University Press.

Brubaker, Rogers. 2006. "The 'Diaspora' Diaspora." *Ethnic and Racial Studies*. 28(1): 1–19.

Burchell, Graham, Colin Gordon, and Peter Miller. eds. 1991. *The Foucault Effect: Studies in Governmentality, with Two Lectures by and an Interview with Michel Foucault*. Chicago, IL: The University of Chicago Press.

Cohen, Robin. 2008. *Global Diasporas*. London: Routledge.

Délano, Alexandra. 2011. *Mexico and its Diaspora in the United States: Policies of Emigration since 1848*. New York: Cambridge University Press.

Dufoix, Stéphane. 2008. *Diasporas*. Berkeley, CA: University of California Press.

Faist, Thomas. 2010. "Diaspora and Transnationalism: What Kind of Dance Partners?" In *Diaspora and Transnationalism: Concepts, Theories, and Methods*, ed. by Rainer Bauböck and Thomas Faist. Amsterdam: IMISCOE Research and Amsterdam University Press. pp. 9–34.

Goldring, Luin. 2002. "The Mexican State and Transmigrant Organizations. Negotiating the Boundaries of Membership and Participation." *Latin American Research Review*. 37(3): 55–99.

Ho, Elaine Lynn-Ee. 2011. "Claiming the Diaspora: Elite Mobility, Sending State Strategies and the Spatialities of Citizenship." *Progress in Human Geography*. 35(6): 757–772.

Karns, Margaret P. and Karen A. Mingst. 2009. *International Organizations: The Politics and Processes of Global Governance*. Boulder, CO: Lynne Rienner Publishers.

Kunz, Rahel, Sandra Lavenex, and Marion Panizzon. eds. 2011. *Multilayered Migration Governance: The Promise of Partnership*. London: Routledge.

Larner, Wendy. 2007. "Expatriate Experts and Globalising Governmentalities: The New Zealand Diaspora Strategy." *Transactions of the Institute of British Geographers*. 32(3): 331–345.

Levitt, Peggy and B. Nadya Jaworsky. 2007. "Transnational Migration Studies: Past Developments and Future Trends." *Annual Review of Sociology*. 33(1): 129–156.

Pécoud, Antoine. 2015. *Depoliticising Migration. Global Governance and International Migration Narratives*. Basingstoke, UK: Palgrave Macmillan.

Portes, A. and J. DeWind. 2004. "A Cross-Atlantic Dialogue: The Progress of Research and Theory in the Study of International Migration." *International Migration Review*. 38(3), Fall: 828–851.

Portes, A., L.E. Guarnizo, and P. Landolt. 1999. "The Study of Transnationalism: Pitfalls and Promise of an Emergent Research Field." *Ethnic and Racial Studies*. 22(2), March: 217–237.

Tölölyan, Khachig. 2007. "The Contemporary Discourse of Diaspora Studies." *Comparative Studies of South Asia, Africa and the Middle East*. 27(3): 647–655.

Vertovec, Stephen. 2009. *Transnationalism*. London: Routledge.

Weiss, Thomas G. 2013. *Global Governance: Why? What? Whiter?* Cambridge, UK: Polity Press.

Weiss, Thomas G. and Rorden Wilkinson. eds. 2014. *International Organization and Global Governance*. Abingdon, UK: Routledge.

Welch, David A. 2013. "What Is 'Governance,' Anyway?" *Canadian Foreign Policy Journal*. 19(3): 253–267. DOI: 10.1080/11926422.2013.845584.

2 State-Led Transnationalism as Governance

Introduction

In the last two decades, several disciplines have contributed to expanding our knowledge of transnational practices in various domains of life. The study of migrant transnationalism constitutes a subset of inquiry within transnational studies, and its development has followed the pioneer work of some sociologists and anthropologists. Basch and colleagues (1994) and Glick Schiller and Fouron (2001), among others, were the ones who initially analyzed important political dimensions and implications of transnational migration, such as the deterritorialization of nation-states, the redefinition of national identity and citizenship, and the expansion of long-distance nationalism. Thus, for a while, our knowledge of the political transformations generated or encouraged by transnational activities largely relied on some notable contributions from fields other than political science. Such emphasis on migrants' agency and the grassroots dimension of transnationalism left politics and public actors relatively less explored.

As a result, this initial focus on the bottom-up character of migrants' networks and on the social implications of several forms of transnationalism, together with the attempt to draw up typologies and clarify conceptual issues, laid the foundations for a research agenda with a disciplinary and methodological bias. Earlier case studies confirmed some assumptions about the development of transnational spaces, largely because they were sampling on the dependent variable. The emphasis on migrants' agency underplayed the dynamic interaction between migrants and their organizations, political authorities, and institutions in both sending and receiving countries. Ironically, it is the embeddedness of these practices in domestic structures that brings states to the center of the stage and, in my view, still requires further investigation.

In this book, I take that challenge seriously, and I aim to make a contribution from a political science and international relations perspective and to encourage inter- and intradisciplinary dialogues. The following sections elaborate on this point and explain the research strategy.

Crossing Disciplinary Boundaries

Although the phenomenon of emigration is not new (e.g., Smith 2003a; Zolberg 2007), political science in general has focused more on the comparative politics of immigration than on the transnational dimension of displacements or the role of sending states (i.e., countries of origin). Migrants' impact on labor markets in the receiving countries and the participation of ethnic minorities in mainstream politics, antiracist movements, and social movements in the host societies have been more investigated than their roles in home politics or their dual engagements (Castles and Davidson 2000; Guarnizo et al. 2003, among others). Within international relations, for decades a traditional emphasis on high politics and state sovereignty led mainstream theories to neglect the study of transnational migration.

I concur with Bauböck (2003), who argues that the field of political science has an important contribution to make: to analyze how transnational phenomena are transcending and modifying politics as usual and how migration is redefining the notions of polity and membership. Bauböck (2005) also emphasizes crucial aspects of migrant experiences today: the existence of overlapping forms of membership and an increasing disconnect between social and political rights—a particularly relevant insight to understand the processes by which the borders of political communities and their territorial bases are being redefined when sending states court diasporas. It is then evident that these processes speak to the core tenets of the field of international relations.

Regarding that subfield of political science, Koslowski (2005:6–9) correctly argues that mainstream international relations theories have neglected the study of migration, downplayed its implications for security and international economics, and concentrated mainly on the politics of immigration in receiving countries. He also reminds us that, although earlier work on interdependence included references to the movement of people, more recent studies on transnationalism have prioritized economic flows to the detriment of the investigation of human mobility. Studies framing the issue in the globalization literature also warn us against overlooking international migration and label it as the "missing leg" of the globalization triad formed by flows of products, capital, and labor (Kapur 2013). Except for notable efforts to conceptualize diasporas within international relations and foreign policy studies (e.g., Adamson and Demetriou 2007; Shain and Barth 2003), it is evident that the field faces challenges when addressing transnational migration, largely because it has not overcome the state-centered and territorial traps (Agnew 1994; Wimmer and Glick Schiller 2003).

It is actually the work of colleagues from other disciplines (e.g., anthropology, human geography) that largely informs our limited understanding of the politics of transnational migration. They have investigated, for instance, the characteristics of unbound nations, new forms of (long-distance) nationalism, and the overlapping of multiple forms of membership and citizenship (e.g., Basch et al. 1994; Glick Schiller and Fouron 2001; Laguerre 1998). Although the state is a central actor in those studies, the analytical focus is understandably not on the state itself. The concern is more with the societal aspects of such processes than with political institutions and techniques of government. In contrast, the use of the term *state-led transnationalism* here denotes my intention to call attention to states' involvement in the construction of transnational spaces.

State-Centered Approaches

Political geographers, among others, have lately produced numerous empirical studies on sending-state outreach policies and elaborated on a number of explanatory factors. Not yet constituting a formal theory (e.g., Agunias and Newland 2012; Ancien et al. 2009; Gamlen 2008), these studies have advanced some propositions, identified best practices, and contributed to establish insightful comparisons, too. In earlier studies, factors such as the international constraints acting on developing countries due to their position in the system; the influence of international norms, state capacities, and the size of the emigrant community; and the role of political parties have been suggested as explanatory factors (e.g., Levitt and de la Dehesa 2003). States' involvement has been generally understood as a response to migrants' demands and their increasing capacity to organize and lobby, which are more likely to happen in the cases of massive migrations that may have a significant political impact, such as Mexicans in the US (e.g., Goldring 2002; Smith 2003b). Some studies emphasize the economic motivation behind states' involvement and its impact in terms of inclusion or exclusion of expatriates, their level of organization, and the transnationalization of social, gender, and regional inequalities (Guarnizo 1998).

In particular, the attempt to capture remittances or to benefit from the lobby capacity of emigrants in the host country (especially in cases of internal or international conflict) have been identified as the main motivations of sending states to court diasporas (e.g., Levitt and de la Dehesa 2003; Østergaard-Nielsen 2003), implicitly assuming that return would not (and should not) be a policy goal. Other studies have focused on regularities in transnational political practices linking sending and receiving states. For instance, Itzigsohn (2000) finds similar patterns across three immigrant communities in the US whose transnational political practices are highly institutionalized and are fostered by three main actors: the sending-state apparatus, political parties in the country of origin, and migrant organizations in the host country. More recent studies condense these factors into analytical frameworks and encourage more comparisons and generalizations (Délano and Gamlen 2014; Ragazzi 2014).

However, the evidence on South American countries does not conform to existing generalizations and does not confirm the assumptions mentioned previously. On one side of the relationship, despite decades of modernization and reforms, states rely on disarticulated, inefficient apparatuses. On the other, migrant organizations are relatively few, participation and mobilization are low and intermittent, and hometown associations are not the locus of migrant activities. Except for Ecuador, the other three South American cases selected here show low dependency on remittances. They all lack political parties with transnational outreach capacity; most Latin American parties, in fact, have undergone a long crisis of representation and discredit and today face serious troubles to rebuild or maintain allegiances. Uruguay, in particular, and, to a lesser extent and with a different modality, Ecuador, have set migration return as a goal. Rather than international norms and constraints, the twists and turns of emigration policies in all cases call for a close examination of state capacities to engage emigrants and live up to promises of inclusion.

Moreover, studying capacities through the disaggregation of bureaucratic and administrative resources and struggles between federal and local levels of governments, as Fitzgerald (2006) does for the Mexican case, is not enough. Emigration policy in South America is usually highly centralized in a few offices around the executive power rather than balkanized. In general, there is little local-level involvement or none at all. Policies are mainly decided by a small government elite in which the executive power has a very prominent (often overwhelming) role. Accounting for these domestic politics variables and specificities is imperative in the selected cases.

Therefore, I analyze sending states' policies toward their emigrants, drawing on several perspectives that allow me to highlight the interplay of domestic and international processes. I draw on studies that frame these initiatives within broader global trends and refocus our attention toward governance and the mechanisms by which states are transforming themselves to adapt to new, more flexible conceptions of borders, citizenship, and national identity (Sassen 1998; Soysal 1994, among others). The emphasis is on political institutions, which, as Bauböck argues, "not only provide 'opportunity structures' for individual or collective transnational practices, but are themselves transformed through transnational relations" (Bauböck 2010:296). In particular, I focus on states' attempts to construct diasporas through discursive and other governance mechanisms, a trend that has been highlighted by studies inspired by Foucault's notion of governmentality (e.g., Kunz 2008; Larner 2007; Ragazzi 2009). Yet, I argue that in the way governmentality is reformulated today within diaspora studies, it cannot account for several cases and may induce misleading conclusions.

Governing Human Mobility

The governmentality framework certainly allows for the analysis of the political nature of these processes and to what extent, and how, emigration policy contributes to reconceptualizing the nation-state and collective identities on a nonterritorial basis. It also permits engagement with the disciplinary component of emigration policies inasmuch as courting involves emigrants in a network of shared responsibilities and self-governing. However, it is argued that the widespread adoption of diaspora policies is best explained by a particular form of governmentality that is deemed "neoliberal," which has presumably swept the entire world, and "glorifies markets and prescribes light-touch, out-sourced forms of regulation that mimic markets and instills values of self-responsibility and participation into networks of active citizens" (Délano and Gamlen 2014:46). Assuming high correlation between economic and migration policies along degrees of openness and closure, a new typology is proposed together with the argument that "the political model of a state (planned economy, welfare state, neoliberal) ultimately best explains the development of diaspora policies" (Ragazzi 2014:87). Interestingly, South American countries are not included in the database from which this typology is drawn, except for Colombia and Brazil, which are both classified in a cluster that does not do justice to their strategies toward emigrants.

I note that, in any case, none of the cases in this volume would support the previous arguments. Their economic and population policies do not clearly fit into the neoliberal model because the governments implementing diaspora policies actually embody the backlash against neoliberalism and a revised version of populist (illiberal) democracy in the region.

The emphasis on the redefinition of the state is germane, though, and is part of the core of my argument. But I note that the literature is oblivious to how recurrent crises and transitional processes (e.g., dramatic financial crises, political instability, institutional breakdown, popular unrest—all factors affecting South American countries in the last few decades) have affected the capacities of states to implement public policies, in general, and transnational policies toward emigrants, in particular. These domestic political processes are relevant because they have required not only the reconstitution of the sociopolitical and economic order, but they have also prompted the recasting of national narratives while repositioning some countries in the global economy and in regional and international politics along variable hierarchies. This indicates the need for the examination of the nature and origin of ideas behind the reimagining of nations and states' roles.

South American countries are also critical cases for examining state capacities to succeed in this policy area because (a) emigration policy has faced constraints coming from the slow and intricate evolution of bureaucratic practices and the diagnosis of the problem at hand, as well as from traditional social notions of state role, national membership, and belonging; and (b) state–society relations exhibit a tragic record of state violence over its citizens and dramatic memories of both violations of human rights (especially during dictatorships in the Southern Cone) and economic debacles to which emigrants refer when responding (with outrage and dissapointment) to state policies. Some of these nations are still struggling to strengthen, consolidate, and improve the quality of democratic institutions. It is not evident, then, how states' initiatives might contribute to recasting their own role and reconceptualizing the notions of nation, state, and nation-state. This has to be investigated at both ends of the relationship.

Postneoliberal Forms of State Transnational Action

Some works within migration studies concentrate on sending-state policies toward highly qualified or wealthy emigrant elites (e.g., Dickinson and Bailey 2007; Ho 2011). Two insights are particularly relevant for this study: (1) although they are called "diaspora strategies," state outreach efforts may be selective, catering to specific segments of the diasporic groups; and (2) they may give place to the emergence of new geographies of national membership. South American cases confirm the first but not the second argument. In Uruguay, for instance, reconfiguring national membership in transnational space has faced serious obstacles. Therefore, processes of reimagining membership are analyzed here as "geographically and historically embedded" (Dickinson and Bailey 2007:761).

Existing studies also highlight that professional and business-class emigrants are helping sending states gain competitiveness in the global knowledge economy in connection to their neoliberal projects; emigrants' main assets are their global networks that might open business opportunities for the country of origin. This in line with the literature that emphasizes sending states' instrumental use of emigration policies to capture migrant resources and with the frameworks of analysis focusing on neoliberal models that place the burden of development on individuals' shoulders and encourage migrant self-help organizations (e.g., Kunz 2008; Mohan 2008) while reluctantly expanding citizenship rights or reappropriating them for the benefit of political elites (Brand 2007).

The South American cases challenge these assumptions in various respects. There is a serious concern with the long-term implications of losing human capital, especially in Argentina and Uruguay. Yet, in contrast to other countries, this concern is compounded by other long-standing structural population issues and conjunctural immigration problems. Thus, emigration policies have to be understood in the context of specific demographic and socioeconomic conditions that shape the continuous outflow and the profiles of various waves of emigrants in each country rather than emigrants' human and social capital alone.

Also, as previously suggested, in all four cases incumbents are fostering a postneoliberal rather than a neoliberal model that combines somewhat contradictory elements: market-oriented principles with highly protectionist economic policies, a strong role for the state in social welfare issues based in human rights and developmental considerations, and neopopulist tendencies that erode the representative, republican dimension of democratic governance.

Hence, bringing the state back for public provisioning and social protection together with this pragmatic combination of governance techniques makes engagement with emigrants and their organizations different from other cases. Still, some of the parties or coalitions in government (which in general face no competition to claim migrant allegiances) have been keen on enacting extraterritorial political rights. Overall, migration policy today is plagued by tensions. Looking at the entire set of immigration laws, political discourses, agreed regional norms, diaspora engagement policies, and border control policies across Latin America, we observe contradictory trends: rhetoric that emphasizes free mobility, universal rights of migrants, antiracism, and anticriminalization of migration together with restrictions on immigrants of certain ethnic origins and security-oriented measures to curb irregular immigration (Acosta Arcarazo and Freier 2015).

In short, South American countries represent critical cases for studying emigration policies. Their specificities contrast with general trends that much of the literature takes for granted and uses to make generalizations. Some notable features of emigration policies in South America include: (a) discursive mechanisms have included but are not targeted exclusively to elites; (b) new reconceptualizations of the citizens abroad are at odds with political practices at home and have failed to fully reincorporate them into the nation; (c) some state strategies have not prioritized financial flows but rather political issues; and (d) rather than capitalizing on migrant transnational networks overseas, states tend to implement a top-down, state-led models on diverse migrant organizations that largely backfire. These and other features make it difficult to fit cases squarely into existing typologies and generalizations.

The connection between diaspora strategies and neoliberal projects is, nevertheless, analytically relevant for another reason: postneoliberalism only makes sense in relation to its predecessor model from which it simultaneously draws and tries to differentiate itself. Identifying the connection has helped to explain policy shifts and emerging public–private partnerships in some cases (e.g., Gamlen 2011). Such a link is a nuanced one, though. Not all countries addressed all dimensions and followed the same phases of neoliberal restructuring.

South American nations are critical cases in this respect, too: they allow us to "think about neoliberalism historically, geographically and culturally" (Larner 2007:343). While some of them have applied draconian neoliberal measures in a relatively short period of time (e.g., Argentina in the 1990s), others have taken a slow, cautious, and selective path (e.g., Brazil and Uruguay). Today, all cases exhibit a pragmatic approach to neoliberal principles within which one pending task stands out: the indefinitely postponed reform of the state, which has old roots and recurrently creates obstacles to policymaking and implementation. Thus, although capitalizing on emigrants' contributions has been part of the attempt to foster development, the legacies of neoliberal attempts and the lack of progress in changing bureaucratic culture and practices impinge on state capacities and keep emigration policies in a stop-and-go cycle of inconsistencies and/or delays.

Finally, geography and regional dimensions seem to differentiate North and South American cases, too. I argue that these factors have implications inasmuch as they affect the capacity of sending states to politically mobilize emigrants. Some authors highlight the increasing politicization of transnational social spaces in the US–Mexico relationship, as well as the externalities of the simultaneous regional integration process, which undoubtedly boosted interdependences and facilitated transnational practices between geographically contiguous sites.

What if borders are not contiguous and there are no supranational institutions to amalgamate national interests? What if mobilization involves long distances?

Lyons and Mandaville (2010) suggest that distance matters in specific ways and that there is a link between domestic political processes and outcomes and transnational practices that engage diasporas with home politics. Yet, they argue: "Politics remain fundamentally about local issues [including migrants' agendas and goals] even while political processes are increasingly globalized" (125). They highlight the "activation" of diasporas as an effective strategy with potential benefits not only to governments but also to other actors. Although their contention that diasporas are the outcomes of political processes (rather than the sources) is debatable, they provide a crucial insight for this study: the pattern and impact of a diaspora's political participation depends on who mobilizes it.

Hence, when looking at responses to emigration policies, I explore whether, how, and with what results sending states may expand or constrain the range of opportunities for migrants' organization and transnational political engagement and whether long distance makes a difference. I argue that sending states may do so, but they have to engage with other states, migrant associations, and international and nongovernmental organizations during the implementation phase of courting, thus contributing to the development of cross-border (public–private) policy networks and new forms of governance. In addition, I trace to what extent long distance adds an additional challenge to the effectiveness of these outreach efforts and makes them more costly.

In sum, South American cases have not only been off the radar for international relations and migration specialists in the North, but they also exhibit several specific features that beg explanation. The case studies presented here provide detailed evidence on the variety of responses within a worldwide trend toward courting diasporas. Exploring the timing, characteristics, achievements, and sources of setbacks in emigration policy unveils the intermestic, multilevel character of state outreach efforts, qualifies and refines existing explanations, expands our understanding of new governance techniques, and provides some insights into the requirements for emigration policies to work effectively. This book aims at making a contribution in those respects.

Methodological Choices

The research strategy adopted in this project is the empirical investigation of migration policies in specific national contexts. I used multiple sources of evidence. I have relied mostly on qualitative methods to collect and integrate such evidence and delineate the case studies. Process tracing helped to unveil the motivation, timing, and choices of decision makers. Institutional analysis situated such a process in the broader set of country-specific institutional structures and domestic politics shaping migration policymaking. Content analysis captured the evolution of policies and political discourses in official documents, statements, legislation, and other texts (e.g., governmental reports and statistics, academic books and articles, international institutions' and nongovernmental organizations' publications, national and international press, websites). This was complemented with various rounds of in-depth, semistructured elite interviewing and personal communications with the most relevant actors and key informants[1] during field research in Mexico, Ecuador, Peru, Argentina, Uruguay, Brazil, France, Spain, and Italy over the last 9 years. One hundred fourteen interviews were conducted; interviewees were selected through a combination of preliminary documentary research and snow-balling.

The interviews included high-rank state officials (ministers, secretaries of state, heads of migration offices, advisors and members of presidential cabinets and other migration-related offices, among others); officials and technical advisors of regional organizations; independent policy consultants with working experience in the public and private sector and/or international institutions; leaders and staff of migrant associations; staff of international institutions and nongovernmental organizations and foundations (e.g., religious and human rights institutions); scholars from various disciplines; and media professionals who specialize in migration and population topics. When long distance made personal meetings impossible, electronic mail questionnaires were delivered and phone/ Skype conversations were conducted; this was necessary in only a few cases. In addition to interviews with elites, I collected migrant testimonies from various sources and conducted personal interviews and written communications with ordinary migrants from two selected emigrant communities in their two primary destinations in Southern Europe: Argentines and Ecuadorians in Madrid and Milan. Zooming in on these sites allowed for a partial assessment of migrant practices and responses to emigration policies, and it contributed to analyzing policy results.

The main research questions refer to the timing and motivations for sending states' actions, as well as the content, modality of implementation, and results of the policies launched. I sought to understand what states did, why they did it, why they did it now, how they did it, and with what results. The cases were treated as single case studies and comparisons are limited to the general traits and trajectory of emigration policies. Thus, the case studies are organized around the main traits and evolution paths to be compared: historical antecedents, political context and timing surrounding the launching or intensification of outreach efforts, policy instruments, and progress toward state goals and/or implementation obstacles. Because any policy involves a relationship, sending states' are always to be understood in reference to the interactions with policy addressees, nonstate actors, and national and local governments in the receiving sites.

There is no attempt to quantify variables and provide generalizations or test theories; rather, the study suggests new explanatory factors, draws lessons, and inspires further comparisons. I deliberately accept the trade-off between deep understanding of complex cases and a parsimonious, generalizable account. I favor the former, despite its limits, in the hopes of capturing the nuances of courting as a dynamic relationship and the meaning policymakers are giving to their decisions and actions. My previous research experience in economic and foreign policymaking in Latin America led me to expect that the advance of policy innovations would be largely contingent on informal and ad hoc adaptations and certain individuals' proactive initiatives, professional experience, and personal involvement rather than a complete, comprehensive, and formal design (e.g., it is not unusual for public officials who hold positions abroad to become informally knowledgeable and willing to motorize innovations). The findings provided in the following chapters, as well as other studies (e.g., Délano 2014:96) prove that assumption right.

Thus, although I agree with those who advocate for more balance between case study and large sample knowledge (e.g., Délano and Gamlen 2014; Ragazzi 2014), I still consider small samples and detailed case studies like the ones presented here necessary to address the types of research questions posed in this study and to unveil the richness and relevance of cases that are relatively underexamined in the literature. In this study, qualitative research methods with a focus on a small sample of understudied cases have been strategic to account for the protagonists' views, which include a general disappointment with the available academic knowledge and practice in the field and, in particular, with states' performances. Therefore, it is not more generalizations based on neat models that are needed, but instead detailed case studies of the vicissitudes of emigration policies. As the old saying goes, "the devil is in the details." These methodological choices made it possible to provide those details and to demonstrate a point made in previous sections: existing typologies would benefit from some refinement.

Preliminary research allowed me to identify four relatively underexamined cases: Brazil, Argentina, Uruguay, and Ecuador. Together with Mexico, these cases share similar patterns of historical socioeconomic development. In all of these cases except Mexico, the process of nation and state building was closely intertwined with immigration flows, not emigration. Today these countries are representative of different emigration dynamics within the region and illustrative of diverse state approaches on how to deal with population problems, economic restructuring, and democratic governance. Although in all cases human rights considerations are evident, the South American cases contrast with Mexico in their use of a postneoliberal discourse that, to some extent, aims at differentiating their approaches from the restrictive, security-related measures being implemented in the North. While Mexico's transnational involvement with emigrants is largely shaped by the bilateral (asymmetrical) relationship with the US and is often secondary to other priorities, South American countries have developed an active multilateral agenda that voices the postneoliberal approach in global arenas, hoping this will re-order priorities, improve cooperation agendas, and enhance their individual and collective bargaining power.

Specific similarities and differences enabled me to tease out the analytical points mentioned in previous sections. The sample includes two small countries with large diasporas (Ecuador and Uruguay) and two large countries with small diasporas (Brazil and Argentina). The references to country size and resources (which are an indication of the country's position in the international politico-economic system) and diaspora size do not have explanatory connotations; instead, they are descriptive references that engage with earlier (albeit still influential) literature in the field and with the counterintuitive findings that I present.[2]

All emigrant communities share some characteristics (e.g., diversity of socioeconomic background, origin, and gender); however, destinations have recently changed for some South Americans (i.e., Southern Europe is preferred over the US, except for Brazilians), and migrant political engagement varies considerably across communities and destinations (e.g., being more intense for Ecuadorians than Argentines, and more so in Spain than in Italy). In addition, state–diaspora relations for Mexicans in the US are cemented by a long history of interactions, a closely knit network of state and nonstate interests, well-established institutions, and particular ways of dealing with asymmetrical power relations. This contrast allows for exploring the reasons why some emigration policies evolve and others fade and why some develop in stages (as Mexico's did, going from assistance to protection, from recognition to linkage, from support to empowerment) and others do not.

For various reasons, my conclusions are limited. Small samples obviously limit the scope of my conclusions and generalizations. The policies analyzed here are a work in progress. They are part of a fluid, constantly changing political dynamic that defies definitive statements. Moreover, a comprehensive exploration of migrant responses across all cases would be necessary to assess results and implications in detail. Such a task exceeds the time frame and resources of this project; that remains for the next undertaking.

Notes

1 I note that emigration policies (and the specific offices running them) are relatively young in South America, where political decision making has always been highly concentrated around the executive power and top ministerial positions. Also, membership and participation in migrant associational life are generally low. Therefore, the number of key informants in each case is relatively small.
2 For instance, at first glance, these two variables might lead to a few intuitive assumptions: states facing emigration of considerable magnitude would be quick and proactive in terms of developing a clear and effective outreach policy, reflecting a consensus among political parties (those in power and those in the opposition); society would be sensitive, attuned to, and probably supportive of such initiatives; and both states and societies would be interested in strengthening nationhood bonds with emigrants and engaging them in national development projects. However, this did not happen in the small countries, and generalizations would be misleading because state-led initiatives followed different trajectories. Ecuador, with a long record of emigration, acknowledged the social problem only in the mid-2000s, and it was a newly created coalition with no roots in the political system the only political force that pushed for a very proactive state policy. In the aftermath of a serious economic crisis, the state devoted considerable resources to expand bureaucratic capacities in this area. Uruguay started to address population and migration problems only slowly and recently, after decades of denial of the devastating effects of massive emigration. According to officials, limited resources are not a major obstacle to progress. Silence about this issue has in fact been a common characteristic in all cases, regardless of the magnitude of emigration and the availability of state resources, which prevents the problem from being considered as such and from entering the governmental agendas. Similar counterintuitive findings show that large states like Brazil and Argentina, which rely on relatively more resources than the smaller ones, have not been the most proactive ones in this policy realm, and their strategies also differ compared one to another.

Works Cited

Acosta Arcarazo, Diego and Luisa Feline Freier. 2015. "Turning the Immigration Policy Paradox Upside Down? Populist Liberalism and Discursive Gaps in South America." *International Migration Review*. Early view online. DOI: 10.1111/imre.12146.

Adamson, F.B. and M. Demetriou. 2007. "Remapping the Boundaries of 'State' and 'National Identity': Incorporating Diasporas into IR Theorizing." *European Journal of International Relations*. 13(4): 489–526.

Agnew, John. 1994. "The Territorial Trap: The Geographical Assumptions of International Relations Theory." *Review of International Political Economy*. 1(1), Spring: 53–80.

Agunias, Dovelyn R. and Kathleen Newland. 2012. *Developing a Road Map for Engaging Diasporas in Development: A Handbook for Policymakers and Practitioners in Home and Host Countries*. Washington, DC: International Organization for Migration and Migration Policy Institute.

Ancien, Delphine, Mark Boyle, and Rob Kitchin. 2009, June. "Exploring Diaspora Strategies: An International Comparison." Workshop report. National University of Maynooth, Ireland.

Basch, Linda, Nina Glick Schiller, and Cristina Szanton Blanc. 1994. *Nations Unbound: Transnational Projects, Postcolonial Predicaments, and Deterriorialized Nation-States*. London: Routledge.

Bauböck, Rainer. 2003. "Towards a Political Theory of Migrant Transnationalism." *International Migration Review*. 37(2), Fall: 700–723.

Bauböck, Rainer. 2005. "Expansive Citizenship—Voting beyond Territory and Membership." *Political Science and Politics*. October: 683–687.

Bauböck, Rainer. 2010. "Cold Constellations and Hot Identities: Political Theory Questions about Transnationalism and Diaspora." In *Diaspora and Transnationalism: Concepts, Theories, and Methods*, ed. by Rainer Bauböck and Thomas Faist. Amsterdam: IMISCOE Research and Amsterdam University Press. pp. 295–322.

Brand, Laurie A. 2007, February. "State, Citizenship, and Diaspora: The Cases of Jordan and Lebanon." Working Paper 146. The Center for Comparative Immigration Studies, University of California at San Diego.

Castles, Stephen and Alastair Davidson. 2000. *Citizenship and Migration. Globalization and the Politics of Belonging*. New York: Routledge.

Délano, Alexandra. 2014. "The Diffusion of Diaspora Engagement Policies: A Latin American Agenda." *Political Geography*. 41: 90–100.

Délano, Alexandra and Alan Gamlen. 2014. "Comparing and Theorizing State-Diaspora Relations." *Political Geography*. 41: 43–53.

Dickinson, Jen and Adrian J. Bailey. 2007. "(Re)membering Diaspora: Uneven Geographies of Indian Dual Citizenship." *Political Geography*. 26: 757–774.

Gamlen, Alan. 2008. "The Emigration State and the Modern Geopolitical Imagination." *Political Geography*. 27(8): 840–856.

Gamlen, Alan. 2011, April. "Creating and Destroying Diaspora Strategies." Working Paper 31. International Migration Institute, University of Oxford.

Glick Schiller, Nina and Georges E. Fouron. 2001. *Georges Woke Up Laughing: Long-Distance Nationalism and the Search for Home*. Durham, NC: Duke University Press.

Goldring, Luin. 2002. "The Mexican State and Transmigrant Organizations. Negotiating the Boundaries of Membership and Participation." *Latin American Research Review*. 37(3): 55-99

Guarnizo, L.E. 1998. "The Rise of Transnational Social Formations: Mexican and Dominican State Responses to Transnational Migration." *Political Power and Social Theory*. 12: 45–94.

Guarnizo, L.E., A. Portes, and W. Haller. 2003. "Assimilation and Transnationalism: Determinants of Transnational Political Action among Contemporary Migrants." *The American Journal of Sociology*. 108(6): 1211–1248.

Ho, Elaine Lynn-Ee. 2011. "Claiming the Diaspora: Elite Mobility, Sending State Strategies and the Spatialities of Citizenship." *Progress in Human Geography*. 35(6): 757–772.

Itzigsohn, J. 2000. "Immigration and the Boundaries of Citizenship: The Institutions of Immigrants' Political Transnationalism." *International Migration Review*. 34(4), Winter: 1126–1154.

Kapur, Devesh. 2010. *Diaspora, Development and Democracy. The Domestic Impact of International Migration from India*. Princeton, NJ: Princeton University Press.

Koslowski, Rey. ed. 2005. *International Migration and the Globalization of Domestic Politics*. London: Routledge.

Kunz, Rachel. 2008, December. "Mobilising Diasporas: A Governmentality Analysis of the Case of Mexico." Working Paper Series "Local Governance and Democracy," Number 3. Institute of Political Science, University of Lucerne, Switzerland.

Laguerre, Michael. 1998. *Diasporic Citizenship: Haitians Americans in Transnational America*. New York: St Martin's Press.

Larner, Wendy. 2007. "Expatriate Experts and Globalising Governmentalities: The New Zealand Diaspora Strategy." *Transactions of the Institute of British Geographers*. 32(3): 331–345.

Levitt, Peggy and Rafael de la Dehesa. 2003. "Transnational Migration and the Redefinition of the State: Variations and Explanations." *Ethnic and Racial Studies* 26(4): 587–611.

Levitt, Peggy and B. Nadya Jaworsky. 2007. "Transnational Migration Studies: Past Developments and Future Trends." *Annual Review of Sociology*. 33(1): 129–156.

Lyons, Terrence and Peter Mandaville. 2010. "Think Locally, Act Globally: Toward a Transnational Comparative Politics." *International Political Sociology*. 4(2): 124–141.

Mohan, Giles. 2008. "Making Neoliberal States of Development: The Ghanaian Diaspora and the Politics of Homelands." *Environment and Planning D: Society and Space*. 26: 464–479.

Østergaard-Nielsen, Eva. ed. 2003. *International Migration and Sending Countries. Perceptions, Policies, and Transnational Relations*. Houndmills: Palgrave/Macmillan.

Ragazzi, Francesco. 2009. "Governing Diasporas." *International Political Sociology*. 3: 378–397.

Ragazzi, Francesco. 2014. "A comparative analysis of diaspora policies." *Political Geography*. 41: 74–89.

Sassen, Saskia. 1998. *Globalization and Its Discontents: Essays on the New Mobility of People and Money.* New York: The New Press.

Shain, Yossi and Aharon Barth. 2003. "Diasporas and International Relations Theory." *International Organization.* 57: 449–479.

Smith, Robert C. 2003a. "Diasporic Memberships in Historical Perspective: Comparative Insights from the Mexican, Italian and Polish Cases." *International Migration Review.* 37(3), Fall: 724–759.

Smith, Robert C. 2003b. "Migrant Membership as an Instituted Process: Transnationalization, the State and the Extra-Territorial Conduct of Mexican Politics." *International Migration Review.* 37(2), Summer: 297–343.

Soysal, Yasemin N. 1994. *Limits of Citizenship. Migrants and Postnational Membership in Europe.* Chicago: The University of Chicago.

Vertovec, Stephen. 2009. *Transnationalism.* London: Routledge.

Wimmer, Andreas and Nina Glick Schiller. 2003. "Methodological Nationalism, the Social Sciences and the Study of Migration: An Essay in Historical Epistemology." *International Migration Review.* 37(3): 576–610.

Zolberg, Aristide R. 2007. "The Exit Revolution." In *Citizenship and Those Who Leave: The Politics of Emigration and Expatriation,* ed. by Nancy L. Green and François Weil. Urbana: University of Illinois Press. pp. 33–62.

3 Emigration Policies in Latin America

Regional Migration Dynamics

Migration flows in Latin America exhibited significant changes in the second half of the 20th century. Changes in socioeconomic conditions, together with political instability and economic restructuring, prompted several waves of outflows, and extraregional immigration (which had been significant until then) receded. In the 1970s, political exiles fled political persecution and repression by military regimes in the Southern Cone. In the 1980s, as economic conditions deteriorated after the debt crisis and subsequent structural reforms, labor outflow increased, mainly from Ecuador, Bolivia, Peru, Argentina, and Colombia. Some outflows intensified in the early 21st century, such as those from Venezuela. The main destinations were advanced economies of the North where migrant networks already existed, such as the US and some European countries, but new destinations were sought too. The US continues to be the main destination for some South American communities (as it is for Mexicans and migrants from countries in Central America and the Caribbean). In the 2000s, an increasing number of South Americans preferred Southern Europe (especially Spain and Italy) and the United Kingdom.[1]

This recreated an old cross-regional migration corridor, this time through the reversal of historical flows: whereas at the turn of the 19th century millions of Southern Europeans moved to South America (mainly from Spain, Italy, and Portugal), flows in the opposite direction were observed a century later. This is not a new phenomenon, but its magnitude gave it visibility and called attention to the social, economic, and political implications.[2] The recent movement of people builds upon old kinship and cultural ties, as well as agreements between sending and receiving countries, that to some extent facilitate exit, transit, residency, and even political engagement by accepting dual citizenship and/or citizenship retention. In some cases, specific agreements (e.g., in the areas of education, social security) may also pave the way for migrant integration in the host societies. Such cooperation is one of the forms that transnational governance has taken in this corridor.

The politics of these processes are complex and indicate the need to look at both national-and regional-level variables. The past three decades were times of accelerated and profound change in the entire region because democratization and economic reforms significantly altered the balance of state–society and state–market relations, with implications for migration dynamics and policies. Those changes did not translate into sustained economic growth and political stability for all countries. There were not only improvements and progress, but also setbacks, cyclical turns, and crises in both fronts. As Texidó and Gurrieri (2012) point out, cycles of economic recovery in some South American nations (e.g., Argentina) and stability in others (e.g., Chile) created incentives for increasing intraregional mobility and, in the last few years, new inflows from other regions, too. Restrictive policies in the North also contributed to changes in migration strategies. The region also exhibits a trend toward feminization of recent migration flows, predominance of economically active workers (between 15 and 64 years old), and a relative increase in the number of skilled workers (Texidó and Gurrieri 2012:15).

Therefore, emigration has become a significant and constant factor of a very fluid population dynamic. This implies a remarkable change for nations that historically imagined themselves as countries of immigration. Addressing this reality (compounded by the increasing visibility of other flows too, such as refugees and human trafficking) is a relatively new challenge for both states and societies in Latin America.

It exceeds the limits of this study to relate all trends in regional migration.[3] The most important indicators for each case study can be found in the chapters that follow. It is sufficient to underline the following here: (a) extraregional emigration continues in all South American countries, though at a slower pace and simultaneous with migration return, which is today a growing concern for some Latin American governments; and (b) current intraregional flows originate mainly in the Andean countries (Colombia, Peru, Ecuador, Bolivia) and Paraguay, while the Southern Cone (Argentina, Brazil, Chile, and, to a lesser extent, Uruguay) has been the main receiver of those flows.

This is relevant because it helps to understand some differences across cases in terms of how they define the problem at hand, set priorities, and move (more or less reluctantly) toward significant changes in emigration policy. In Ecuador, the size of the diaspora in relation to the total population makes it more visible and politically consequential; there we observe the most intense emigration policy. Uruguay also has a large diaspora, but it is mostly composed of highly skilled workers who, together with foreign workers, are crucial for the country's development goals; thus, engaging with the diaspora is parallel to efforts to entice return and an incipient interest in potential immigration. Countries with relatively small emigrant groups, such as Argentina and Brazil, have joined the global trend toward courting diasporas, but in a limited, gradual, and even intermittent fashion. Argentina, in particular, as it became the receiving country for most intraregional flows, lately shifted attention and resources away from emigration and toward immigration.

However, migration dynamics are only part of the explanation, and they do not explain per se the kind of responses governments choose to give to new realities. There are other factors to take into account if one is to explain cases that do not fit in existing typologies. I note that domestic politics within the region have colored those choices and the migration debate more broadly. A backslash against neoliberalism swept the region in the last decade (also known as the *pink tide,* in reference to a turn to the left whose radical character is dubious), creating the ferment for inward-looking, nationalist, populist, and moderately contestatory policies.[4] This is the background against which new approaches to migration issues have lately developed in South America, setting that area of the region apart from Mexico. As the following chapters explain, postneo-liberal and neopopulist discourses were instrumental in the construction of new governing coalitions, in the articulation of their domestic and foreign policies, and in the timing and content of emigration policies.

Attuned with this new political orientation, constitutional and legislative updates or changes have been introduced or are in the making in all countries, and these have implications for migration dynamics; namely these are principles and norms against discrimination and human trafficking and in favor of immigration, refugee protection, and equal treatment for nationals and migrants, as well as norms to facilitate the regularization of migrants' residency statuses and the exercise of migrants' rights that still coexist in some cases with past restrictive measures (Ceriani Cernadas 2011; Escobar 2007, among others). As it is explained later, regional norms were agreed upon following these same principles. As a result, norms, institutions, and programs to preserve nationhood bonds with citizens residing abroad, to protect and/or expand emigrant's rights, and to encourage migrant engagement with the homeland have become embedded into new normative frameworks at the national and regional levels. This proves the relevance and long-term implications of changes in sending states' approaches to emigration.

Each country, however, exhibits a distinct trajectory not only in relation to migration policy but also in how, and to what extent, it has completed and consolidated the political and economic transformations previously mentioned. Thus, it is under discussion whether Latin American states can actually make that normative consensus effective (i.e., to what extent migrants can exert the newly acquired rights on the ground). All sending states have courted their diasporas lately, but, as the selected case studies demonstrate, the trajectories of emigration policies are still short of full engagement and largely constrained by the legacies of unfinished processes of reform of the state and changing state–society relations. Notwithstanding legislation update, the terms of inclusion and exclusion are currently being redefined in practice for those members of the nation residing abroad. That is why I argued in Chapter 1 that engagement has to be problematized and that courting might or might not become engagement.

Mexico is a very telling case in this respect. The longest and most advanced experience of courting diasporas in the region is observed there. Mexico presents some specificities and differences with the South American cases that make comparisons difficult. Still, I argue that Mexico offers precious clues about how the interplay of domestic and international factors shapes the results and possible evolution of emigration policies. I include the details of this case in Chapter 9, where I resume the issue of results and responses.

Migration Policies Within Regional Spaces

The emigration policies analyzed here are not the only area in which South American countries have innovated recently. Together with increasing state-led transnationalism, there has been a revival of regional attempts to push regional integration further within the framework of existing regional agreements and/or through the creation of new regional institutions.[5] At the same time, sociopolitical issues (including all questions related to human mobility and citizens' rights) have ranked high on the agendas of those organizations and have been taken to negotiations with counterparts in Europe (CELAC 2012). The advance in the harmonization of migration norms and member states' obligations to comply with those norms prompted national legislation updates and other adjustments in order to fully implement multilateral agreements. Thus, the emerging normative consensus has been reinforcing the incentives for innovation in migration policy in general at the national level. Emigration policies are part and parcel of those broader changes.

Indeed, over the last decade, a considerable number of general and procedural norms have been agreed on among MERCOSUR members, and related conceptual, procedural, and institutional innovations occurred within this policy domain, including major agreements on free movement and equal rights for nationals of member states, norms on residency, and ongoing negotiations to elaborate a statute on regional citizenship. The same principles were voiced in the forums and summits between representatives of Latin America and the European Union, which since 2008 have taken the form of a structured dialogue to develop a comprehensive approach to the management of cross-regional migration flows.[6] Thus, the regional level becomes analytically relevant because the regional consensus attained in South America lately on how to manage international migration has impinged on the content, timing, and evolution of emigration policies, as well as on the cross-regional dialogues that shape transnational migration governance.

Such consensus gained momentum only in the last decade. Within the regional integration process initiated in mid-1980s, people's mobility was initially conceptualized in terms of market mechanisms (i.e. as a necessary complement to the free circulation of capital, goods, and services within an enlarged area). Only towards the end of the 1990s was the discussion of common social and labour issues intensified (Novick, Hener, and Dalle 2005; Pérez Vichich 2007). A new commission in charge of labour migration was created and member states committed to uphold migrant workers' equal rights, start harmonizing national norms on mobility, exchange information and coordinate actions on border controls, and compile data about migration flows. In 1999, the Economic and Social Consultation Forum was created as an incipient mechanism to incorporate the views of social actors (e.g., businesses, union organizations) in the policymaking process.

The Residency Agreement for Nationals of MERCOSUR Member States, signed on 6 December 2002, was a turning point in the harmonization of migration policies. The agreement reflects the renewed political impetus given to integration and marks the beginning of a period in which several accords on citizens' rights to residency, circulation, and other civil, social, and cultural rights were negotiated. This agreement, which was ratified by all member states in 2009, reflects governments' intentions to redirect the integration process toward placing a strong emphasis on social issues as a remedy for the excesses of the previous market-centered approach.

The agreement states the need to harmonize national legislation and establishes common norms for the regulation of residency issues, including requirements, procedures, and residents' rights. It also proposes "MERCOSUR nationality" as the criterion for residency (i.e., nationals of a member state are entitled to legal residency in any other member state). Article 9 focuses on civil, social, cultural, and economic rights for migrants and their families, including the rights to work, to petition, to mobilize, to form associations, to maintain their religious practices, to family reunion, to send remittances transfer, to pursue children's education, and to be treated equality vis-à-vis nationals regarding labor legislation, wages, and working conditions.[7]

The Residency Agreement served as the inspiration and basis for other norms. The Santiago Declaration About Migration Principles, adopted in Santiago de Chile on 7 May 2004, for instance, establishes basic principles of migration management to be adopted regionally and recognizes migrants' rights and migrants' multiple contributions to the development of home and host countries. The Residency Agreement has also served to structure MERCOSUR's stance in other regional and global fora (Alfonso 2012) and as the basis for the elaboration of a Citizenship Statute. Such a project includes facilitating the free circulation of migrant workers, deepening the civic and social dimensions of the bloc, and strengthening citizens' rights. Though still in early stages, it promises the deepening of social regional integration.

The new normative framework has had repercussions beyond MER-
COSUR. Another rapidly growing scheme of integration in the region,
UNASUR (Union of South American Nations), has built upon MERCO-
SUR's achievements in this area when it established in its constitutive
treaty of 2008 the development of South American citizenship as one of
the main goals of the organization, underlining the importance of migration issues, free human mobility, and citizens' rights. Several political declarations followed that reinforced this commitment and the intention to
promote a regional approach to be taken to negotiations with countries of
the North. The decision to start working toward South American citizenship was adopted in late November 2012, together with the creation of a
working group to elaborate a report and strategic guidelines.[8] This shows
that MERCOSUR advances in this area might have a broader regional
and global effect. Moreover, it highlights that migration policymaking
at different levels (regional, national, global) is closely intertwined, thus
suggesting that those links are analytically relevant.

The results of activities of the working group above are not available
at the moment of this writing. Nonetheless, top officials' oral testimonies
confirmed that the incipient construction of regional citizenship is envisioned along the following dimensions, though the political component of
them is not being discussed yet.[9] First, regarding who has political membership, the principle of nationality (based on *jus solis*) in any member
state, as per the Resident Agreement mentioned previously, would ren-
der all citizens members. However, regional norms are still silent about
enfranchising those members. Political rights are not included in the list
of norms regulating the circulation and life of citizens within MERCO-
SUR.[10] The decision MERCOSUR/CMC/DEC. no. 64/10 of December
2010, which aimed at a plan of action for the creation of a citizenship
statute, briefly states that such a plan would assess how to make progress
in the granting of political rights to citizens of a member state residing in
any other member state, including the possibility of electing members to
the bloc's parliament.[11]

Second, with reference to which rights are granted, the list of civil,
social, cultural, and economic rights stipulated by the Residency Agreement would be the core of the new institution of regional citizenship.
Third, as for how interest intermediation is structured, regional institutions are silent about channels and mechanisms of representation. The
few and relatively young institutions of representation within MERCO-
SUR (i.e., the Economic and Social Consultation Forum and the Joint
Parliamentary Commission—the latter replaced by the Mercosur Parliament in 2005, effective in 2007) are not mentioned in the documents
establishing the creation of a South American citizenship.

Fourth, it is still unknown how the bloc would foster regional identity.
References to a preexistent South American identity are included in some
documents, but its features and future expansion are not elaborated. For

instance, the UNASUR Decision cited previously is clear on the intention to initiate citizenship construction "from its migration dimension" (art. 1), and it refers back to the organization's constitutive treaty to set the goal of consolidating "South American identity through the progressive granting of rights to nationals of a member state residing in any of the other member states in order to attain South American citizenship." The document also argues that "free human mobility within the region is one of the fundamental elements in the construction of South American citizenship."

In short, thus far, the existence of regional identity is taken for granted, and portable rights are proposed as the basis for regional citizenship creation. The question of whether this is enough for building up a substantive, meaningful regional citizenship by which South Americans can exercise their rights transnationally remains open. However, such a political project is in sync with the rights-based discourse that underlies emigration policies and provides additional ideational and institutional support to state-led transnational initiatives. It is then germane to identify the factors that made significant regional integration in the migration policy area possible in such a relatively short period of time. These factors might well foreshadow the likelihood of further progress and provide some clues on the fate of still incipient emigration policies. The next section addresses this point.

Impetus and Sustainability of New Migration Norms

As I explained elsewhere in detail (Margheritis 2013), migration has entered the regional agenda in response to some facts and encouraged by the action of certain national and transnational actors. New political discourses and institutions exhibit the political commitment of governments to tackle problems created by increasing human mobility within the bloc. Epistemic communities and relatively close policy networks provided necessary input, consensus, and impetus to regional negotiations. Argentina's proactive stance, together with Brazil's acquiescence, facilitated agreements in a relatively short period of time. The brief consideration of each of these factors helps in analyzing the links between national and regional policies.

Migration dynamics within the Latin America in general, and the Southern Cone in particular, have lately acquired new characteristics that contrast with those of previous decades (Martínez Pizarro 2008; Martínez and Stang 2006; Martínez and Vono 2005). Among other things, a renewed dynamism in intraregional flows became evident in the 1990s, with Chile and Argentina being the most important migrant receiving countries. Various factors encouraged this development, namely differentials in labor demand and wages and exchange rate differentials that momentarily improve migrants' capacities to save and send remittances, reinforced by existing migrant networks. Argentina, in particular, has been the main receiving country of intraregional migration for the last three decades, attracting 68% of the intraregional flows at the beginning of the 2000s (Maguid 2007:262).

Intraregional migration to Argentina persisted despite the fact that the neoliberal reforms of the 1990s implied significant changes in labor markets and working conditions and led to rising unemployment and poverty. Unemployment peaked in the mid-1990s, and currency convertibility ended with a dramatic crisis in December 2001, forcing migrants to adapt to a more unstable and precarious scenario, but without prompting massive returns to their countries of origin (Maguid 2007). Despite a renewed emphasis on social policy after the crisis and remarkable rates of gross domestic product (GDP) growth in the last decade, conditions of poverty and marginality have intensified in the last few years. Argentina has thus exposed the contradictions of populist promises and increasing levels of inequality.[12] In addition, as it will be explained in Chapter 6, Argentina has had a long tradition of social discrimination against dark-skinned, low-class nationals and aliens, creating the ferment for social unrest that may emerge in times of electoral competition. The conflict about the (migrant) occupation of public lands in December of 2010, for example, illustrates the interplay of regional and domestic social politics and policymaking.[13] To prevent social disorder, Argentine governments have lately adopted an inclusive discourse toward immigrants and the country became the leader of legislative changes at home and at the regional level to more effectively regulate human mobility.

The inclusion of human mobility in the regional agenda was also encouraged by the research of think tanks, academics, and regional bureaucracies that emphasized the importance of multilateral management of migration issues, the acknowledgement of shared responsibility and potential gains coming from cooperation and regulation, and the need to seek consensus between countries of origin and destination. Experts have framed these ideas in terms of governability (CEPAL 2006; Gurrieri 2005; Mármora 2003, among others), defining migration as a multilateral, rather than a strictly domestic, problem. This was attuned to governments' concerns with states' capacities to deal with border controls and tensions generated by migration flows.

In addition, existing disappointment with MERCOSUR's performance in the economic area (e.g., trade disputes, impossibility to advance toward the common market stage) opened a window of opportunity to act quickly in the migration policy realm, which gathered more consensus than other integration areas, such as trade.[14] Officials perceived migration to be among the issues that required less expertise, generated limited controversies, and were amenable to pragmatic and quick resolutions. They were also aware that the effectiveness of policies depended on multilateral cooperation and, therefore, they focused on moving negotiations forward.[15]

One of the mechanisms to do so was to channel MERCOSUR's policy-making process through two tracks: the economic-commercial one, which was the original focus of the bloc and still keeps aiming at the formation of the long-postponed custom union; and the politico-institutional one, which largely relies on the political will of member states and impulses given by intergovernmental negotiations. This politico-institutional track has acquired more relevance in the last decade[16] not only as an operational division of labor for daily routines, but also as negotiation paths that advance at different paces.

This division has been reproduced at the level of domestic bureaucracies in the two leading states, that is, the foreign ministries of Brazil and Argentina.[17] The proactive stance by the executives in Brazil and Argentina reinforced these changes and showed presidents' agreement not only on pushing MERCOSUR beyond the economic area, but also on linking South American style regional integration to governments' claims in international forums for a reformulation of global rules of governance. Both former presidents Néstor Kirchner and Luiz Inácio "Lula" da Silva worked to repay their countries' debts to the IMF—a move aimed not only at financial gains but also at pleasing left-wing supporters. The Copacabana Act signed by Kirchner and da Silva on 16 March 2004 explicitly linked their domestic and regional policy goals. It reinforced the countries' commitments to both multilateral cooperation and economic growth with equity at home, showing that it is precisely the connection between human—or labor—mobility, economic growth, and equity that pushes sociopolitical issues to the top of the regional agenda. The declaration also summarized their demands, among other things, for the elimination of subsidies in developed countries, the relaxation of IMF conditionality on governments' spending, and the right to discriminate in government procurement in favor of national and regional investors.[18] In sum, these administrations tied the regional dynamic to the fate of their domestic constituencies, and the presidents became the voices of the (moderate) contesters of the Washington consensus.

Accordingly, former presidents da Silva and Kirchner reaffirmed their commitment with the integration process in 2003 (Martínez and Stang 2006), although the seeds of convergence around a new model of development were planted earlier: the administrations of Fernando Henrique Cardoso and Fernando De la Rúa had already coincided on the need to reestablish state capacity to shape economic processes and increase policy coordination. Toward the end of his mandate and holding the pro tempore presidency of MERCOSUR, Cardoso attempted to push regional integration further as a last sign of his commitment to the project, and this accelerated negotiations for the Residency Agreement (Alfonso 2012:48). By 2007, da Silva and Kirchner labelled the bilateral relationship a "strategic alliance" encompassing common positions on national, regional, and global economic and political matters.[19] The administrations that followed in both countries (Cristina Fernández de Kirchner in Argentina and Dilma Rousseff in Brazil) have maintained such political agreement and carried it within UNASUR. Thus, the relaunching of MERCOSUR in the 2000s and the creation of UNASUR became rooted in a deeper process of redefinition of developmental goals and strategies. These strategies involve a partial questioning of neoliberal principles, the reassertion of the role of the state, and the encouragement of region-building as a political platform to strategically place South American economies in a better standing within global affairs (Phillips 2001, 2003). In line with those ideas, national strategies also involve innovation in the ways these countries address diaspora issues.

As usual, ideas did not travel by themselves, but rather they were embedded in performative acts and institutions. Presidential speeches and migration norms incorporated a distinctive characteristic in the last few years: the rhetorical emphasis on framing migration within human rights and development considerations and on articulating this with the identity of the bloc vis-à-vis global structures and processes. These elements were taken from the institutions and documents listed later, showing that migration policy networks and epistemic communities had an impact on the negotiation of migration policies because they met the two conditions specified in the literature: (1) their ideas were compatible with the beliefs and goals of the top decision makers and (2) they gained access to those actually making decisions (Haas 1992; Risse-Kappen 1995).

Indeed, framing migration policies around human rights and defining migration as a right clearly differentiates the South American approach from securitization and xenophobic trends in the North (Domenech 2007). On this point, former Brazilian president da Silva stated: "In MERCOSUR, we do not criminalize immigration"; he added, "While in other regions immigration is criminalized, here we build an open space."[20] Recent agreements within MERCOSUR have built upon this human rights–based approach, drawing on principles and ideas debated in several meetings of other regional networks and their publications, such as the Regional Conference on Migration and the South American Conference on Migration.[21] The latter has been crucial in disseminating those ideas and forging a consensus around the notion of migrants as subjects of rights and key actors in social transformations (Alfonso 2012:34–35; Texidó and Gurrieri 2012). Those meetings served to spur the ideas and policy recommendations of a number of research institutions, think tanks, and international organizations for the last 15 years.[22] Common themes emerged from all debates and declarations: the defense of human rights, the need to update migration policies and facilitate human mobility, the importance of improving consular services as part of a policy toward expatriates based on states' protection of migrants' rights, the condemnation of massive deportations and xenophobic attitudes, the promotion of intra- and interregional cooperation, the improvement of border controls, and the importance of expanding consultation forums. As the following chapters explain in detail, all these ideas informed outreach efforts toward emigrants.

Ideas then went beyond debate often to reach out to top policymakers and representatives of member states in global forums, thus having an impact on domestic, regional, and international decision making. For instance, the Declaration of Buenos Aires, endorsed by member states participating in the South American Conference on Migrations on 18 August 2013, summarized the regional consensus and recommended taking such concerns to discussions within the United Nations.[23] The synergies created by these forums and state bureaucracies are also worth noting. Grugel (2005) documents a number of initiatives (including research, publications, debates, networking, and national and transnational advocacy) by technicians and activists to advance claims for social citizenship and provide MERCOSUR with a social agenda. Some of these experts developed intense advocacy activities and close links with political parties and state officials that give them leverage over arguments that justify decisions and increase their impact on agenda setting. Experts' participation in transnational networks facilitates drawing on those experiences to recycle and propose ideas that may not be up for public debate but are reproduced in policy realms, contributing to the elaboration of shared understandings within those relatively close circles (Bellettini and Carrión 2008; Botto 2009, 2011).

In sum, the processes mentioned previously account for the (largely informal) process of socialization of regional elites and formation of policy consensus. Both dynamics are also crucial in explaining why and how harmonization of migration policies happened. Whereas social pressures and disputes among state offices have been suggested as a source of conflict in the trade area and, consequently, a constraint on regional integration (e.g., Gómez-Mera 2009), intrabureaucratic consensus and relative isolation of a few decision makers, together with the input provided by migration policy networks, help explain the relatively fast and consistent progress in the migration area. Most important, similar dynamics have affected the policymaking processes of initiatives toward diasporas. The chapters that follow include further evidence of this point.

The last source of impetus comes from the agency of the bloc's leading members. This is not surprising in a regional integration process that is mostly reliant on intergovernmental negotiations and in which low institutionalization is still the preferred option. Yet, it is not the most powerful member or the one holding clear and continuous leadership. The second largest leader, Argentina, has been working as an agenda-setter for migration management, indirectly shaping the pace, content, and institutional developments within this area of regional integration. Official documents and several policymakers involved in regional negotiations agree that Argentina has promoted and initiated the elaboration of projects and encouraged the discussion of the vast majority (around 90%) of the migration-related norms agreed upon within MERCO-SUR.[24] It is worth noting that this leadership role is compounded by the fact that Argentine legislation has been a model for the recent passing of similar laws or bills submitted in Uruguay, Paraguay, Chile, and Brazil.[25] In other words, Argentina has not been leading the intergovernmental negotiations on migration because of its relative power, but because of its initiative capacity within the regional policymaking process and the emulation effect of its national migration policy.

Argentina's proactive stance also helps to examine in detail how MER-COSUR members' foreign policies relate to domestic politics, as well as the tensions and contradictions of the Southern Cone approach to migration. Its activism at the regional level is only one dimension of the redefinition of its entire migration policy since 2003, when Migration Law no. 25871 was passed (see Chapter 6 for details). Consistent with the regional consensus, this law conceptualizes migration as a right, it is based on a broad notion of human rights (including equal rights for nationals and aliens, as well as a number of social rights for immigrants), and it makes explicit references to the regional dimension.

In Domenech's terms (2009), this law embodies a transition from the rhetoric of *exclusion* to the rhetoric of *inclusion*. The same author identifies the emergence in early 2000s of a new Argentine migration policy that "situates international migrations as part of international relations between countries, based on the notion of cooperation and as a key component of regional integration policies" (2009:34). Along a similar line, Alfonso (2012: 52) argues that, toward the mid-2000s, "when in Argentina under Néstor Kirchner the role of the state as a fundamental agent of development was vindicated and social inclusion and the defense of human rights were priorities, the criterion of 'MERCOSUR nationality' was an ideal tool to design the new migration policy." Yet, although the official discourse refers to an open door policy, the rationale of the 2004 plan to regularize the residency status of immigrants from neighboring countries (generally known as *Patria Grande*, meaning enlarged homeland) reveals the government's intention to collect information about residents in an irregular status; only then would the state be able to extract resources from them through taxes or contributions to the social security system. The assumption is that only by having official records of those immigrants could the state regulate and control a social sector that generates costs, competes with local labor for jobs, and could eventually alter the social order.[26] In the words of a former migration official involved in this policy: "an open migration policy that facilitates regularization is more functional to the concepts of security and labor transparency than a close, expulsive migration policy." (Alfonso 2012:16).

Despite a long-standing dispute for leadership within the bloc, Brazil has acquiesced to (rather than led) most of these initiatives. Secondary sources, as well as officials and specialists consulted for this study, agreed off the record that Brazil does not have many incentives to lead because immigration is not a pressing domestic issue for the country today, while Argentina is always eager to fill the leadership vacuum and take credit for progress in nonconflictive areas. Also, Argentina's proposals reflect a common bilateral concern with broadly defined governability and security issues (including both transnational crime and, mainly, domestic social order). This convergence is expressed in former Brazilian Foreign Minister Celso Amorin's words: "a politically stable, socially just and economically prosperous South America is a goal that must be pursued not just from a natural sense of solidarity, but also for the benefit of our progress and well-being" (quoted in Malamud 2011:7). Thus, the bloc leaders have shared a basic political understanding in this policy area. Coordinated action of the two foreign affairs bureaucracies (and, to a lesser extent, those of the ministries of interior) did the rest to articulate joint positions.

Analysis and Conclusions

The evidence presented in the previous sections indicates that MERCO-SUR made rapid progress in developing regional migration norms that are carried forward by UNASUR's regional citizenship project. This was possible due to a number of interrelated factors that have been largely neglected by the existing literature on South American regional integration and migration policy.[27] This chapter has situated the courting of diasporas in the framework of broader political processes and norms that embody the ways states are currently governing human mobility, including but not restricted to emigrants. This demonstrates that even if courting is still short of becoming full engagement, it is part of a broader dynamic that supports its continuity and might trigger further developments. From an analytical point of view, the regional dynamic helps to explain the politics of courting and situates courting within the context of transnational governance. Specific contributions of this analysis include the following.

First, this chapter shows that domestic socioeconomic conditions in individual states and unprecedented flows of intraregional migration with potential disturbing effects pushed human mobility up not only in the governments' agendas but also in the regional agendas and negotiations in the 2000s. The potential disturbing effects of such inflows become more prominent in the context of unstable socioeconomic conditions and unfinished processes of democratic consolidation. Such instability may create social demands and incentives for governments to recast their supporting coalitions around new ideas. This is in itself an analytical contribution because, while regime vulnerability and the instrumental use of regional cooperation to strengthen fragile democracies in the mid-1980s have been acknowledged (e.g., Parish and Peceny 2002), the impact of a pervasive context of instability on policymakers has not been contemplated in the theoretical discussion of regional integration and international migration.

Second, this chapter highlights that there has been a rhetorical and institutional regional turn away from market-oriented policies and toward sociopolitical issues in the past decade. This move is embodied today in national and regional coalitions and norms as the leaders in office agree on the need to bring the state back in to regulate socioeconomic relations and address long-postponed social issues; they also converge on the idea of linking domestic growth, equity, and regional governance. Leftist governments of different orientations have framed their interventionism in terms of remedies to past market-oriented policies and an assertive, distinctive voice in regional and global affairs, including migrants' protection and rights. These facts indicate that: (a) emigration policies based on human rights considerations are to be framed in such policy and discursive convergence; (b) postneoliberalism is leading to a new form of governability and has to be examined as such; and (c) the interaction between domestic politics and regional processes—a point further investigated in each case study—is analytically relevant.

Third, the previous analysis indicates that governmental discourses and practices have sought consensus, cooperation, and multilateral management of migration problems in the last 15 years. Such rhetoric has emphasized a distinctive approach to migration nurtured by advocacy groups and based not only on human rights considerations but also on the positive links between people's mobility, national development, and regional integration. Beyond regional blocs, the same ideas are further consolidated in the documents issued by other forums, namely the South American Conference on Migrations.[28] The role of transnational public–private policy networks has been crucial in this respect: even if informal and nonbinding ties prevail in those networks, they have a feedback effect on cooperation and domestic policy innovation. From an analytical point of view, this highlights that ideational arguments need to be taken seriously to account for the role of transnational policy networks and such hybrid forms of institutionalization that might keep regional policymaking moving forward and reinforce emigration policy convergence.

In other words, ideas have found effective carriers and feedback mechanisms, and they are becoming embodied in a regional normative consensus. This creates a propitious and fertile ground to apply similar principles and ideas in all dimensions of migration policy, including efforts to reach out to and protect citizens abroad and to demand reciprocity and equal treatment for them in host countries. To the extent that the consensus reinforces a positive view of regional migration, even states with low stakes in this policy area are likely to endorse state-led transnationalism. And indeed, these developments are seen as a win-win situation; anchoring initiatives in the human rights discourse is attuned with current times and would only yield political benefits at the domestic and international levels.[29] I gather from interviews that officials in all countries see no down sides to these policies, and they underestimate the potential for politicization. Their testimonies supports the view that the adoption of a technical view of migration issues has contributed to a narrative that depoliticizes its nature (Kunz 2011; Pécoud 2015). Moreover, in the view of some officials who often participate in regional negotiations, if South America advances toward a political union, as UNASUR aims to, the concern with emigrants might ultimately disappear or be subsumed in that broader project because, at least for migrants residing within the region, their rights, interests, and claims would be addressed and protected by such a union.[30]

Fourth, in the meantime, until such a goal materializes, the biregional dialogue is another arena in which these ideas are promoted. Sending and receiving countries have acknowledged shared responsibility and have agreed on the need to cooperate on the basis of a global approach to international migration. Tensions between the European Union's attempt to tighten rules regarding illegal immigration and Latin American countries' emphasis on migrant rights have been at the core of those conversations (CELAC 2012). Nevertheless, those ideas have been incorporated in declarations and various documents. The intention to cooperate subsists, and since 2009, it takes the form of the so-called Latin American and Caribbean-European Union Structured Dialogue on Migrations,[31] following up on the agreement of heads of state in their 2008 summit in Lima, Peru. The goal is to seek common solutions, guarantee the exercise of human rights of all migrants, and improve the management of international migration. The EU invested €3 million to fund a project on the strengthening of this dialogue.[32] Collaborations have revolved around several topics and have advanced so far through three general meetings.[33] The project provides one more piece of evidence of the public–private policy networks that feed transnational migration governance, because this ambitious endeavor is implemented not only by governmental offices but also by a partnership with the International Organization for Migration (IOM) and the *Fundación Internacional para Iberoamérica de Administración y Políticas Públicas* (FIIAPP, Ibero-American International Foundation of Administration and Public Policies).

In sum, the study of sending-state policies toward their emigrants cannot be confined to the state level of analysis as if it were a matter of solely unilateral initiatives. The commitment of South American states to managing migration multilaterally and cross-regional initiatives are good examples of emerging forms of governance at the transnational level. The emphasis on the shared responsibility of home and host countries, as well as on new arenas of public–private multilateral collaboration, suggest the need to analyze emigration policies in the context of new forms of state–society relations across borders, with profound implications for the exercise of citizens' rights and, ultimately, the quality of democratic governance.

Notes

1 The OIM estimates that in the past decade Europe has received 3.1 million South Americans, mainly coming from Ecuador, Colombia, Brazil, Argentina, and Peru. Eighty percent of them went to Spain (cf. Texidó and Gurrieri 2012:23). For a detailed analysis of trends within the Latin American-Southern Europe corridor, including differences within subregions and countries of origin, see CELAC (2012).
2 Today, it is estimated that immigrants of Latin American origin constitute 36.7% of the total immigrant population in Spain and 19.5% in Italy (CELAC 2012:27).
3 For information on the entire region, see Martínez Pizarro (2011) and SICREMI (2012). For details on individual countries, see SICREMI (2011).
4 On this process see, for instance, Cameron and Hershberg (2010), Levitsky and Roberts (2011), and Weyland et al. (2010).
5 For the most part, this section focuses only on MERCOSUR (Spanish acronym for Latin American Southern Cone Market) and UNASUR (Union of South American Nations). The latter is still a young regional organization that is taking baby steps on regional migration and citizenship based on the principles and norms adopted by the former. Argentina, Brazil, and Uruguay are founding members of MERCOSUR, together with Paraguay. Ecuador's membership is being discussed. All four countries analyzed in the following chapters are members of UNASUR.
6 For a list of all events shaping such common biregional agendas, see CELAC (2012), Chapter 5.
7 See Agreement of Residency for Nationals of MERCOSUR Member States, Bolivia, and Chile, MERCOSUR/RMI/CT/ACTA no. 04/02.
8 See UNASUR/CJEG/Decision no. 8/2012.
9 Interviews with officials who participated of that group meetings: Gabriel Servetto, chief official (ministro de segunda), Directorate of International Migrations, Ministry of Foreign Affairs of Argentina, and Nora Pérez Vichich, advisor, Directorate of International Migrations, Ministry of Foreign Affairs of Argentina, both in Buenos Aires, June 13, 2014; Ambassador Rodrigo do Amaral Souza, director, Department of Immigration and Legal Affairs, Ministry of Foreign Affairs of Brazil, Brasilia, May 28, 2014.
10 See Cartilla del Ciudadano del MERCOSUR, Edición 2010, Comisión de Representantes Permanentes del MERCOSUR, available at www.mercosur.int/innovaportal/file/2431/1/cartilla_ciudadano_mercosur_-_esp.pdf, accessed March 3, 2014.
11 See www.mercosur.int/innovaportal/file/2808/1/DEC_064–2010_ES_Estatuto%20de%20Cidadania.pdf, accessed March 3, 2014.
12 Just to mention an example, surveys of 864 poor settlements in the Buenos Aires suburban area conducted by an NGO indicate that over the last 5 years, 90 new shantytowns have formed, most of them originated in the seizing of public lands. The population living in very precarious conditions in those areas increased 55% in the last 10 years as a result of internal (from poor provinces) and foreign immigration; it involves today over half a million families, most of them formed by immigrants from neighboring countries (mainly from Paraguay and Bolivia). See *La Nación*, "En Cinco Años se Instalaron 90 Nuevas Villas en el GBA," October 5, 2011. More broadly,

statistics compiled by the 2004–2012 period show that 55% of the economically active population do not have formal jobs and access to social welfare benefits. Poverty affects 25% of the urban population, and because the most dynamic part of the economy "does not need" these sectors, their situation is worsening and becoming structural. It has been argued that conditions of social inequality, marginality in terms of the access to the formal labor market, and structural poverty have intensified in that period and translate in practice into "subcitizenship" for around four million people whose subsistence depends on state subsidies but who have no chance of real inclusion (cited in Pikielny, Astrid. 2014. "Agustín Salvia: El Gobierno ha Multiplicado los Efectos de la Desigualdad Social en un Contexto de Crecimiento." *La Nación.* January 5, Enfoques: 1).

13 I am referring to the occupation of public lands in Buenos Aires by thousands of poor people (mostly immigrants from slums in suburbs of the capital city), a failed forced eviction, violence, and domestic political infighting between the national and local governments that were triggered by the argument (by Buenos Aires' mayor) that the squatters were a direct consequence of the national government's overly permissive immigration policy. In the midst of institutional paralysis and the proliferation of around 30 squatters around the country, President Cristina Fernández de Kirchner resorted to the regional level to frame the dispute in terms of discrimination and to legitimate a number of principles and policies implemented in the last few years. During the bloc's summit of December 16–17, 2010, in Foz de Iguazú (Brazil), she urged MERCOSUR members to issue a declaration stating the bloc's condemnation of xenophobia; top officials took a stand against discrimination and linking immigration to crime, and negotiations for an agreement on the citizenship statute gained momentum. See *Clarín,* December 15–16, 2010, and *La Nación,* December 17, 2010.

14 Interview with Rubén Ruffi, director, MERCOSUR Political Directorate, Ministry of Foreign Affairs of Argentina, Buenos Aires, August 15, 2010.

15 Interviews with Nora Pérez Vichich, advisor, Directorate of International Migrations, Ministry of Foregin Affairs, Buenos Aires, August 13, 2010, and Adriana Alfonso, former director, National Directorate of Migrations of Argentina, Buenos Aires, August 10, 2010.

16 See details on MERCOSUR's official site: www.mercosur.int/index.jsp.

17 Within the Brazilian Foreign Affairs Ministry, the MERCOSUR Department is divided into two units: Divisão de Coordenaçaõ Econômica e Asuntos Comerciais do MERCOSUL and the Divisaõ de Asuntos Políticos, Institucionais, Jurídicos e Sociais do MERCOSUL (see www.itamaraty.gov.br/o-ministerio/conheca-o-ministerio/organograma). In 2010, MERCOSUR issues within the Argentine Ministry of Foreign Affairs were conducted by two directorates, the political and the economic one; bureaucratic units were renamed recently as Directorate of Economic and Commercial Affairs and Directorate of Institutional Affairs. There is also a new unit for Special Representation for Regional Economic Integration and Social Participation. See www.mrecic.gov.ar.

18 *The Economist,* December 20, 2005.

19 *MercoPress,* April 28, 2007.

20 See *Clarín,* December 17, 2010.

21 For details on the origin, evolution, and impact of these multilateral fora, see Ramírez and Alfaro (2010) and Hansen (2010).

22 Among others, the IOM (International Organization for Migration), CELADE (Population Division within the UN Economic Commission for Latin America and the Caribbean), CEMLA (Latin American Migratory Studies Center from Argentina), INCAMI (Catholic Chilean Institute for Migration), FCCAM (Catholic

Argentine Migration Commission Foundation), ILO (International Labour Organization), the UN Human Rights Commission, and FLACSO (Latin American School of Social Sciences, which has offices in several Latin American countries).

23 See http://csm-osumi.org/Archivos/DocCSM/DECLARACION%20DE%20 BUENOS%20AIRES_28agostoFINAL%20(1).pdf, accessed July 18, 2014.

24 Interviews with Facundo Nejamkis, member of the Minister's Cabinet, Argentine President's Office, and former official at the Commission of Permanent Representatives of MERCOSUR, Buenos Aires, August 4, 2010; Federico Agusti, director, International Affairs Office, National Directorate of Migration, Ministry of Interior, Buenos Aires, August 8, 2010; and Nora Pérez Vichich, advisor, Directorate of International Migrations, Foreign Affairs Ministry of Argentina, Buenos Aires, August 13, 2010. See also Foro Especializado Migratorio del Mercosur, Memoria Institucional, available at: www.migraciones.gov.ar/foro_migratorio/pdf/memoria_institucional.pdf.

25 For details, see Zurbriggen and Mondol (2010) and Texidó et al. (2003).

26 For details on this plan, see Nejamkis and Rivero Sierra (2010).

27 For instance, most studies on South American regional integration focus on the economic dimension of the project and are oblivious of migration issues, as well as of ideational factors; also, the impact of advocacy networks has been studied in various policy domains (e.g., Keck and Sikkink 1998) and regional integration processes (Peterson 2004 for the EU, among others) but remains largely underexplored in the case of MERCOSUR and UNASUR.

28 All the Conference's documents can be found at http://csm-osumi.org/?v= DocCSM.

29 Interview with Federico Agusti, Buenos Aires, August 8, 2010.

30 Interview with Gabriel Servetto, Buenos Aires, June 13, 2014.

31 See www.consilium.europa.eu/uedocs/cms_data/docs/pressdata/en/misc/108821. pdf, accessed May 3, 2015.

32 For details, see https://ec.europa.eu/europeaid/regions/latin-america/eu-celac_ en, accessed May 3, 2015.

33 See www.andes.info.ec/en/news/celac-gets-ready-bilateral-dialogue-eu-migration-and-post-15-agenda.html, accessed May 3, 2015.

Works Cited

Alfonso, Adriana. 2012. "Integración y Migraciones. El Tratamiento de la Variable Migratoria en el MERCOSUR y su Incidencia en la Política Argentina." Cuadernos Migratorios no. 3. Buenos Aires: Organización Internacional para las Migraciones.

Bellettini, Orazio and Melania Carrión. 2008. "Partidos Politicos y Think Tanks in Ecuador: ¿Unión Fallida o a la Espera de Conocerse?" Paper presented to the Overseas Development Institute, September.

Botto, Mercedes. 2009. "The Role of Epistemic Communities in the 'Makability' of Mercosur." In *The EU and World Regionalism: The Makability of Regions in the 21st Century* ed. by Philippe Lombaerde and Michael Schulz. Surrey, UK: Ashgate Publishing. pp. 171–185.

Botto, Mercedes. 2011, August. "Think Tanks en América Latina: Radiografía Comparada de un Nuevo Actor Politico." Documento de Trabajo no. 60. Buenos Aires: FLACSO.

Cameron, Maxwell A. and Eric Hershberg. eds. 2010. *Latin America's Left Turns: Politics, Policies and Trajectories of Change.* Boulder, CO: Lynne Rienner Publishers.

CELAC. 2012, December. *Compendio Estadístico sobre Migraciones entre CELAC y UE.* Santiago de Chile: Comunidad de Estados Latinoamericanos y Caribeños.

Ceriani Cernadas, Pablo. 2011. "Luces y Sombras en la Legislación Migratoria Latinoamericana." *Nueva Sociedad.* 233, Mayo–Junio: 68–86.

Comisión Económica para América Latina y el Caribe (CEPAL). 2006. "Cuatro Temas Centrales en Torno a la Migración Internacional, Derechos Humanos y Desarrollo." LC/L.2490. CEPAL, Trigésimo primer período de sesiones, Montevideo, Uruguay, 20–24 de Marzo.

Domenech, Eduardo E. 2007. "La Agenda Política Sobre Migraciones en América del Sur: El Caso de la Argentina." *Revue Européenne des Migrations Internationales.* 23(1): 71–94.

Domenech, Eduardo E. 2009. "La Visión Estatal Sobre las Migraciones en la Argentina Reciente: De la Retórica de la Exclusión a la Retórica de la Inclusión. In *Migración y Política: El Estado Interrogado,* coord. by Eduardo E. Domenech. Córdoba, Argentina: Universidad Nacional de Córdoba. pp. 21–70.

Escobar, Cristina. 2007. "Extraterritorial Political Rights and Dual Citizenship in Latin America." *Latin American Research Review.* 42(3): 43–75.

Gómez-Mera, Laura. 2009. "Domestic Constraints on Regional Cooperation: Explaining Trade Conflict in MERCOSUR." *Review of International Political Economy.* 16(5): 746–777.

Grugel, Jean. 2005. "Citizenship and Governance in Mercosur: Arguments for a Social Agenda." *Third World Quarterly.* 26(7): 1061–1076.

Gurrieri, Jorge. 2005. "El Proceso Consultivo en América del Sur: La Conferencia Sudamericana sobre Migraciones." Expert Group Meeting on International Migration and Development in Latin America and the Caribbean. Population Division, Department of Economic and Social Affairs, United Nations Secretariat. UN/POP/EGM-MIG/2005/06. Mexico City, November 30–December 2.

Haas, P.M. 1992. *Knowledge, Power, and International Policy Coordination.* Columbia: University of South Carolina Press.

Hansen, Randall. 2010. "An Assessment of Principal Regional Consultative Processes on Migration." Geneva, Switzerland: OIM, Migration Research Series, no. 38.

Keck, Margaret E. and Kathryn Sikkink. 1998. *Activists Beyond Borders: Advocacy Networks in International Politics.* Ithaca, NY: Cornell University Press.

Kunz, Rahel. 2011. "Depoliticization through partnership in the field of migration: the Mexico-US case." In *Multilayered Migration Governance. The promise of partnership,* ed. by Rahel Kunz, Sandra Lavenex and Marion Panizzon. London and New York: Routledge. pp. 283-310.

Levitsky, Steven and Kenneth M. Roberts. eds. 2011. *The Resurgence of the Latin American Left.* Baltimore, MD: The Johns Hopkins University Press.

Maguid, Alicia. 2007. "Migration Policies and Socioeconomic Boundaries in the South American Cone." In *Migration Without Borders: Essays on the Free Movement of People,* ed. by Antoine Pécoud and Paul de Guchteneire. Paris: UNESCO Publishing; New York: Berghahn Books. pp. 259–280.

Malamud, Andrés. 2011. "A Leader Without Followers? The Growing Divergence Between the Regional and Global Performance of Brazilian Foreign Policy." *Latin American Politics and Society.* 53(3): 1–24.

Margheritis, Ana. 2013. "Piecemeal Regional Integration in the Post-Neoliberal Era: Negotiating Migration Policies within MERCOSUR." *Review of International Political Economy.* 20(3), June: 541–575.

Mármora, Lelio. 2003. Políticas Migratorias Consensuadas en América Latina. *Estudios Migratorios Latinoamericanos.* 17(50), April: 111–141.

Martínez, Jorge and Daniela Vono. 2005. "Geografía Migratoria Intraregional de América Latina y el Caribe al Comienzo del Siglo XXI." *Revista de Geografía Norte Grande.* 34: 39–52. Santiago de Chile: Pontificia Universidad Católica de Chile.

Martínez Pizarro, Jorge. ed. 2008, September. "América Latina y el Caribe: Migración Internacional, Derechos Humanos y Desarrollo." LC/G. 2358-P. Santiago de Chile: CEPAL.

Martínez Pizarro, Jorge. ed. 2011, May. "Migración Internacional en América Latina y el Caribe. Nuevas Tendencias, Nuevos Enfoques." Santiago de Chile: CEPAL.

Martínez Pizarro, Jorge and María Fernanda Stang. 2006. "El Tratamiento Migratorio en los Espacios de Integración Subregional Sudamericana." *Papeles de Población.* 48: 77–106. Toluca, Mexico: Universidad Autónoma del Estado de México.

Nejamkis, Lucila and Fulvio A. Rivero Sierra. 2010. "Patria Grande: Consonancias y ¿Disonancias? Entre Políticas Públicas, Prácticas Políticas y Discursos. In *Migraciones y Mercosur: Una Relación Inconclusa,* dir. Susana Novick. Buenos Aires: Catálogos. pp. 73–94.

Novick, Susana, Alejandro Hener, and Pablo Dalle. 2005, December. "El Proceso de Integración Mercosur: De las Políticas Migratorias y de Seguridad a las Trayectorias de los Inmigrantes." Documentos de Trabajo no. 46. Buenos Aires: Instituto de Investigaciones Gino Germani, Universidad de Buenos Aires.

Parish, Randall and Mark Peceny. 2002. "Kantian Liberalism and the Collective Defense of Democracy in Latin America." *Journal of Peace Research.* 39(2): 229–250.

Pécoud, Antoine. 2015. *Depoliticising Migration. Global Governance and International Migration Narratives.* Basingstoke, UK: Palgrave Macmillan.

Peterson, John. 2004. "Policy Networks." In *European Integration Theory,* ed. by Antje Wiener and Thomas Diez. New York: Oxford University Press. pp. 117–136.

Pérez Vichich, Nora. 2007. "Fundamentos Teóricos del Tratamiento de la Movilidad de Personas en MERCOSUR." *Entelequia: Revista Interdisciplinar: Monográfico.* 7: 255–270.

Phillips, Nicola. 2001. "Regionalist Governance in the New Political Economy of Development: 'Relaunching' the MERCOSUR." *Third World Quarterly.* 22(4): 565–583.

Phillips, Nicola. 2003. "The Rise and Fall of Open Regionalism? Comparative Reflections on Regional Governance in the Southern Cone of Latin America." *Third World Quarterly.* 24(2): 217–234.

Ramírez G., Jacques and Yolanda A. Alfaro. 2010. "Espacios Multilaterales de Diálogo Migratorio: El Proceso Puebla y la Conferencia Sudamericana de Migración." *Andina Migrante.* 9: 2–13. Quito, Ecuador: SIMA/FLACSO.

Risse-Kapen, Thomas. 1995. *Bringing Transnational Relations Back In: Non-State Actors, Domestic Structures, and International Relations.* New York: Cambridge University Press.

SICREMI. 2011. "Migración Internacional en las Américas. Informes nacionales." Primer Informe del Sistema Continuo de Reportes sobre Migración

Internacional en las Américas. Washington, DC: Organización de los Estados Americanos.

SICREMI. 2012. "Migración Internacional en las Américas. Informe Anual." Segundo Informe del Sistema Continuo de Reportes sobre Migración Internacional en las Américas. Washington, DC: Organización de los Estados Americanos.

Texidó, Ezequiel and Jorge Gurrieri. 2012. *Panorama Migratorio de América del Sur 2012*. Buenos Aires: Organización Internacional Para las Migraciones.

Texidó, Ezequiel, Gladys Baer, Nora Pérez Vichich, Ana María Santestevan, and Charles P. Gomes. 2003. "Migraciones Laborales en Sudamérica: El Mercosur Ampliado." *Estudios Sobre Migraciones Internacionales*. 63. Ginebra: Oficina Internacional del Trabajo, Programa de Migraciones Internacionales.

Weyland, Kurt, Raúl L. Madrid, and Wendy Hunter. eds. 2010. *Leftists Governments in Latin America: Successes and Shortcomings*. New York: Cambridge University Press.

Zurbriggen, Cristina and Lenin Mondol, coords. 2010. *Estado Actual y Perspectivas de las Políticas Migratorias en el MERCOSUR*. Montevideo, Uruguay: FLACSO Uruguay/Logos.

4 Ecuador

Cultivating Transnational Links

Introduction

Ecuador is a tiny country of 283,520 square kilometers of land with a total population of 15.49 million people.[1] As explained later, around 10% of the total population was involved in the last massive emigration wave in the early 2000s, a figure that represented nearly 20% of the economically active population at the time. *Todos somos migrantes* (we are all migrants) became the slogan of a very active transnational policy developed by the Ecuadorian state a few years later.

Although this policy builds on some precedents and emulates similar policies in other countries, the initiative represents a departure from old ways of conceptualizing migration in Ecuador and differs from other cases. It includes several measures and programs aimed at reaching out not only to the emigrant community but also to migrants' associations in Ecuador and the public in general. It also involves the creation of new migration-related institutions within the state apparatus and new relations among bureaucratic units to deal with the issue. This has been done at a relatively fast pace. President Rafael Correa (2007–present) became personally involved in this policy; the references to the migration problem have been a constant in his political discourse. His administration has aimed at making this new policy orientation an integral part of its foreign policy and promoting it within Andean regional institutions and other international fora. The slogan touches on sensitive questions of national identity and calls for an active response from all sectors of society. Only very recently has migration policy been moving toward a more comprehensive, integrated approach that aims at addressing dimensions other than emigration, such as questions related to immigration, transit, and return.

Thus, the questions of why the Ecuadorian state has developed such an active and innovative migration policy under the Rafael Correa's administration, why they have done so now (i.e., only under this government), and what the political and policy implications for this are beg explanation.

Socioeconomic Conditions, Political Instability, and Emigration Waves

Ecuador returned to democracy in August 1979, right when the oil boom was generating positive expectations about development, economic growth, and distribution of wealth. Over three decades later, economic problems persisted, large sectors of the population found their expectations unmet, and political practices cast doubt on the strength and transparency of democratic institutions. The years between 1995 and 2005 were particularly critical in terms of political instability and worsening of economic conditions. Six presidents alternated in office in that period (or eight if one counts those who occupied the presidency for a few days).[2] This was compounded by accusations of corruption, social unrest, strikes, riots, and virulent street protests that reflected the loss of credibility and support of political elites. A combination of factors contributed to a dramatic economic crisis toward the end of the 1990s, with the concomitant losses in terms of wealth and jobs: the fall of oil prices in 1998; the decline in GDP growth and increasing fiscal deficit and external debt; deep recession and the difficulties of stabilizing the economy, which was on the verge of hyperinflation; the effect of the oscillation in atmospheric conditions in the tropical Pacific (known as *El Niño*) on the agricultural sector; the depreciation of the currency; default on part of the external debt; and, finally, the collapse of the banking system (Jácome 2004).

By all accounts, these processes impacted migration trends. Among other things, emigration increased considerably in the late 1990s and acquired different characteristics than in previous decades, bringing the issue to the public debate and to governments' attention. The most recent massive wave of out-migration from Ecuador took place between 1998 and 2004. It differed from previous ones in several respects: (a) instead of gradual and incremental migration, large outflows (nearly equivalent to those of the previous three-decade-long wave) occurred in the space of a few years in what became to be known among locals as "the big stampede"; (b) rather than individual decisions, it mainly reflected family projects; (c) in opposition to the rural emigration from small towns in the southern provinces of Azuay and Cañar and indigenous migrants from Otavalo, this time urban migrants (mostly from middle- and low-middle sectors whose living conditions worsened) led the emigration; (d) the number of women (and of women leading family displacements) increased significantly; (e) emigrants' profiles were more diverse not only in terms of gender but also age, educational level, and professional/occupational background (the most recent wave is predominantly female, younger, more educated, and more heterogeneous in terms of working experience); (f) the main factor affecting the decision to migrate was the deterioration of national economic conditions, accentuated by political instability and financial crises; and (g) the preferred destination was

Spain, leaving the United States in a second position for the first time in decades (Acosta et al. 2006:67–88; FLACSO/UNFPA 2006; Herrera et al. 2005:31–70; Ramírez Gallegos and Ramírez 2005).[3] As a result, Ecuadorians in Spain became the largest immigrant Latin American community, and the Ecuadorian state started to implement a series of measures to reach out to them.

The social, political, and economic implications of these emigration trends are considerable and help us understand states' initiatives. Some small cities (e.g., Loja, Riobamba) and important sectors of large cities (e.g., Guayaquil, Quito) were seriously affected by the outflow of people. Social life there has been transformed by the changes in family ties and practices. As mentioned, at the end of the 1990s, the flow represented 8% to 10% of the total population and 20% of the economically active population.[4] Remittances increased from $794 million in 1998 to $2.3 billion in 2005, thus becoming the second foreign exchange earner (behind oil exports) and crucial in families' incomes (Herrera 2007:190). Therefore, migration became an issue that, for better or worse, directly or indirectly touched almost every individual and family in Ecuador.[5] Migrants became relevant actors in a society that has been changing rapidly. They have been portrayed at times as the lucky fellows who would materialize everybody's dreams of social progress—cultural ambassadors and important channels for the country's projection in the international scene—and, alternatively, as victims of a process of decay, backwardness, and collective frustration. Either way, they became a constituency whose allegiance nobody could claim thus far. The migration problem progressively made its way into some politicians' discourses, namely Correa's. As in other sending countries, the phenomenon was supported and, to some extent, reinforced by the development of transnational networks and practices through which emigrants redefined their sense of belonging, associational links, commitments, customs, and identities.

A New Approach to Emigration

Early steps toward a state-led policy were the 1998 National Plan of Human Rights, elaborated by the Ministry of Foreign Affairs, including a chapter on migrants; a number of bills and projects discussed in Congress; and the increasing salience of the issue in media and academic and social organizations' discussions toward the end of that decade. This was compounded by the creation of new migrants' associations in Spain and their sister institutions in Ecuador led by emigrants' relatives, a discussion I resume in Chapter 8.[6] As Eguiguren Jiménez (2009) indicates, a few big changes occurred at that time that had implications for the policies that followed: in contrast to previous decades of silence about the migration problem, the issue rose to the top of the agendas for both public and private institutions, public authorities defined it as an area of state intervention, and the crisis was identified as the primary cause of massive emigration.

During the first half of the 2000s, several other milestones paved the way for further state involvement, such as the implementation of a National Plan of Ecuadorians Abroad (also designed by the Ministry of Foreign Affairs) in 2001, which aimed at improving the performance of consulates and, consequently, the services provided to citizens living abroad, as well as the general management of migration-related issues such as irregular or illegal status, cultural links, electoral participation, plans to return, remittances, deportation, and so forth. An agreement with Spain was also reached the same year for the regularization of Ecuadorian immigrants and regulation of future flows. Other important antecedents included the creation of the Fund for Support, Savings, and Investments for Migrants and their Families in 2002, which provided assistance to indebted migrants or those who planned an investment in the home country; the creation of the Corporation of Aid to Ecuadorian Migrants in 2003 (which dissolved later the same year); and the implementation of new requirements for Colombian immigrants concerning criminal records in 2004 (Arízaga 2005; Vono de Vilhena 2006). These three initiatives originated in the presidency while Congress was simultaneously considering several bills concerning the regulation of migration flows, including the proposal of a comprehensive law that would help Ecuadorian migrants and their families. When analyzing those projects, Eguiguren Jiménez (2009:40) identifies another important change at the level of discourse: the intention to protect and compensate migrants for the risks and costs of emigrating and the recurring reference to migrants and their families as new subjects of legislation. In addition, in 2006, Ecuadorians abroad were able to vote in national elections for the first time (a right introduced in the Constitution by the 1998 reform).

Since then, significant ideational and institutional changes followed suit at a relatively fast pace, indicating the increasing importance and political relevance of the migration issue, as well as the intention for Ecuador to innovate on this policy area and become a leader or model for other countries in the region. In only two years (2005–2007) the efforts to design, institutionalize, and implement a new and comprehensive migration policy intensified. The topic was incorporated in the National Plan of Foreign Policy for 2006–2020 (known as PLANEX 2020), which redefined the goals of foreign policy and included emigrants' protection among them; it also made explicit the government's intention to have a fluid dialogue with Ecuadorians abroad and offer protection to them and their families.

The plan was ratified under the government of Rafael Correa, whose presidential campaign emphasized, in opposition to other candidates' lack of ideas on the subject, a concrete proposal of a migration policy, including political representation of expatriates in legislative bodies and the creation of a special office to take care of the well-being of Ecuadorians residing abroad. As explained later, these initiatives implied a redefinition of the role of migrants. In this respect, Correa parallels the case of former Mexican president Vicente Fox, who explicitly addressed Mexicans in the United States in his presidential campaign as heroes (in opposition to former pejorative characterizations) who represented not only an important sector of his constituency but also a crucial part of the Mexican nation (Kunz 2008:12–13).

In a similar fashion, Correa courted the diaspora during the electoral campaign, promised that his administration would be the "migrants' government," and held several meetings with associations when campaigning abroad. He also framed the issue in terms of "that national tragedy called migration" (in reference to the expulsion of Ecuadorians from their homeland) and argued that the implementation of neoliberal policies was the cause of it (Inaugural Speech to Congress in Lucas 2007:295, 304).

This was also in line with similar discursive mechanisms recently used in neighboring countries. For instance, like Correa, former Peruvian president Alejandro Toledo convoked the diaspora to a process of national (political, social, and economic) reconstruction in 2001 and named it the *Quinto Suyo*, in reference to the fifth imaginary province residing outside the national territory; Bolivian president Evo Morales has frequently appealed to nationhood bonds and the idea of one single nation, regardless of where nationals reside, when requesting help from those abroad to reconstruct the country; and in 2002, former Brazilian president Fernando Henrique Cardoso convoked emigrants to return to their homeland, linking nationals to their place of origin and arguing that the country needed them (Domenech 2009; Green 2008:423; Tamagno and Berg 2003). Yet, Ecuador differs from other cases in the region. Overall, Correa's approach to emigrants is relatively less focused on strengthening cultural links and capturing emigrants' votes, which are relatively few and elusive (see Chapter 8), than on linking migration to national problems and using human rights-centered discourse as a way of strengthening the identity of his political coalition.

Thus, under his administration, a number of initiatives and bureaucratic changes have been prioritized, indicating the intention to have a proactive and innovative stance in this policy realm. It is worth noting that, following a trend starting in the early 2000s with the so-called Tables of Dialogue on Migration and involving private and public actors, during Correa's campaign and immediately after taking office, the first stage of migration policy-making involved an intense process of consultation with NGOs, religious institutions, migrants' associations, local authorities, the media, and academic institutions. (This stands in contrast to other examples of state-led transnationalism in South America in which intense consultation of a broad array of social groups is not the norm except, to some extent, in Brazil.)[7]

The president's sister, Pierina Correa, coordinated some of these initial activities. However, given the characteristics of the decision-making process and the president's leadership style (explained in the next section), together with the lack of regular consultation today, Correa's initial purpose seems related to sensing social demands and catering to some key groups rather than promoting substantive participation and inclusion.

This ambivalence toward political participation is consistent with the form of populism (negligent of institutions, personalist, antipolitics, and clientelistic) he promoted in general (Freidenberg 2008). It is also consistent with the initiatives of other leaders in the region who came to office in the midst of similar circumstances. The Kirchners' governments in Argentina since 2003 are a case in point (see details in Chapter 6). Suffice it to say here that, also an outsider with no teams or consolidated supporting coalition, Néstor Kirchner tied state-led transnationalism to a re-foundational political project aimed at social reparation after the devastating 2001 crisis. He capitalized on social disappointment with institutions and elites whose policies encouraged emigration, thus forging his distinctive political identity through opposition to past incumbents and policies. He also appealed to the symbolic content of the human rights discourse and traumatic social memories to gather the support of specific constituencies and propose "reparatory" measures; like Correa, he was the main spokesman of this position.

At the level of ideas, migration started to be framed in the language of human rights in Ecuador. Although there is a reference to the importance of preserving community and cultural ties, like in most cases of state-led transnationalism worldwide, the emphasis is on the protection and dignity of emigrants' rights. According to Koller (2009–2010:62), the reasons to use rights as the cornerstone of the political discourse are to be found in Correa's goals: to raise the international profile of Ecuador as a country of both immigration and emigration, to reinforce the political legitimacy of his government, and to manage migrants' interests. More specifically, four rights have been the focus of this approach: free circulation, the right to choose not to migrate, fair social and labor conditions, and the right to preserve cultural identity (Vono de Vilhena 2006). Increasing activism of social and religious organizations that met to discuss the problem contributed to shaping these notions and channeled not only ideas but also pressure to place the issue more saliently in the governmental agenda.

It is worth noting that, by all accounts, the role of NGOs has been crucial in the initial agenda-setting process, while political parties offered only partial, vague, or no proposals on the subject. Also, several of those social actors and intellectuals became public officials in charge of migration policy in Ecuador; thus, the ideas driving migration policy are also rooted in their advocacy for a reform of the state and a development process based on the notion of *sumak kawsay* (good living in Quichua).[8] Again, by linking migration to indigenous claims, old ethnic cleavages, and the historical evolution of political and economic institutions, Ecuador differs from other cases of state-led transnationalism. The reasons for doing so are found in Correa's need to build a supporting coalition and the identity of his emerging political party.

Regarding institutions, the initiative that has attracted the most attention and is portrayed as a sign of how innovative Ecuador wants to be in this policy area was the creation of the National Secretariat of the Migrant in 2007 (thereafter SENAMI, its acronym in Spanish), a new office created by Presidential Decree #150 within the organizational structure of the presidency (and reporting directly to the president) but enjoying for some years an ambiguous ministerial status. (I will come back to the bureaucratic and political implications of this point later.)

The SENAMI may partially be seen as the ultimate result of the restructuring of consular services initiated early that decade when emigrants' flows increased considerably and consular offices multiplied, incorporated technical personnel, and changed bureaucratic procedures to respond to an overwhelming number of demands. The new office superseded its predecessors: the General Directorate of Support to Ecuadorians Abroad, the Under-Secretariat of Migration and Consular Affairs, and the Under-Secretariat of Migration and Consular Relations—all of them within the Ministry of Foreign Affairs and mostly focused on providing services, assistance, and advising to migrants trying to regularize their legal situations or solve labor-related problems.

This institutional development contrasts with the path taken by neighboring countries. For instance, the Under-Secretariat of Peruvian Communities Abroad was created within the Peruvian Ministry of Foreign Affairs in 2001; this and other measures, including the creation of Consultation Councils to promote dialogue and cooperation between communities abroad and consular authorities, paved the way for a more clear definition of a migration policy in that country toward 2005 (SIMA 2009; Tamagno and Berg 2003). But overall, Peru (as well as Bolivia, Colombia, Argentina, and Brazil) has maintained a more traditional approach: while the government has been supporting the creation of a transnational space, it has done so through traditional mechanisms, such as the consular offices and services, and following an approach based on assistance rather than rights. Peruvian officials, for instance, consider this a more fruitful way to address the migration problem than the Ecuadorian politicization of the issue, and they do not frame emigration in terms of crisis, loss, and tragedy, although the number of Peruvian emigrants has increased lately.[9]

In sum, issues related to nationals abroad usually fall within the foreign ministry; no other Latin American country has an institution with such a level of autonomy and salience in the bureaucratic structure— not even Mexico, which probably has the widest and most institutionalized network of relations that link federal agencies, local governments, hometown associations, and other migrant groups. As it will be explained in Chapter 9, the *Instituto de los Mexicanos en el Exterior* (IME, Institute for Mexicans Abroad), established in 2003, is a decentralized agency of the Ministry of Foreign Affairs, which has carried out the Mexican Communities Abroad Program since 1990.[10]

Instead, the SENAMI embodies the strategy used by the Correa administration to position the issue of migration at home and abroad and to link it to the reform of the entire state apparatus. According to several testimonies, it also reflects the negative view the president has of consular offices, which he formed through first-hand (apparently disappointing) experiences when he was a student in the United States. The initial goals of the new secretariat were: the international diffusion of a migration policy based on the idea of rights, the promotion of migrants' and their families' human development, the strengthening of ties between migrants and home society, the support of voluntary return, and the promotion of multiculturalism and universal citizenship (SENAMI 2007). Since its creation, the secretariat has been actively diffused information about migration in general, expanded its personnel and facilities, opened offices in other countries,[11] and launched a considerable number of programs and activities that address various dimensions of migrants' lives.

The SENAMI carried out these tasks according to the detailed declaration of intentions, goals, and a schedule established in the secretariat's master document, the National Plan of Human Development for Migrations, 2007–2010,[12] in which migration policy is explicitly linked to the "citizens' revolution" proposed by Correa, the protection of migrants' rights is presented as a key guiding principle, and migrants' contributions to the economic and social development of the country are recognized. Moreover, the specific goals, performance criteria, and policies to be implemented were presented in close relation to the National Plan of Development proposed by the National Secretariat of Planning and Development (SENPLADES) and to foreign policy positions and actions, thus indicating the role of migration policy within an ambitious reform of the state.

A comprehensive analysis of the performance of the SENAMI exceeds the limits and purpose of this work. Suffice it to say that, according to the Ministry of Coordination's evaluation, the SENAMI has correctly followed the new organizational standard procedures contained in the National Development Plan and has attained the proposed goals and budget considerations established in the governability system (known as SIGOB) that oversees the performance of public institutions,[13] although its roles and achievements tended to be loaded to gain political visibility and avoid being absorbed by any ministry.[14] Most important for the perspective of this study, the SENAMI's performance at the regional and international levels is revealing of the motivations and timing behind this policy. The Correa administration has aimed at setting a migration agenda within the Community of Andean Nations (CAN) during Ecuador's presidency pro-tempore (2007–2009) and, to a large extent, the initiatives were welcomed because they might help to revive this 40-year-old institution that has lost its sense of purpose and influence in the region. Among other things, Ecuador led discussions within the Andean Forum for the elaboration of a Plan of Human Development of Migrations reflecting Ecuador's concern with migrants' rights instead of the traditional security and economic concerns. In other words, Ecuador "Andeanized" its migration policy.[15] Ecuador has also taken the same proposal to other international forums within South America and beyond (e.g., MERCOSUR, UNASUR, the World Social Forum on Migrations, and the South American Conference on Migrations); the goal has been to work as an agenda-setter, to promote a redefinition of the migration problem in terms of human rights, and to lead a regional bloc that might set the issue in multilateral discussions and negotiate collectively vis-à-vis receiving countries. In addition, SENAMI's officials advised governments in other countries (e.g., Paraguay, Morocco, Honduras). It is too early to assess how the SENAMI's recent incorporation to the institutional structure of the Ministry of Foreign Affairs will impact such international projection –a point that is addressed later in this chapter.

Another controversial measure was the attempt to encourage savings and productive investments, to tax emigrants' assets, and to channel remittances to entrepreneurial activities in Ecuador. Again, the SENAMI played a role in the implementation of some of these initiatives,[16] which were seen as excessive state interventionism in individuals' finances and their relationships with their families.[17] Moreover, this attempt was also phrased in a normative discourse that portrays migrants as economic agents and links them to a national project of reconstruction and development. This reinforces, in the social imagination, old ideas about migration as a means to attain a dream—that of progress by way of a trip to the North, the place of modernity, success, and development. As Vallejo (2004) suggests, the state's responses to transnational migration reflect some deep structural and normative changes in the subjective notion of development: in the neoliberal era, the agency of progress is transferred from the state to the individual because the state can no longer fulfill that promise. Thus, emigration is much more than a response to unemployment and poverty; it represents the redefinition of personal trajectories in close connection to a national political and economic project.

Finally, two other major developments taken as indicators of Ecuador's commitment to an innovative migration policy are (1) the inclusion in the 2008 constitution of numerous articles about human mobility and migration-related issues and (2) migrants' formal representation in the legislative process. The new constitution is considered a milestone in the process of guaranteeing migrants' rights. Among other provisions, it includes the state's commitment to defining and implementing a migration policy that will support those rights; it promotes no discrimination against migrants; it proclaims the ideal of universal citizenship and its promotion at the regional (Latin American) level; it promises migrants and their families protection and assistance in their transit and place of destination; it offers them voting rights and political representation; it encourages the strengthening of family and nationhood links; and it promotes the investment of migrants' resources in activities that would benefit them and the country as well (SENAMI 2008). Some of these clauses reflect the proposals submitted by Ecuadorian migrants residing in Italy and Spain to the National Constitutional Assembly early in 2008.[18] Moreover, six seats within the assembly were awarded for elected representatives of Ecuadorians living abroad; these were divided into regions (two representatives for those residing in Europe, two for those in the United States and Canada, and two for those in Latin America). In this respect, Ecuador follows the international trend of granting to emigrants political representation and a voice in home politics.

Problems and Tensions in the New Migration Policy

A number of contradictions and tensions emerged from the Ecuadorian state's attempt to engage in innovative transnational policies. Some of them are related to the political rationale behind such policies, others make evident some policy inconsistencies in conceptual and ideological terms, and others still question the degree and character of innovation.

First, the official migration discourse is inconsistent and not honored in practice. Although the discourse advocates for the defense of human rights in general and the protection of migrants' rights abroad in particular, it turns to securitization of migration issues when it comes to immigrants from neighboring countries, especially Colombia, with whom diplomatic relations have been strained in the last few years and negative stereotyping applies.[19] Moreover, it advocates for a strong role of the state and interventionism to promote national development while targeting the establishment of universal citizenship, a somewhat idealized and vaguely defined concept that inherently goes against the notion of sovereign territorial nation-states because it can only be attained within a different kind of political organization that eventually supersedes states. Also, although Correa's political discourse gathers old ideas about development and good living, is critical of neoliberal policies, and often refers to 21st century socialism, economic policy in Ecuador has remained within market-oriented principles, dollarization, and a largely unchanged distribution of wealth. In other words, collective interests are invoked, but economic and migration policies rely on an individual-centered notion of development.

Second, although SENAMI was created under the assumption that centralization in a single institution would lead to better coordination of actions and higher efficiency, it hardly lived up to that goal. Top-ranking officials in this office argued that this institution represents a more modern, progressive, and inclusive approach in comparison to traditional migration policies that fall within the sphere of foreign affairs ministries.[20] All people interviewed agreed that despite good intentions, considerable resources, and sound programs, the SENAMI was constantly caught in political battles largely because its jurisdiction, role, and status were still contested and overlapped with those of the Ministry of Foreign Affairs and other bureaucratic units. There were attempts to solve this problem (several drafts of a formal agreement between the ministry and the secretariat circulated, establishing a clear mission and set of functions for the latter, as well as areas of cooperation between the two) with no success. Overlapping of functions, dual criteria in decision making, and lack of coordination have been persistent problems up to the end of SENAMI's autonomous period.[21]

Indeed, a new chapter of SENAMI's evolution started in November 2012 when Correa reappointed Lorena Escudero as national secretary (a controversial figure who held that same position between 2007 and 2010). He also confirmed that the transfer of the headquarters to a large new building under construction in the city of Azogues was launched,[22] and a new status for SENAMI was announced. As per Presidential Decree #20 of June 10, 2013, the secretariat was transformed into the Vice Ministry of Human Mobility and incorporated in the administrative structure of the Ministry of Foreign Affairs.[23] This new status became effective in September 2013.[24] The new building took longer than expected to be finished.[25] As per the presidential decree above, a new vice minister was appointed and the internal structure of the vice-ministry was defined: The Vice-Ministry is composed of three Under-Secretariats: of Migration and Consular Services; Ecuadorian Migrant Community, and Assistance to Immigrants. Two new units to address specific issues are to be added: Protection of the Migrant Community and Assistance to Returnees.[26]

Some of the SENAMI's programs are expected to be taken over by other ministries and agencies while its offices and activities abroad are being absorbed by consulates. In addition, a more integrated approach to migration problems has started to emerge lately: discussions around a bill to pass a human mobility law took place last year. These forums revived the dialogue with migrant associations at home and abroad, among other social actors, and conveyed the government's intention to further improve consular services, reach out to emigrants, defend their rights, and address problems generated by other flows, too, such as immigration, transit, and return.

It remains to be seen if these changes bring recurrent problems. Until now, frequent institutional changes and policy inconsistency have affected not only the practice but also the content of migration policy, since SENAMI tended to emphasize rights while other units focused on consular services (e.g., the Ministry of Foreign Affairs) or security issues (e.g., the Ministry of Government). The source of these problems is to be found in a factor that resonates in several other Latin American cases: unfinished and ill-defined efforts to produce drastic changes within the state apparatus. Such efforts gained momentum and specific intensity under Correa, thus illustrating a feature that differentiates Ecuador from Uruguay and from other cases, too.

The third tension lies in the fact that the proposed reform of the state is mostly a work in progress with uncertain effects. The main responsibility for it was been assigned to the National Secretariat of Planning and Development (SENPLADES), which is committed to a rapid and drastic reformulation of the role and capacities of the state along the developmental, interventionist, and nationalist lines that guide Correa's citizens' revolution (Ramírez Gallegos and Minteguiada 2007). Thus, changes affecting the migration policy area have included the disaggregation of functions along a larger number of ministries and the creation of new ones to coordinate all of them in 2007[27]—all of which are subject to a complex and endless bureaucratic reorganization that aims to apply highly technical principles and evaluation mechanisms to all agencies under the previously mentioned governability system. However, all officials interviewed agreed on the vagueness of this new organizational structure and the uncertainty about whether this has improved the efficiency and transparency of the public administration. They also agreed on the negative impact of high centralization of decision-making power at the level of the presidency, Correa's tendency toward micromanagement, and his discretionary, very demanding, technical-oriented, and quasi-authoritarian style. This is certainly compounded by the fact that political reforms have been almost a constant in Ecuador in the last three decades, giving place to permanent uncertainty, weak institutionalization, intense political disputes (often including disputes about the norms to rule political practices), and increased inefficiency in the public administration (Pachano 2007).

The underlying logic of the ministerial reorganization is that the state had to be re-founded through the so-called ruptures, and this would make coordination and the institutionalization of policies possible so that they become long-term, consistent *políticas de Estado* (state policies). However, public officials interviewed found it difficult to define this strategy in clear terms and even showed some confusion about their public role (that is, they talk of their positions as belonging to the state apparatus at times, and they also talk of the state as an external actor as if their offices were not included within it). As mentioned previously, some of them were previously activists and/or members of NGOs and have a technocratic profile; thus, they reflect a partial renewal of bureaucratic cadres that, according to several people interviewed, gather a considerable number of relatively young, recently graduated professionals. In addition, many of them are women (in a social context that remains relatively conservative and sexist). For most of these young officials, this is their first experience working for a public institution, and some still work as consultants for private organizations, which may partially explain the confusion about the public–private sphere.[28]

In particular, all people interviewed agreed on the identification of interbureaucratic struggles (fueled by the generational gap between young, recently arrived technicians who often ignore and underestimate standard procedures and old bureaucratic cadres) as a factor that has policy implications. In particular, these clashes have been considered one of main obstacles to the successful implementation of a migration policy. Some officials would argue off the record that inexperienced technicians and activists transformed the SENAMI into a quasi-NGO in terms of the management style and the number and type of programs it pursued. In addition, although a special status was negotiated and approved for the SENAMI's officials working abroad, there are many other procedures around which tensions and conflicts arose daily between the SENAMI and the Ministry of Foreign Affairs in the past years, sometimes leading to the resignation of appointees and undermining policy continuity and consistency.[29] Some officials interviewed also mentioned that institutional changes advanced so fast that there was not much time for policy design and improvement; they feel overwhelmed by deadlines and the demands coming from the presidency, as well as growing expectations from emigrants, their associations, and society at large.[30] There have been constant rumors about dismissals and appointments, and turnover of officials was relatively higher than in other bureaucratic units (the head of the secretariat changed three times in the two initial years; the renewal of lower-ranking appointees was more frequent, mostly because of internal infighting). Correa's personal involvement tended to add confusion (e.g., he announced the plan discussed next without consulting with the specialists, taking everybody by surprise). It is expected that the recent institutional changes explained previously will translate into a more comprehensive, integrative, and consistent approach to the entire migration policy, in line with the broader label adopted: human mobility—that is, not just emigration but all types of migration flows.[31]

Fourth, the Voluntary Return Plan was launched in 2008 and was the source of several controversies. The plan was included in the initiative called "Welcome Home," and it aimed to encompass both physical return and the recuperation of emigrants' capacities; it recognizes migrants as subjects (i.e., agents) of development; and it facilitated not only the trip back but also the search for jobs and economic activities that may make the return sustainable in the long run.[32] Besides facing some implementation problems (e.g., delays, bureaucratic obstacles), this and related initiatives presented some inconsistencies. On the one hand, the SENAMI framed return in the context of broader ideas that have been shaping its migration approach: a project of national reconstruction in which emigration is seen as temporary; the need to include those who are absent; the notion that *patria* (fatherland) is "made by all of us"; and the idea that migration is an option, not an escape valve—the slogans being *estamos arreglando la casa para que vuelvan* (we are rebuilding the house so that you can return), *somos todos migrantes* (we are all migrants), and *bienvenidos a casa* (welcome back home).[33] On the other hand, the reliance of the Ecuadorian economy on remittances as a second source of foreign exchange and the limited capacity to offer jobs and good wages to potential returnees cast doubts on the viability and desirability of such a plan. It places postneoliberal arguments at odds with the "privatization" of the notion of development mentioned in the previous section. In other words, the government criticizes neoliberalism and, at the same time, implements policies based on an individual-centered, market-oriented liberal principles.

Analysis and Conclusions

In terms of the dimensions of policy trajectory that this project compares, the case of Ecuador offers some similarities and contrasts with other South American countries. As in most other cases, the historical antecedents of state interest in emigration are scarce, and the time of launching courting attempts coincides with the aftermath of a crisis and the formation of a new political governing coalition with a postneoliberal discourse.

A long crisis of political representation and persistent political instability is the background against which the redefinition of the migration problem and the attempt to construct and court the diaspora occurred in Ecuador. These conditions help to explain the political maneuvers involved in policy innovations. A new migration policy started to take shape when Rafael Correa became a presidential candidate, and it gained momentum once he took power. This policy built upon the activism of social organizations of various sorts and was presented as a necessary response to an unprecedented, critical situation (i.e., massive emigration). It fit perfectly the political needs of a loose electoral coalition that had neither political identity nor technical cadres to draw upon. The use of a highly symbolic and sensitive issue affecting almost the entire population allowed Alianza PAIS (Patria Altiva y Soberana, the coalition supporting Correa) to amalgamate diverse groups and views on the matter, differentiate itself from other political forces (the ones identified with the crisis that provoked emigration), and tie migration policy to an antipolitics and antineoliberal discourse. As one of the main protagonists put it, "Migration might not be a priority but is a flag."[34]

Regarding the policy instruments, this case exhibits similarities with others in the type of measures (e.g., rhetorical shift, institutional developments, enfranchisement, linkage programs) but differs considerably in the scope and intensity of diaspora engagement mechanisms. The top-down initiatives explained previously created a subject for new policies, a new constituency on the basis of migrant identity rather than party identity, and a realm on which the state has expanded its interventionism. For the most proactive part of the process, a new institution with relatively high institutional status and considerable resources carried out courting at home and at the destination. SENAMI, with offices in the main receiving countries and a powerful mandate, embodied then the most ambitious form of state-led transnationalism across long distances. The new policy also represents a shift in the relationship between state and society to the extent that it frames migration in a broader, long-term, re-foundational national project that, despite the central and highly paternalistic role reserved to the state, puts the burden of development on the shoulders of individual citizens. Moreover, the new approach has revolved around migrants' rights and, based on that discourse, it has been a tool to enhance Ecuador's international profile in regional organizations within and beyond South America.

Therefore, this case confirms the importance of the role of the state in shaping social involvement in transnational policies, as Ecuador has developed an intense outreach activity at destinations, too. It also suggests revisiting and refining arguments about the size, economic impact, and level of mobilization of the emigrant community. No doubt, the concern with remittances and investments by returnees played a role in bringing the issue to the top of the agenda. However, the volume of emigrant flows (and its importance in terms the possibility of capturing remittances or votes) is only one of the incentives for a sending state to develop transnational policies. Ecuador points out some other relatively underexplored variables that help explain the timing, motivation, and impact of state-led transnationalism.

First, the positive and negative connotations the diaspora evokes in the social imagination (i.e., hope in the possibility of progress and success, together with generalized disruption of the social fabric) give policy-makers the possibility of appealing to very sensitive issues and redefining the identity and role of nationals abroad; in Ecuador, such redefinition entailed their becoming key agents in the transformation of the country and the subjects of rights. By doing so, the state not only develops a new area of intervention, but also provides the resources through which emergent political forces (like Alianza PAIS), brought to power by precarious electoral coalitions, may acquire identity and reach out to diverse constituencies.

Second, the central role of the executive power as an agenda-setter (rather than political parties, as most of the literature emphasizes), stands out. This is typical of highly centralized presidential systems with weak institutions which facilitate the conversion of the president's stance into a rapid advance of his initiatives—more so in the midst of serious crisis of political representation. In this respect, Correa follows old political practices in the region. Despite his technocratic profile and preference for bureaucratic reform, he has concentrated decision-making power and has cultivated a personalistic and caudillo-like style. His personal involvement raised the profile of migration issues, tied them to national causes, and complicated and accelerated the timing of policy implementation. Some of these features mirror political processes in Uruguay, where the importance of the president's role is confirmed. Argentina and Brazil also support this point by showing what happens when the president is not the engine of the innovation process.

Third, the existence of specific political projects that may benefit from innovations may accelerate change. This is particularly so in neo-populist governments led by outsiders or nontraditional politicians who claim to embody an ambiguously defined *pueblo* (the people) and a re-foundational political project (usually in the aftermath of a dramatic crisis). Correa provides a good example of the political representation mechanisms that characterize neopopulism in Latin America today, notably in Argentina within the small sample considered here. In other words, he is the atypical leader that filled the void left by the collapse of political institutions, appeals to an antipolitics discourse, and dispenses with intermediaries in his relationship with mass constituencies. While building on these tools to construct his political project, he anchored migration on human rights, linked it to indigenous claims and old ethnic cleavages, and, as mentioned, made good use of migration as a flag.

These characteristics of the political regime are closely linked to a fourth factor: the impact of unfinished and fragile democratization processes on states' capacities and policy content and outcomes. The ongoing reform of the state in Ecuador is not just a caprice of a new generation of public officials attuned to diverse notions of development and an old paternalistic view of the state. It is a late response to the need to adapt governance techniques in a new era, one that under postneoliberal discourses still expects the state to provide the solutions to its own collapse. As in all other cases, state adaptation is at the forefront of the explanation. The inconsistencies and tensions identified in emigration policies reflect the desperate compromise of transitional democracies between providing public goods and privatizing socioeconomic development. As it is explained in the following chapters, a different equilibrium has been attained in other South American countries.

Finally, the evidence shows that Ecuadorian state-led transnationalism not only shares some traits with other cases in terms of the mechanisms used to reach out to the diaspora, but it also departs from other countries in pursuing a leadership role in the region, acting as a model, and brokering proposals that might be taken to negotiations with receiving countries. Only Argentina has acted along similar lines within regional organizations, though in a more limited and intermittent fashion. This points out a fifth important variable that supports the arguments made in Chapter 3: the role of foreign policy, multilateral agreements, and international (especially regional) organizations in shaping a normative consensus about the content of transnational policies, leading to policy convergence across countries.

Notes

1 2012 World Bank figures. See http://data.worldbank.org/country/ecuador, accessed May 2, 2014.

2 I am referring to Abdalá Bucaram (1996–1997), Fabián Alarcón (1997–1998), Jamil Mahuad (1998–2000), Gustavo Noboa (2000–2003), Lucio Gutiérrez (2003–2005), and Alfredo Palacio (2005–2007). Vice President Rosalía Arteaga was president for 2 days in February 1997. The 2000 coup brought to power a *junta* (a collective body formed by some military and indigenous leaders) for a short time.

3 At the same time, Italy has become the second preferred destination in Europe and third in the global ranking.

4 Numbers peaked in 2000 and started to decrease in 2004, though they have remained considerably higher than in previous decades.

5 This is compounded by the fact that inflows of migrants from neighbor countries also increased in that decade, mainly in the form of forced or economic migration from Peru and Colombia. Yépez del Castillo and Herrera (2007:189) argue that this rendered Ecuador the Andean country with the highest rate of both emigration and immigration at that time.

6 This is the case of two of the most active and largest organizations: Rumiñahui Association, created in 1997, and Llactacaru Association, founded in 2001; both have offices in Ecuador and Spain. For details, see Chapter 8.

7 Interview with Pablo de la Vega, technical secretary ad hoc of Working Table on Labor Migrations, coordinator of Documentation Center on Human Rights (*Segundo Montes Mozo S.J.*), Quito, May 14, 2009.

8 The idea of good living draws on indigenous peoples' holistic understanding of well-being and calls for new ethical standards in the pursuit of development in which economic progress is subordinated to the laws regulating nature and some criteria based on the respect for human dignity, equality, solidarity, and improvement of quality of life. Thus, development is a goal and a work in progress at the same time, aiming at the full expansion of the individual and collective potential—a category that is in a permanent state of construction. The state is seen as the agent that promotes development and corrects market failures. Both states and markets have to be redefined politically in order to build up "a society with a market, instead of a market society" (Acosta 2008).

9 Interview with Juan Del Campo, director of migration policy, Ministry of Foreign Affairs of Peru, Lima, May 29, 2009.

10 See www.ime.gob.mx.

11 The SENAMI opened offices in other countries where most of the Ecuadorian diaspora resides (United States, Spain, Italy, and Venezuela) to offer information and services to migrants, protect their rights, and strengthen national bonds and identity. The status and functions of these offices were the source of controversies because they overlapped and often conflicted with consular offices and activities. As it is explained in the last section of this chapter, under the recent reform of the SENAMI, these offices continue working within consulates.

12 See www.senami.gov.ec/index2.php?option=com_docman&task=doc_view&gid=108&Itemid=98.

13 For details, see www.mcds.gov.ec.

14 Interview with María Isabel García, advisor on migration area, Ministry of Coordination on Social Development, Quito, May 15, 2009.

15 Interview with Guido Mendoza Fantinato, head of the Migration and Labor Program, General Secretariat, Andean Community of Nations, Lima, May 27, 2009.

16 For example, the fund "El Cucayo," launched in July 2008, provides advising and seed money to return migrants who are willing to start an economic activity in Ecuador. The funds usually range from $15,000 for individual projects up to $50,000 for collective projects.

17 Interviews with Gloria Jiménez, president of Rumiñahui association, Quito, May 15, 2009; Luis Sánchez, member of the technical commission, Rumiñahui association, Quito, May 15, 2009; and Patricio Carrillo, head of Llactacaru association, Quito, May 13, 2009.

18 See www.migrantesenlinea.org/enlinea.php?c=2009.

19 Ecuadorians see Colombians as unreliable and prone to engaging in criminal activities.

20 Interviews with Arturo Cabrera Hidalgo, undersecretary, SENAMI, Quito, May 11, 2009, and Lorena Altamirano, director of service to migrants, SENAMI, Quito, May 12, 2009.

21 Interview with Hernán Holguín, undersecretary of citizenship and solidarity, SENAMI, Quito, May 12, 2009.

22 Azogues is situated in the province of Cañar, one of the regions most affected by emigration. Thus, the moving was presented as a sign of policy decentralization and an incentive to reactivate the local economy. See www.migrante.gob.ec/presidente-correa-constata-avances-en-la-construccion-del-edificio-para-atencion-de-los-migrantes/, accessed May 29, 2013.

23 See http://decretos.cege.gob.ec/decretos/decretos.aspx, accessed June 12, 2013.

24 See www.ecuadorinmediato.com/index.php?module=Noticias&func=news_user_view&id=204688&umt=lorena_escudero_renuncio_al_viceministerio_movilidad_humana_tras_culminar_transicion_senami_audio, accessed July 8, 2014.

25 The construction started in November 2012, cost over $5 million, and undergone several delays. It was expected to be finished in July 2014. See www.elmercurio.com.ec/434366-azogues-en-julio-estara-el-edificio-del-viceministerio-de-movilidad/#.U7wbuPldVid, accessed July 8, 2014. However, it was inaugurated only in mid-September 2015. See www.eltiempo.com.ec/noticias-cuenca/168522-presidente-inaugura-obras-en-azogues/, accessed October 10, 2015.

26 See http://cancilleria.gob.ec/es/integracion-de-la-senami-al-nuevo-vice-ministerio-de-movilidad-humana/, accessed 07/08/14; and http://cancilleria.gob.ec/es/cancilleria-crea-dos-dependencias-a-favor-de-la-proteccion-a-los-migrantes/, accessed July 8, 2014.

27 See www.presidencia.gov.ec/articuloh.php?ar_codigo=35&ca_codigo=53&ca_padre=0&tipo=1.
28 Interviews with Lorena Altamirano, Quito, May 12, 2009; Ursula Troya, director of bilateral and multilateral affairs, SENAMI, Quito, May 12, 2009; and Paulina Larreátegui, former director of migration policy, SENAMI, Quito, May 13, 2009.
29 Interviews with Carlos Lopez Damm, ambassador, general coordinator, Ministry of Foreign Affairs of Ecuador, Quito, May 13, 2009, and Jacques Ramirez, undersecretary of consular services, Ministry of Foreign Affairs of Ecuador, former advisor at SENAMI, Quito, May 13, 2009.
30 Interview with Jacques Ramírez, Quito, May 13, 2009.
31 See interview with the vice minister at www.telegrafo.com.ec/noticias/informacion-general/item/ahora-tendremos-mas-de-80-casas-del-migrante.html, accessed July 8, 2014.
32 The program aimed at facilitating return by providing information and advice on practical and legal matters. According to Deere (2013:58–59), 7,947 persons had benefited from this program up to 2012; the information they received was not the main determinant of the decision to return, although in some cases this and related programs, such as the Plan Cucayo, accelerated the move and/or encouraged investment in resettling business activities.
33 Interview with Susana López, consultant for OIM, coordinator of the Political Analysis Unit within the SENAMI, Quito, May 19, 2009.
34 Interview with Susana López, Quito, May 19, 2009.

Works Cited

Acosta, Alberto. 2008. "El Buen Vivir, una Oportunidad Para Construir." *Revista Ecuador Debate*, December 28.
Acosta, Alberto, Susana López, and David Villamar. 2006. *La Migración en el Ecuador. Oportunidades y Amenazas*. Quito: Centro Andino de Estudios Internacionales, Universidad Andina Simón Bolívar, and Corporación Editora Nacional.
Arízaga, Leonardo. 2005. "La Política del Estado Ecuatoriano Hacia los Emigrantes Nacionales." In *Emigración y Política Exterior en Ecuador*, ed. by Javier Ponce Leiva. Quito: Ediciones ABYA-YALA and FLACSO. pp. 21–55.
Deere, Carmen Diana. 2013. "Gender, Remittances and Asset Accumulation in Ecuador and Ghana." Paper prepared for the Economic Empowerment Section, UN Women, New York, under the TOR "Evidence-Based Policy Paper on Gender, Remittances and Development."
Domenech, Eduardo E. 2009. "Avatares de la Política Migratoria en Bolivia: El Estado y los Emigrantes Como Nacionales en el Exterior." In *Migraciones Contemporáneas: Contribución al Debate*. La Paz: CIDES-UMSA/CAF/Plural. pp. 259–288.
Eguiguren Jiménez, María M. 2009, September. "Sujeto Migrante, Crisis y Tutela Estatal: Construcción de la Migración y Modos de Intervención del Estado Ecuatoriano." Master's thesis, Sociology Program, Facultad Latinoamericana de Ciencias Sociales, Sede Ecuador.
FLACSO/UNFPA. 2006, December. *Ecuador: Las Cifras de la Migración Internacional*. Quito: Fondo de Población de las Naciones Unidas and Facultad Latinoamericana de Ciencias Sociales.

Freidenberg, Flavia. 2008. "El Flautista de Hammelin. Liderazgo y Populismo en la Democracia Ecuatoriana." In *El Retorno del Pueblo: Populismo y Nuevas Democracias en America Latina*, ed. by Carlos De la Torre and Enrique Peruzotti. Quito: Flacso/Ministerio de Cultura del Ecuador. pp. 189–237.

Green, Paul. 2008. "Family and Nation: Brazilian National Ideology as Contested Transnational Practice in Japan." *Global Networks*. 8(4): 418–435.

Herrera, Gioconda. 2007. "Ecuatorianos/as en Europa: De la Vertiginosa Salida a la Construcción de Espacios Transnacionales." In *Nuevas Migraciones Latinoamericanas a Europa. Balances y Desafíos*, ed. by Isabel Yépez del Castillo and Gioconda Herrera. Quito: FLACSO Ecuador, OBREAL (Observatorio de las Relaciones Unión Europea-América Latina), Universidad Católica de Lovaina y Universitat de Barcelona. pp. 189–215.

Herrera, Gioconda, María C. Carillo, and Alicia Torres. eds. 2005. *La Migración Ecuatoriana. Transnacionalismo, Redes e Identidades*. Quito: FLACSO and Plan Migración, Comunicación y Desarrollo.

Jácome, H. and I. Luis. 2004, January. "The Late 1990s Financial Crisis in Ecuador: Institutional Weaknesses, Fiscal Rigidities, and Financial Dollarization at Work." IMF Working Paper WP/04/12. Washington, DC: International Monetary Fund, Monetary and Financial Systems Department.

Koller, Sylvie. 2009–2010. "Équateur: La Politique des Droits." *Problèmes d'Amérique Latine*. 75: 61–73.

Kunz, Rahel. 2008. "Mobilising Diasporas: A Governmentality Analysis of the Case of Mexico." Working Paper Series "Glocal Governance and Democracy" 03. Institute of Political Science, University of Lucerne, Switzerland.

Lucas, Knitto. 2007. *Rafael Correa. Un Extraño en Carondelet*. Quito: Planeta.

Pachano, Simon. 2007. *La trama de Penélope. Procesos Politicos e Instituciones en el Ecuador*. Quito: FLACSO/International IDEA/NIMD.

Ramírez Gallegos, Franklin and Analía Minteguiaga. 2007. "El Nuevo Tiempo del Estado. La Política Posneoliberal del Correismo." *OSAL*. 8(22), September. Buenos Aires: CLACSO.

Ramírez Gallegos, Franklin and Jacques P. Ramírez. 2005. *La Estampida Migratoria Ecuatoriana. Crisis, Redes Transnacionales y Repertorios de Acción Migratoria*. Quito: Centro de Investigaciones CIUDAD, UNESCO, Ediciones ABYA-YALA.

SENAMI. 2007. "Validación de la Agenda Política de la SENAMI." Workshop's minutes, November 23. Quito: Secretaría Nacional del Migrante.

SENAMI. 2008. "Constitución de la República del Ecuador. Texto Integral Sometido a Referéndum el Día 28 de Setiembre de 2008." Quito: Secretaría Nacional del Migrante, Gobierno Nacional de la República del Ecuador, Agencia 69 Editores.

SIMA. 2009, April. *Andina Migrante 3*. Boletín del Sistema de Información Sobre Migraciones Andinas. Quito: FLACSO Sede Ecuador.

Tamagno, Carla and Ulla D. Berg. 2003. "El Quinto Suyo: Conceptualizando la 'Diáspora Peruana' Desde Abajo y Desde Arriba." In *Comunidades Locales y Transnacionales: Cinco Estudios de Caso en el Perú*, ed. by Carlos I. Degregori. Lima: IEP. pp. 1–19.

Vallejo, Andrés. 2004. "El Viaje al Norte. Migración Transnacional y Desarrollo en Ecuador." In *Migración y Desarrollo. Estudios Sobre Remesas y Otras Prácticas Trasnacionales en España*, coord. by Angeles Escrivá and Natalia

Ribas. Córdoba, Spain: Consejo Superior de Investigaciones Científicas and Instituto de Estudios Sociales de Andalucía. pp. 111–147.

Vono De Vilhena, Daniela. 2006. "Vinculación de los Emigrados Latinoamericanos y Caribeños con su País de Origen." Serie Población y Desarrollo #71. Santiago: CEPAL.

Yépez del Castillo, Isabel and Gioconda Herrera. eds. 2007. *Nuevas Migraciones Latinoamericanas a Europea: Balances y Desafíos*. Quito: FLACSO/OBREAL/ Universidad Católica de Lovaina/Universitat de Barcelona.

5 Uruguay
From Denial to Formal Overtures

Introduction

Uruguay occupies a relatively small area of South America; it is the home of over three million people, most of whom reside in urban settings along the coast. Montevideo alone, the capital city, hosts almost half of the total population.[1] This demographic distribution is the result of long-term trends, namely internal migration from the countryside to the main cities encouraged by economic changes, modernization, and urbanization. In particular, internal displacement of people has often been the first step in a long journey that extends beyond the country's borders; a significant part of the total population (between 15% and 18% in the mid-2000s) moved abroad. Thus, in terms of migration flows Uruguay passed from being a receiving country up to the 1950s to a sending country since then. Low population growth, depopulation of large areas of its territory, and emigration became structural problems in the following decades, posing obvious limits to any development and growth strategy. The intensification of political and economic problems since the 1960s rendered the balance of migration flows negative, a trend that has persisted until today and has intensified in times of severe economic crises (i.e., the early 1980s and the 2000s).

However, it was not until the mid-2000s that the magnitude of the problem was acknowledged and population and migration problems entered the governmental agenda and political discourse. A new set of innovative measures and institutional changes gained momentum only in the last decade, with an "official launching" of initiatives to court the diaspora in 2005 under president Tabaré's Vázquez's first term in office (2005–2010). Some of these measures are similar to what other Latin American countries are doing in this respect, but not all of them. Yet, the scope and sustainability of these measures are still subject to controversies. This raises questions concerning the factors prompting this policy shift, the timing, the degree to which this is a departure from past policies, and the sources of setbacks and controversies surrounding current migration policy change and debate.

Population and Migration Policies:
Brief Historical Overview

Similar to other Latin American countries, Uruguay constructed its idea of being an independent nation-state around the confluence of people, state, and territory. Yet, Calvo and Mieres (2007:18) argue that, from the demographic point of view, Uruguay is an atypical case: it did not go through peaks of population growth, and an early decline in mortality and birth rates gave it a demographic profile more similar to the advanced countries than to its developing neighbors, though it still shared with the latter the struggle to overcome economic underdevelopment. Such demographic evolution contributed to a generalized perception of a lack of population problems and, consequently, to the absence of specific policies. The problem is today compounded by a low fertility rate, concentration of population in a small coastal area, continuous population aging and emigration, and low immigration inflows.

Until the mid-20th century, scarce or slow population growth was compensated with an open door immigration policy.[2] However, the insertion in world markets through a model of primary commodity exports mainly based on extensive farming until the 1930s, and a relatively successful but short-lived industrialization process in the following decades, reduced the quest for labor-intensive activities and, to some extent, eluded the continuous depopulation problem (Finch 1982). Since the 1960s, as the import substitution model declined, there was a reversion of migration flows.[3] Political violence and authoritarianism in the 1970s provoked a significant wave of political exiles, while economic opening brought deindustrialization, unemployment, and deterioration of wages and working conditions in general. Thus, the migration balance became negative, and the demographic and migration profile of the country changed: immigration decreased and remaining inflows have come from neighboring countries rather than from Europe; emigration increased considerably, including mostly young educated men and new destinations. However, the state was silent and oblivious of increasing emigration, and the social dimension of the emigration phenomenon remained scarce and fragmented (Pellegrino in Calvo and Mieres 2007:84–85).

The emigration trend continued even after the return to democracy in 1985, showing that moving abroad had become a socioeconomic strategy in dire times for middle- and upper-class young sectors of the society (those who already had financial resources, information, and links with the destination).[4] Only recently have new flows of immigration from neighboring countries and return migration been observed, though they are of uncertain magnitude and are not documented in the statistics yet.[5] Although loss of human capital has been a concern, some reviews of the literature show that these concerns did not go beyond denouncing the problem, they did not lead to further elaboration of diagnosis and solutions, and, overall, the problem was minimized or forgotten (Aguiar 1982:23–24; Coraza de los Santos 2003).

Citizens Abroad: The Profile of the Last Wave of Emigrants

The profile of those who left since 2000 differs from previous waves of emigration. Given the 2001 crisis, Argentina was not the preferred destination early in that decade as it had been overwhelmingly in the past. Spain and the US captured most of the outflows, followed by other countries such as Italy, Argentina, Mexico, and Israel. The age of emigrants has decreased (most are men between 20 and 30 years old), and their educational levels have increased. Over a third of emigrants have completed secondary school and 21.9% hold a college/university degree (or similar), which is higher than the average in the nonmigrant population (OIM 2011b:53–70).

The 1998 economic crisis, aftermath recession, and unemployment are listed among emigrants' primary motivations to leave. Nevertheless, the level of wages and the lack of possibilities for social mobility would be better indicators of motivations (Pellegrino and Vigorito 2005) because regardless of the employment situation at time of departure, the underlying concern is a more subjective, nuanced factor: the gap between expectations and real living conditions. Ethnographic research documents a generalized perception among Uruguayan emigrants, especially among the young: the country is not only small but also a boring place to live; it has been stagnant, frozen in time for too long and progressively emptied of its most vital, dynamic people, thus becoming the land of the elderly; and there is no future to look forward to (Pastorini 2007:48–52; Trigo 2003:25–30). These ideas nurtured dual illusions: fulfillment can only be achieved abroad, and the nation deserves to go back to its glorious path. It has also been assumed that emigrants' memories of a country where full employment, prosperity, social mobility, and access to education were real possibilities have led to a relatively high level of attachment and engagement with Uruguay's present and future (including significant political mobilization recently), even if at a long distance (Portillo 2006). Extensive transnational networks have not only facilitated the process of exit and integration in the host society but also reinforced the sense of belonging to a dispersed population and having open choices to respond to adverse economic circumstances (Pellegrino and Vigorito 2005:65). The links with home country are deemed intense in terms of the frequency of communications with family and relatives at home, level of information about developments in the home country, and visits to Uruguay. Remittances, though, are not a strong component of those links.[6]

Early Steps Toward an Emigration Policy

Early antecedents to the current migration policy are to be found in some attempts to address the problem of exiles in the postauthoritarian period and encourage migrant return. Those efforts sow the seeds of the current linkage policy. They illustrate the difficulties of addressing the needs of a heterogeneous diasporic group and rooting emigration policy in one single institutional base. The creation of the National Commission of Repatriation (Ministry of Education and Culture) in March 1985 was guided by the intention to facilitate return, regardless of migrants' levels of qualification or backgrounds. It was created by Chapter VI of the Amnesty Law no. 15,737,[7] and it succeeded in bringing back a good number of professionals that were formerly exiles. The commission acted in collaboration with civil society organizations, such as the national Commission for the Reunion of the Orientals and the Ecumenical Service for Re-Insertion, which provided funds and assistance. The National Commission for Migration was also created in 1985 (and re-created again in 1997) and charged with elaborating proposals to encourage both immigration and return. According to Taks (2006:146), it is only in the late 1980s when scholars and practitioners started to agree on their claim for a clear and broader migration policy that should be considered a priority.

However, this consensus did not translate into a comprehensive policy strategy, nor was it institutionalized yet. Proof of that is that the measures launched by the Ministry of Foreign Affairs around the time of democratization show that there was more commitment and engagement from the main public university and international organizations than from the state offices. Moreover, bureaucratic practices stood in the way of innovation, anticipating a challenge that would become clear years later. Consular services still followed police-like bureaucratic and intelligence practices learned during the authoritarian period when emigrants were escaping political persecution. Portillo (2006:319) suggests that democratization implied the end of those practices, but the same officials remained in their positions and no specific emigration policy was implemented; therefore, in his view (i.e., in the view of those who led innovation later), a neglectful style of consular service has persisted. As explained later, this institutional inertia accounts for some obstacles during implementation.

Another impetus came from studies on highly qualified emigrants in the late 1960s and 1970s. Although official discourses continued to consider the exodus as a temporal trend in those decades (Aguiar 1982:29), academic arguments (e.g., Petrucelli 1979) started to resonate in journalistic accounts. The loss of skilled workers gained renewed attention in the mid-1990s (Pellegrino 2001, 2002, among others). Consequently, some initiatives targeted scientists and technicians in particular. Again, in contrast to other countries, these initiatives promoted migration return rather than solely brain circulation. The Program for the Development of Basic Sciences, launched in 1986 to encourage collaboration with national scholars residing abroad in the creation of master's and doctoral programs, created conditions for the return of some scholars. Also, the Universidad de la República (the most important national public university) engaged in the Program of Fellowships for the Return and Re-Insertion of Scientists Abroad. The creation of a regional branch of the Pasteur Institute in 2006, spearheaded by researchers linked to that institution in France and other countries, contributed to return, too (Pellegrino and Vigorito 2009).

The idea of brain exchange and linkages took shape only recently. The Universidad de la República became further involved in 2000, when the General Directorate for International Cooperation at the Ministry of Foreign Affairs initiated contacts to launch the Linkage Program with Highly Qualified Uruguayans Residing Abroad, also in collaboration with the International Organization for Migration (IOM). Workshops and consultation meetings with distinguished members of the emigrant community were held. As a result, several instruments were put in place between 2001 and 2004: a website, a database of Uruguayans abroad, a newsletter, and regular meetings and workshops.[8] Two other related units were created in 2001: the National Commission for Linkages with Uruguayans Residing Abroad and an Advising Committee to said commission that was formed by members of the Ministries of Foreign Affairs, Interior, and Education and Culture and some scholars.

In the last decade, the idea of designing a comprehensive policy toward the emigrant community (not just highly skilled migrants) progressively yet slowly advanced. A major step forward was the report submitted by the Advising Committee to the National Commission in 2003, which acknowledged that the previously mentioned initiatives were short of producing "tangible results in terms of policies or implementation institutions" (4), and contained around 40 recommendations to give shape to a national migration policy. This document provides a record of almost all antecedents since 2001, makes a brief diagnosis of the problem, contextualizes the Uruguayan exodus of highly trained technicians and professionals in regional and global terms, and suggests that return and linkage might well be complementary policies.[9] Given the long record of denial of population and emigration problems, I argue that the adoption of some of these recommendations was not part of a deeper transformation already underway, as in other cases (e.g., Gamlen 2011), but it represents a significant and sudden departure from previous neglect and a case of policy innovation.

Main Features of the New Emigration Policy

A breaking point in migration policymaking came in 2004, largely because of the intense mobilization of Uruguayans abroad to take part in the national election. Between 20,000 and 40,000 citizens (approximately 1% to 2% of the electoral roster) returned to the country to cast their ballots (Moraes Mena 2009:113). The Frente Amplio (Broad Front, a coalition of socialist, communist, Christian-democratic, and independent parties) won with 50.4% of the votes,[10] thus avoiding a *ballotage* and making evident that just less than 1% may make a difference. The outcome illustrates the relevance of emigrants' heterogeneous profiles: migrant activism was the result of intensive collaborative work by international networks of individuals and migrant associations to facilitate and finance the trips; a good number of the members of these associations were former political exiles who had been involved in politics for a long time and supported parties within the Frente (Coraza de los Santos 2003:90–91, 96–97), while others were younger, recent emigrants. The effort received wide media coverage, which increased the visibility of the emigrant community, generated some public debate, and pushed migration up in the political agenda.

The issue had been in the electoral campaign agenda before the elections as part of the coalition's broader, postneoliberal approach to national development in which social policy ranks high. Such a strategy pursues a broad definition of development and links social inclusion, equity, and democratization to sustained economic growth. Population and emigration policies thus became integral part of development. "The current situation may be considered a demographic emergency," argued the Frente Amplio in its programme.[11] Moreover, as previously explained, the state has a central role in development that is far from being left only to the market forces. The state is then committed to the creation of conditions that would reduce incentives to emigrate (which would indirectly increase the motivation to return, too) and would strengthen the links with citizens abroad. Migrant mobilization to participate in elections also "created a commitment for the Frente with that sector of the electorate"[12] and triggered a number of responses after the victory.

A few features defined the new policy. First, local specialists and practitioners named the new initiatives *políticas de vinculación* (linkage policies), thus presenting the construction of links as the main motivation for the government's efforts. Second, in opposition to previous initiatives, the Frente Amplio government emphasized migrant political engagement and targeted the entire emigrant community, not just professionals and scientists. Third, discursive mechanisms were put to work to convey the new intentions. Rhetoric actually went beyond linkage to engage with the definition of nation; former president Tabaré Vásquez named Uruguayans abroad the *patria peregrina* (peregrine nation) in his inaugural speech on March 3, 2005, with an emphasis on the word *patria*.[13] Fourth, new institutions were created, national legislation was updated, and emigrants' political participation and enfranchisement were promoted.

The new governmental techniques included the creation of a new office within the Foreign Affairs Ministry in 2005: the General Directorate for Consular Affairs and Linkage, which is in fact an expansion and an upgrading of the old General Directorate for Consular Affairs position. Following the example of other countries, the office became popularly known as the 20th Department, that is, the extraterritorial jurisdiction that symbolically represents Uruguayans abroad.[14] In 2008, the General Directorate expanded and divided into two subunits: the Directorate of Consular Affairs and the Directorate of Linkage. Within the former, the Office for Assistance to Compatriots is in charge of all sorts of paperwork and support to Uruguayans abroad (e.g., legal assistance to prisoners, health care in case of accidents, remains repatriation in case of death). Within the latter, the Office of Return and Welcome has broader duties related to cultural issues, and it channels the concerns of those who are willing to return (OIM 2011b).

These units represent a new institutional development, a sort of island in the midst of public offices that tend to resist change. They have kept expanding slowly since 2005, and by 2012 they employed over 30 people. Besides linkage, their work has mainly focused on facilitating some red tape for migrants and returnees, such as certification of university degrees and other documents, legal assistance, and reinsertion orientation. Still, "there are issues that these offices cannot solve because they fall within other areas of migrants' lives such as health, education, or housing; coordination with other state offices is necessary and not always achieved. . . . In fact, too high expectations about what the state can do have been created; there was an inflation of expectations at the moment of launching the policy."[15] These units soon became overwhelmed by demands of all sorts, and they struggled with, on the one hand, a reality that changes too fast and poses new challenges constantly and, on the other hand, the inertia and resistance to innovation within the state apparatus. The heads of these offices expected to overcome the short-term demands soon and to be able to address all dimensions of migration in a comprehensive manner, perhaps under a more complex and autonomous bureaucratic structure, but this has not happened yet.[16] Their narratives constantly oscillate between wide-open possibilities for innovation and dynamism and a constraining state structure, because "the diplomatic corporation does not come along, it is obsolete, and the reform of the state has been discussed but advances very slowly."[17]

Obstacles have been identified and tackled, with partial success. Some issues emerged from the persistence of the old bureaucratic practices mentioned in the previous section. To enhance policy consistency and overcome some resistance to changes from old bureaucratic cadres, a retraining of bureaucratic cadres (particularly within the Ministry of Foreign Affairs) was attempted. A specific course on migration management was introduced in the curricula of the foreign affairs training program. It is aimed at helping officials develop skills to deal with linkage issues and problems that go beyond traditional consular affairs. However, this resocialization takes time to be fully incorporated and translate into new practices. It has proved difficult to advance consistently in other areas, too. To upgrade and recategorize migration and population issues, for instance, there was an attempt to relocate the Directorate of Migrations in 2007 (out of the police, where it has been based), with no success. This was a missed opportunity to produce a significant shift away from the border control and security-oriented approach to migration that traditionally prevailed in the police and the Ministry of the Interior and to generate synergies with other state offices. In addition, offices in charge of migration return exist in both the Ministry of Foreign Affairs and the Ministry of Labor. "The rationale for duplicating offices and functions has not been explained."[18] Also, there has been an effort to intensify planning and coordination of migration-related programs and to work on migrant data systematically, which might facilitate policy continuity. In other words, despite difficulties, the state attempted to increase its capacities to reach out to migrants. A voluntary register of Uruguayans abroad was created, the use of online mechanisms to gather information and communicate with migrants was encouraged,[19] and contacts and consultation with migrants' organizations were expanded.

Yet, rather than a partnership model of state–diaspora relations, a top-down approach was followed. Consultation councils were created in 2005 to achieve the goals previously mentioned. These are associations of migrants with elected representatives who maintain a close link with consular authorities in their places of residency. The state encouraged the emergence of these interlocutors and their organization (explicitly naming the council leaders "interlocutors" in the online listings and other documents), thus treating them as the legitimate voice of emigrants, the representatives of their interests and claims, and the main channel for migrant political participation.[20] In addition, a good number of preexisting migrant associations are still active in several receiving countries.[21] Five general meetings (in 2006, 2007, 2009, 2011, and 2013) have taken place among representatives of the government, members of civil society (e.g., business firms), and all consultation councils to discuss migrants' concerns, ideas, and projects, including the councils' own organization, expansion, and role, as well as the planning of an agenda for future collaboration.

However, the results of the councils' performance are mixed. Former director of the Directorate of Consular Affairs and Linkage, Álvaro Portillo (2006), emphasized the autonomous, pluralist, and flexible character of these institutions. Yet, the councils initially gathered members from old migrant associations (i.e., those originally created by political exiles and that were, presumably, too close to the left-wing coalition in power). The government's encouragement to organize was interpreted as a co-optation mechanism that would lead only to a top-down dynamic, and the old associations' influences were seen as tainting the relationship, introducing a political bias in the initiatives, and preventing other (younger, recent) emigrants from participation (Moraes et al. 2009:310–312). In general, then, "councils were not welcome as we expected and in some cases they generated conflicts."[22] "Addressing the heterogeneity of the diaspora has [also] been an issue. The councils overlapped with existing institutions. In some destinations they generated divisions and conflicts."[23] All informants, including officials involved, agree on the need to reform them or to create a more flexible structure to channel linkages, but those changes have not happened yet.

The adaptation of governance techniques also included another major step in placing the state as guarantor of rights and regulating population and migration issues: the passing of Law 18,250 in December 2007 (effective January 2008), which recognizes migration as an inalienable right (article 1) and declares the right to family reunion and equal treatment of migrants vis-à-vis their co-nationals.[24] Chapter V of this law created two new institutions: the National Junta (collective body) of Migration, formed by representatives of three ministries (Interior, Foreign Affairs, and Labor and Social Security) to advise the executive power and to elaborate and coordinate migration policies, and the Advising Consultation Council of Migration (formed by members of social organizations and unions) to advise the Junta. The law also stipulates the migration-related functions of all other public offices across several ministries involved in the management of migration issues and establishes general norms on residence and circulation of people. Chapter XIV is devoted to Uruguayans abroad.[25] While the relevance of this law lies in the institutionalization of the new policy orientation, the gap between norms and practices limits the impact of normative developments. The lack of extensive parliamentary debate and quick approval of the bill, as well as public opinion indifference, show that "migration issues still generate faint echo and politicians hardly know how to approach them."[26]

Political enfranchisement is illustrative of the difficulties of reimagining membership in the context of constraints posed by long-term conceptions of the polity and a territorially based nation. The Frente Amplio governments encouraged the granting of absentee voting rights to Uruguayans residing abroad. The issue has been framed in the country's strong democratic tradition that pursued (and, to some extent, consolidated) an inclusive political model in the first half of the 20th century. The initiative resonated with reparatory arguments aimed at reintegrating the nation after the disruption of this tradition by the military dictatorship, which triggered massive emigration and suspended political participation

(Moreira and Pellegrino 2001). Absentee voting rights have been a central claim raised by Uruguayans abroad, as reflected in the consultation councils' discourse; they argue that policies have to be based on modern and updated concepts of nation and citizenship that transcend territorial borders. The enactment of this right is seen as the measure that would make all other linkages relevant; the right to vote, as the ultimate form of participation, gives meaning to all other (cultural, economic, social, etc.) ties and membership practices.[27]

To incorporate voting rights for citizens residing abroad would require a constitutional amendment to allow for absentee ballot by postal or other means.[28] Hence, three bills were discussed in parliamentary commissions. Congress finally voted down a revised bill in October 2007. The project was subject to a referendum on October 25, 2009, for which the Frente Amplio developed an intense campaign in collaboration with the consultation councils and other organizations within and outside the country, again with no success (only about 37% of voters supported the initiative).[29] This was a major setback for the new policy, and it led to intense debate about future initiatives. Public officials argued off the record that the Frente Amplio would relaunch the project, expecting to make emigrants' absentee voting rights effective by the 2014 presidential elections. This did not happen, but social mobilization has increased lately. The project is now being discussed again.[30]

Finally, in contrast to other Latin American countries, public officials interviewed for this study agreed on the fact that economic motivations did not rank high in this case. State initiatives to capture economic resources from emigrants have been very limited. The low level of remittances does not encourage efforts in that sphere, although forms of lowering the cost of money transfers and facilitating other bank transactions have been explored.[31] Instead, following a trend identified by other studies (see Chapter 2), Uruguay has attempted to capture knowledge resources: the program called Circulation of Highly Qualified Uruguayans (CUAC in its Spanish acronym) within the Ministry of Foreign Affairs works in collaboration with the National Agency for Research and Innovation and the Universidad de la República to compile information about scholars, artists, and entrepreneurs abroad and create a network of potential partners at home.[32] Yet, Uruguay has not yet joined those countries that effectively tap into overseas transnational networks. Relying on migrants to promote consumption of national products abroad, as well as investments at home and other economic activities, has been in the official discourse (i.e., migrants as marketing agents or entrepreneurs who facilitate economic businesses), but no significant programs have been implemented.

In sum, most of these measures are in line with general trends in emigration policies across regions (namely state efforts to use rhetorical, institutional, and engagement mechanisms to reach out to citizens abroad and involve them in national development projects), but they present specific characteristics that depart from general trends in several respects. By all accounts, these policies imply a significant progress in the approach to population problems in Uruguay. But, at the same time, they fall short of being efficient and comprehensive enough to represent a solution. Emigration and population policies are considered a work in progress by scholars and practitioners alike, a necessary, albeit partial and insufficient, step in addressing a complex and changing phenomenon. Off the record, some informants would blame politicization and neglect of technical expertise (i.e., consultation with and appointment of specialists has decreased in favor of political appointees, especially under José Mujica, 2010–2015); others would focus on institutions. "The institutional structure is still too weak; it can hardly go beyond receiving demands."[33] "It is hard to say that there is a state policy, though some programs are indeed implemented."[34] Why? What stands in the way of further progress toward a consistent and comprehensive emigration policy? What explains the vicissitudes of this policy? The next two sections offer some answers.

From Implementing to Institutionalizing the New Policy

The Uruguayan case confirms that state emigration policies require the political commitment of specific actors to prosper. As in Ecuador, it is not the state as a unitary apparatus or as political parties but rather specific actors and offices (i.e., the president, foreign minister, special migration units) that politically push transnational initiatives. Emigration policy also requires an articulation between symbolic and rhetoric initiatives and concrete measures to entitle and engage emigrants. In addition, this case underlines that emigration policies are contingent on a dynamic of acceptance/resistance molded by historical bureaucratic practices within the state and society's imaginary notion of nation and belonging.

As explained in Chapter 2, the literature has taken note of a rhetorical shift toward friendly characterizations of expatriates (Ho 2011; Østergaard-Nielsen 2003; Ragazzi 2009, among others) but it says little of what it takes to succeed in that realm and what the implications are. Uruguay offers an example of a shift that was part of a confusing, ineffective, and perhaps too vague discourse that undermined the state–diaspora relationship and policy credibility. According to Portillo (2006:321), the first head of the new office in charge of emigration affairs, the phrase *patria peregrina* was coined to convey a dynamic idea of *patria* without borders and on the move. However, the label has not taken hold either in the public (official) or in the migrant organizations' discourses. It is hardly heard in Uruguay nowadays. A *peregrine* is a traveler, a wanderer in a foreign place, or a pilgrim to a sacred place in a foreign land, but I found no evidence of any religious connotation in the use of the expression by President Tabaré Vázquez. To call migrants peregrines is, then, to characterize them as nomads that are settled neither here nor there. Hence, the term peregrine is at odds with the idea of homeland, which is essentially associated with a fixed place of origin and belonging, and it does not help to define new, nonterritorial boundaries of the nation-state because the idea of constant movement conveys a sense of vagueness and indeterminate borders. The expression is also oblivious of the fact that makes sense of a linkage policy: migrants being "here and there", or in other words, the dual character of migrants' lives, which conflates both ruptures and persistent attachments. Calling migrants peregrines is to deny an important part of their experience: migration is usually a journey to find a new place in a foreign destination, to become incorporated into the host society, and in some (but not all) cases, to remain simultaneously connected to the home country. This is usually a hard journey that transforms individuals' identities, perceptions, and life experiences and creates new attachments (even if they are temporary) instead of staying on the move forever—a particularly traumatic process in the case of political exiles.[35] In short, regardless of the intensity of dual engagements, contemporary migrants reside in a certain place and are, to different extents and modalities, relatively stable members of a foreign community. As such, they have acquired identities and agency that go well beyond that of travelers.

Failing to tap into that reality has significant implications in the case of Uruguay. Although a persistent process of emigration has cemented the idea of a dispersion among Uruguayans, of being part of a process that has kept pulling people out of the country for decades, the idea of nation and state as coterminous is still very strong in the Uruguayan social imaginary. Hence, *patria peregrina* is an expression that has not resonated with the vicissitudes of Uruguayans abroad and has failed to give them an identity, thus jeopardizing the chances of constructing them as subjects and interlocutors. This is a point not addressed in other case studies that focus on successful attempts to reimagine diasporas and redefine membership through discursive and cultural mechanisms (e.g., Dickinson and Bailey 2007).

Moreover, this terminology has casted doubts on the conceptualization of the problem and policy intentions because it involves a redefinition of borders when, in fact, political and social ideas about the nation remain strongly tied to territory in Uruguay. The debate on extraterritorial voting rights illustrates this point and the importance of matching rhetoric with entitlements. The official political discourse emphasized notions of national identity and unity, collective commitment with nation-building, citizens' interest in contributing to a shared future, and a sense of responsibility toward the country's fate. But, in fact, Uruguayan political parties have held a completely different view of the issue: the Colorado party argued against emigrants' voting rights on the basis that physical presence in the territory at the moment of suffrage ultimately contributes to reinforcing the nationhood bond, and the Frente Amplio considered extraterritorial voting as one of the principal manifestations of democracy strength and attempted to expand civil and social rights to all citizens, regardless of their place of residency. Similar distinctions have been made by other political forces, including those within the governing coalition.[36] In other words, two views clashed: one identified the nation with the territorial state, and the other acknowledged the existence of an unbound nation, part of which resides beyond the borders. In sum, this is a divide about different forms of conceptualizing the nation, establishing who belongs to it and who does not (Taks 2006:151).

Migrant organizations' discourse also attests to that divide. Leaders of some of those organizations were initially ambiguous about the benefits and costs of mobilizing around this issue, but they enthusiastically supported the referendum campaign as the time approached. They argued that the existing legislation marginalizes migrants who do not have the economic means to travel to cast their vote or who have an irregular status in the destination country, thus denying them political rights and keeping them as "citizens of nowhere" (Moraes Mena 2009:114, 119). The discourse used by migrant associations further connected the individual and sociopolitical dimensions of migration by making references to the social, economic, and political reasons for emigration, evoking emigrants' constant "presence" (i.e., involvement) in the country despite geographical distances, and calling the government's initiative a "just and necessary vindication." Such rhetoric also invoked a notion of citizenship that goes beyond territorial boundaries and requested the adaptation of democratic institutions to a new historical circumstance, arguing that "Uruguay cannot marginalize us. The Uruguay of Abroad claims for integration into the construction of a new Uruguay."[37] In short, migrant claims have been about belonging to the nation and inclusion, which the ongoing policy cannot guarantee yet. It is too early to tell if recent rhetorical innovations calling for inclusion and migrant involvement in the country's future will work better.[38] The government's capacity to match rhetoric with entitlements has then become the ultimate test for the new emigration policy.

Such a capacity has been thus far constrained by domestic political factors. The ability to introduce changes largely remains concentrated in a few hands (presidents or top officials), which makes the sustainability of those changes contingent on the individuals' dispositions, styles, and leadership. "The president brings up the issue and a few actions from some state agencies follow, with few resources, though. That is it."[39] Congress does not show any capacity to initiate changes. It rarely engages in discussions about the topic. Approving Law 18,250 (mentioned previously) without debate is one more indicator that migration is not within the political parties' priorities. Public opinion was largely indifferent to the passing of the bill. Population issues in general are either addressed vaguely or are absent in electoral discourses (Taks 2010:172). In other words, Uruguay does not support assumptions about sending-state apparatuses and/or political parties as drivers of transnational migration policies and engagements (e.g., Itzigsohn 2000). Instead, presidents Vázquez and Mujica have been the spokespersons and engines of the new policies. The former launched some of the main measures; the latter reinforced and intensified some of them "mostly through gestures such as meetings with former political exiles during his trips abroad, because policy remains largely informal rather than formal."[40] Thus, presidents have also been crucial in signaling the commitment of their governments with the new policy orientation and giving it continuity.

Yet, as policy sustainability is contingent on individual dispositions and styles, it may be subject to frequent ups and downs. For instance, Mujica's leadership and performance were contrasted with his predecessors' and questioned. The press and recent public opinion surveys confirm a criticism I gathered in interviews for this study: Uruguayans charged Mujica with talking too much about projects and ideas that never materialize (including major reforms, like the reform of the state) and characterize his administration as "much ado about nothing" in reference to the lack of implementation of initiatives (e.g., Ladra 2012). Top officials would admit off the record that the president's style is a serious obstacle to grounding the new policy on a more permanent and consistent basis. Also, the president tends to be more concerned about immigration than emigration lately, though his discourse in that respect has also generated criticisms.[41]

A few other actors occasionally raise the visibility of the policy. Former foreign affairs minister (under Mujica's administration) Luis Almagro Lemes "is personally committed; he is moved by political conviction,"[42] and, therefore, he placed the issue high on his agenda and encouraged the expansion of some measures. He was well informed because of his own personal experience living abroad. Thus, Uruguayans abroad were one of the three priority areas under his tenure. "President Mujica comes along and supports the policy; in contrast, the Minister gives it priority."[43] Almagro emphasized the long-term character of the new policy and the promise of reversing the emigration trend that it carries (Almagro 2012). "His bet is on showing that this government can stop emigration; this would be his major political gain."[44] Although his ministry hosts the main offices devoted to migrants' needs and claims and is the epicenter of some initiatives, the cooperation of other bureaucratic agencies within the state apparatus has become increasingly necessary to address emigrants' and returnees' demands.

Setbacks and Obstacles to Innovation

It is, indeed, in the bureaucratic practices that a major obstacle to policy consistency resides. "There is an institutional culture that is very difficult to change. The reform of the state is missing."[45] Lack of coordination,

conflicting goals and interests within very small circles, and different perceptions of the problem (e.g., as a social welfare, purely administrative,
or economic issue) by various offices are unanimously cited as obstacles
to efficient and consistent policies. Top officials lament that the offices
responsible for the management of population and migration issues do
not share the same diagnosis of the problem and the same degree of commitment to address it properly. Therefore, they argue that "the main
problem is not resources but lack of sensitivity within the state; there is
no much echo of the Foreign Affairs Ministry's efforts in the rest of the
state" and "other offices do not show any sensitivity toward the situation
of emigrants and returnees alike." [46] Other voices claim that key offices
are in the hands of political appointees rather than specialists with some
technical expertise. Then, resources are wasted and a number of inconsistent programs exist, while a comprehensive policy still awaits concrete
and effective implementation.[47] These factors leave migration policies
subject to constant *vaivenes* (the word I most often heard during field
research, meaning ups and downs, comings and goings), undermine the
prospects of institutionalization, and cast doubts about the sustainability
of the new approach in the long run.

   The main source of these shortcomings is to be found in persistent
deficiencies in the public administration due to lack of, or partial, reform
of the state apparatus. Such reform has been on the agendas of Latin
American countries since the debt crisis of the 1980s. It was encouraged by the Washington consensus policy recommendations to stream-
line public accounts and create an adequate institutional framework for
market-oriented structural reforms. However, Uruguay departs from the
literature linking neoliberal projects and emigration policies because it
never fully embraced the "rolling back the state" wave and postponed
a comprehensive reform of the state. Only some tepid attempts have
been made since the mid-1990s. The reasons are to be found in the ideational and institutional limits that said reform has faced. Panizza (2002)
underlines the central role of the state in the national imagination as the
architect, engine, and embodiment of modernization (including political
modernization and a long democratic tradition) to explain the opposition
to radical neoliberal reforms in Uruguay and the preference for selective, gradual, and partial reforms that contrast with the path taken by
Argentina, Chile, and Peru in the late 1980s and early 1990s. The defense
of the "Uruguayan way" has then been rooted in historical antecedents
and guided by specific ideas and choices: acceptance of state reform as
an inevitable and necessary change, respect for a timing that responds
to an idiosyncratic progressive adaptation rather than to the urgency
and imposition of foreign actors, deliberate attempts to avoid social and
bureaucratic resistance and vetoes, and rejection of simplistic ideological views and of the state-market dichotomy as polarizing and exclusive
terms. In other words, state reform in Uruguay entailed an institutional

reconstruction of the state rather than a dismantling. This preserved an active state role in social welfare that allowed left-wing incumbents to pragmatically adopt a (postneoliberal) reformist position in the 2000s.

Other studies and testimonies call attention to certain conjunctures and the dynamics of domestic politics in the last few years. "The reform of the state did not progress as expected; those processes are very slow and compounded by a high turnover of officials."[48] Chasquetti (2008) analyzes the outcome of the ambitious reform package reannounced by former President Vázquez in March 2007 (2 years after the first announcement at the time of his inauguration), which included tax, health, education, and state reform, among others. He argues that the executive was the agenda-setter then and relied on legislative majority to push for these initiatives. However, slow progress and obstacles to reforms were mainly political: difficulties in achieving a compromise within the ruling party about the content of reforms, uncertainty and concerns about the president's negative to reform the constitution to allow his reelection (and the consequent internal infighting to decide the composition of the next ticket), and criticisms from opposition parties and social sectors (e.g., unions) that raised the costs of implementation.

In that context, proposals to transform traditional consular practices to accommodate linkage goals can only advance slowly and in a piecemeal fashion. In this respect, emigration policy illustrates well Narbono's argument (2011): the Frente Amplio have addressed one of the components of state reform, the one that refers to the definition of roles and functions of the state in economic development and social equity (and they did so along proactive, distributive, and inclusive lines that resonate with the historical central role given to the state), while it has tackled the complementary reform of the public administration only partially through various unfinished projects to change the system of selection, promotion, and career development of public officials. This second aspect of the reform of the state is very much a work in progress, and there is a still a long way to go to professionalize the management of public affairs and overcome discretionary and client-oriented practices within the public administration. The difficulties of changing those practices accounts for the modest progress of emigration policy. In other words, on the state side, the limits to official initiatives reside in (a) traditional and conflictive views of bureaucratic units that pursue diverse political (partisan or other) goals and strategies and (b) bureaucracies' tendencies to constantly launch new pet projects because officials' turnover is very frequent and new appointees need to legitimize their roles through new ideas, discretionary appointments, and redistribution of resources.

On the societal side, emigration policy finds little impetus due to (a) the relatively low capacity of migration-related and other nongovernmental associations to work as agenda-setters and exert strong pressure or veto power and (b) the resilient character of imagined notions of nation.

Important developments in this area include the creation of the *Consejos Consultivos* mentioned previously and of the Network of Support to Migrants in 2010, which was formed by several associations working in favor of migrants' rights. According to a recent OIM report (2011b: 8), the activities of this network (e.g., meetings, discussion fora) have contributed to broadening the public debate and calling the government's attention to migration issues. The OIM itself, together with the United Nations Population Fund, has played a key role in providing support for those activities, working with governments and civil society on various programs, advising, coordinating seminars and workshops, and publishing some of the most updated information. Yet, there seems to be a gap between technical discussions and policy implementation. "As in other countries, the impact of recommendations usually depends on political willingness, sustained commitment, and institutional resources."[49]

The role of academia, amplified by some media and international organizations' publications, has had a similar, limited impact. A group of scholars from various disciplines have been at the forefront of diffusion of information and generation of public debate on population and migration issues since the late 1980s; their work has provided inputs to decision-makers and some of them have been personally involved as consultants, reviewers, advisors, or part-time public officials (Comisión Sectorial de Población 2011). Their expertise and academic reputations have contributed to legitimizing some ideas and proposals, such as the linkage policy explained previously. In particular, the Program on Population at Universidad de la República has been training specialists and prospective public officials and publishing a good number of studies from a policy-oriented perspective.[50] Interviewees indicate that it is common knowledge in the local milieu that the majority of the faculty at this institution have an ideological affinity with the current coalition in government. However, scholars perceive their own roles as limited to providing information (i.e., inputs for decision makers or the media) and intermittent, depending on each administration's preferences for technical support (which clearly declined under Mujica).[51] Although the government encourages consultation, the relationship with social actors is still limited to a few players (e.g., associations like *Asociación de Familiares y Amigos de Migrantes "Idas y Vueltas,"* the *Asociación Cultural y Casa de los Inmigrantes "César Vallejo,"* the *Red de Apoyo al Migrante*, or the local chapter of the Scalabrinians) who have only sporadic participation and is driven by governmental actions. In short, "civil society is still an incipient actor."[52]

Finally, oral testimonies pointed to one important impediment to civil society leadership in the entire set of migration and population problems: it operates in the context of a society with discriminatory attitudes toward immigrants with a different racial or ethnic backgrounds (i.e., non-White, indigenous) and toward those who left the country and, presumably, do not understand the hardships of staying and are not entitled to the benefits of belonging. "Society is relatively hostile to returnees."[53] "There is some rejection of those who are abroad. As a popular saying goes: *los de afuera son de palo* (those who are outside [the family, the nation, or other] exist only in a figurative sense, but have no say on decisions)."[54] The idea of a nation as a self-contained entity and of being a relatively homogeneous and predominantly White or *mestizo* society of European descent is still very strong in the Uruguayan national identity, and this translates into a pejorative language and behavior toward immigrants from neighboring countries with darker skin or indigenous traits.[55] The media has reported some discriminatory measures, and experts warn that, in the advent of high volumes of immigration, the Uruguayan society has to work on accepting it as a positive change.[56] Therefore, potential inflows of immigrants from Bolivia or Paraguay, for instance, are not yet welcome, although they represent a much needed input in the declining labor force. Likewise, any migrant association aiming to represent the interests and rights of emigrants, foreign-born nationals, or newcomers faces the challenge of pushing for inclusion amidst those negative perceptions and attitudes and reworking the meaning of national identity and membership.

Analysis and Conclusions

In terms of historical antecedents and timing for innovation, Uruguay joins other South American cases: silence and neglect prevailed until recently. Only in the past decade have governments made significant efforts to court Uruguayans living abroad. The new policies, although they build on previous initiatives and extensive studies addressing the costs of inaction, represent a significant departure from a long record of underestimation and neglect of population and migration problems. As in Ecuador and Argentina, the coming to power of a new coalition set the stage for innovation. The immediate factor that prompted this policy shift was the mobilization of Uruguayans abroad around the time of the 2004 elections and its role in the Frente's victory, which created an unavoidable commitment to address that constituency's demands.

This was compounded by factors also present in other cases: the last two presidents' leadership roles, the profile of the emigrant group, and the nature of the Frente's political project, namely a development strategy in which the state has a prominent role and a progressive social agenda that brings human rights considerations to the forefront. An emphasis on linkages and absentee voting rights promised not only to reinforce nationhood bonds but also to make effective a notion of citizenship that goes beyond territorial borders and redefines the idea of the nation. The difficulties of reforming legislation to enfranchise expatriates is a characteristic of this case that sets it apart from the general trend in the region toward expanding political rights and extraterritorial voting.

In other words, the redrawing of the boundaries of the nation-state along nonterritorial bases is still an incipient process in Uruguay. Thus, in terms of goals, courting has been relatively successful in extending the scope of state actions, but it has failed to extend the borders of the polity to fully incorporate Uruguayans abroad. The sustainability of this policy is contingent not only on the state's capacity to reform itself but also on society's ability to acquire a greater voice and more organizational capacity, as well as to engage broader sectors with the reconstruction of national membership along pluralistic and nonterritorial lines.

From an analytical point of view, this case study contributes to the discussion on emigration policies in a number of ways. It expands our knowledge of the significant variation in sending states' policies toward emigrant communities by providing detailed evidence of why, how, and when state-led transnational policies develop in a country that differs considerably from the better-known cases in the existing literature; that is, it is a very small country that had historically neglected emigration problems and has a distinct demographic structure, a prolonged negative migration balance, a relatively small but highly qualified diaspora, and a long tradition of democratic inclusiveness. It adds to the comparison, too. While Uruguay shares with other cases the use of similar policy tools (e.g., new specialized offices and rhetoric, linkages), it differentiates itself in its emphasis on migration return, emigrants' political rights, and the difficulties in consistently advancing and institutionalizing emigration policy, even though there is serious political commitment to do so. The ups and downs of courting the diaspora illustrate the intermestic character of state-led transnationalism and the need to explore enabling and constraining factors within both the state and society in order to make emigration policies work more effectively.

This case study also qualifies and refines existing explanations and brings new elements to the discussion of potential applicability to other cases. Like Ecuador, Uruguay underlines the importance of some relatively underexplored domestic factors concerning the profile of the emigrant community, specific political projects, key decision makers, the state reformist approach, and social notions of citizenship and belonging. I argue in the concluding chapter that these factors are relevant not only to the explanation of emigration policymaking in Uruguay but also, more broadly, to our understanding of state– and society–diaspora relationships.

As mentioned in Chapter 2, the profile of the emigrant community is usually placed in a secondary role; size and potential economic contribution take priority. The case of Uruguay suggests that the levels and types of skills and the heterogeneity across various emigration waves may be as relevant as diaspora size. Uruguay also shows that human and social capital with transnational reach may be coveted by the state but, in contrast to other cases, emigrants' main contributions are expected to be made *in situ* rather than abroad. This is one of the ways in which this case underlines the importance of territoriality.

In addition, if various waves of emigration are examined, different state political motivations become evident, as does the importance of specific political projects. Paradigmatic cases of diaspora have biased the literature toward the study of broad, long-term processes of nation-building or nation-wrecking. Instead, Uruguay points out the relevance of political conjunctures such as democratic transitions or nation reconstruction after crises, that is, processes that involve an immediate "reparation" commitment with some sectors of society and may trigger policy innovation—a factor further illustrated by the Argentine case in the next chapter. This explains subtle variations: the Uruguayan state has committed to generating the conditions for return, rather than only capitalizing on migrant overseas networks, as other countries have done.

In addition, exploring formal levels of authority within the state, as other studies do, may not be enough. Intrabureaucratic and informal politics in transitional countries with strong presidential systems point to a few individual actors (presidents, ministers) who have an overwhelming voice in emigration policymaking. They, rather than the entire state apparatus or other political actors such as political parties or local governments, are in the driver's seats. As in Ecuador and Argentina, this "personalization" of policymaking seems crucial to understanding the many detours that policies may take and the difficulties of embedding policy initiatives in a firm institutional base; it also underlines that policy instruments are intertwined, and their effectiveness may be negatively affected if, for instance, presidential rhetoric is too vague or not matched with resource allocation and institutional commitments.

This case also shows that the connection between neoliberal projects and diaspora strategies is not a linear, straightforward one. Instead, a contextual and historical analysis of neoliberal and postneoliberal paths is necessary to identify synergies and/or tensions. Uruguay confirms that in contexts of unfinished democratic consolidation, partial or ineffective reform of the state undermines policy consistency and implementation and questions policy sustainability in the long term. Moreover, the strong role of the state advocated by postneoliberal governments may reinforce top-down approaches and jeopardize the chances of building state–diaspora partnerships. This is a point that will be revisited in connection to migrant responses to state-led initiatives (see Chapter 8).

Finally, while studies on long-distance transnationalism mostly emphasize the deterritorialization and wide-open possibilities of nation reimagining, Uruguay is a case of reterritorialization of the emigration debate. It suggests exploring conflictive notions of nation, belonging, and citizenship-related entitlements largely rooted in historical processes that have shaped the social imagination (i.e., the meanings of who is considered part of the nation and who legitimately participates in political decisions). Ironically, these notions are at odds with the human rights considerations pursued today, and together with relatively weak civil society organizational capacity, they function as brakes in the passage from courting to more permanent and substantive engagement.

Notes

1 The area of the country is 176,215 square kilometers. According to the 2011 census, the population is 3,286,314; approximately 95% of the total population resides in cities; and 1,319,108 people live in the capital city of Montevideo. See data from the National Institute of Statistics of Uruguay at www.ine.gub.uy/censos2011/index.html, accessed September 20, 2012.
2 Population at the time of independence (1828) was estimated at 74,000 (OIM 2011b:43). Immigrants mostly from Spain, Italy, and France account for the population growth in the second half of the 19th century. Total population was 1,042,700 at the peak of the European immigration wave (1908) and went up to 2,538,779 in 1960. Since then, the annual rate of population growth has been between zero and 1% (see World Bank data at http://databank.worldbank.org/data/views/reports/tableview.aspx, accessed February 6, 2014).
3 The migration balance turned negative in 1960–1964: –6,000 people, that is, –0.47% of the country's population. It reached –147,000 (–10.49%) in 1970–1974, and decreased again in the following two decades. It dropped below –10 % again in 2002 (Taks 2006:2; OIM 2011b:56). The mortality rate has been relatively constant since the 1950s, and the birth rate has consistently declined since then. (See details in OIM 2011b:56.)
4 While the GDP grew in the last two decades, unemployment increased, reaching 17% in 2002 and decreasing later to a 5.4% in 2011 (OIM 2011b:33–34, 46). This reflects broader fluctuations in the levels of economic activity, employment, wages, and benefits that contributed to regular waves of out-migration. Uruguayans abroad are estimated at around 600,000 people, (18% of the total population in 2006) (OIM 2011b:57). See the same source for further details on different forms of measuring the emigration phenomenon, historical trends, and the profile of emigrants.
5 Estimates are based on reports prepared by the Ministry of Foreign Affairs indicating that the number of returnees tripled since 2009, reaching around 350 people per month in 2011 (Ministerio de Desarrollo Social 2012:92).
6 The volume of remittances has tended to increase, but it remains relatively low: $95 million in 2009, which equaled 1.4% of the GDP and reached only 2.4% of total households that year, with a monthly average of $150 remitted (OIM 2011b:83–82). The most recent figure is for 2013, when remittances amounted to $108 million (cf. www.pewhispanic.org/2013/11/15/remittances-to-latin-america-recover-but-not-to-mexico/ph-remittances-11-2013-a-16/, accessed July 25, 2014).
7 See www.parlamento.gub.uy/leyes/AccesoTextoLey.asp?Ley=15737&Anchor=, accessed October 1, 2012.
8 See www.vinculacion.gub.uy/informacion.htm, accessed October 5, 2012.
9 The analysis relies heavily on the work of the local leading expert, Professor Adela Pellegrino, as well as on the policy advice of international organizations such as the United Nations Conference on Trade and Development,

the United Nations Educational Scientific and Cultural Organization, and the IOM. The report recommendations included the creation of a specialized office to address the needs of all Uruguayans abroad, the expansion of consular activities, the compilation of information about migration problems, the granting of absentee voting rights to citizens residing abroad, the revision and update of legislation, and the promotion of all types of ties with nationals abroad. See www.vinculacion.gub.uy/Informe%20Comite%20Asesor.htm, accessed October 1, 2012.

10 Cf. www.corteelectoral.gub.uy/gxpfiles/elecciones/Elecciones%20Nacionales% 202004.htm, accessed October 12, 2012.
11 See Programmatic Plan 2010–2015 approved by the V Extraordinary Congress of the Frente Amplio, Cro. Zelmar Michelini, December 13–14, p. 160, available at www.frenteamplio.org.uy/files/Programa%202010–2015_1.pdf, accessed October 16, 2013.
12 Interview with Mariela Dardanelli, independent consultant, former official at the Ministry of Labor and Social Security, Montevideo, April 25, 2012. Personal communication with José Peralta, journalist specializing in migration, Montevideo, April 25, 2012.
13 He addressed three social sectors in particular: the youth, women, and those living abroad. Regarding the latter, he emphasized that "the peregrine nation is peregrine but, above all, is nation" and invited them "to work together for the construction of an Uruguay where to be born would not be a problem, to be young would not be suspicious, and to become old would not be a punishment" (author's translation). See www.lainsignia.org/2005/marzo/ibe_014.htm, accessed February 7, 2013.
14 Uruguay's territory is divided into 19 departments or administrative jurisdictions.
15 Interviews with Jorge Muiño and Andrés Peláez, directors, General Directorate of Consular Affairs and Linkages, Ministry of Foreign Affairs, Montevideo, April 25, 2012.
16 In the meantime, last year's governmental efforts have focused on modernizing consular services, encouraging further legislation update, and providing support to returnees and information to prospective immigrants and tourists, among other things. See www.mrree.gub.uy/frontend/page?1,dgacv,DGACV AmpliacionVinculacion,O,es,0,PAG;CONC;2013;31;D;principales-avances-en-gestion-consular-y-vinculacion-2013;1;PAG, accessed July 10, 2014.
17 Interview with Jorge Muiño and Andrés Peláez, Montevideo, April 25, 2012.
18 Interviews with Alba Goycoechea, head officer, OIM, Montevideo, April 25, 2012, and Mariela Dardanelli, Montevideo, April 25, 2012.
19 The office's website compiles all kinds of news and information related to linkage. Over the last 2 years, the site has been changing considerably in format and content to expand coverage of new linkages with emigrants, provide more information to both emigrants and returnees, and generate dialogue with the emigrant community in general. See www.d20.org.uy/.
20 The online list posted by the 20th Department includes 44 active councils around the world but, unfortunately, it is not updated. See www.d20.org.uy/Lista-de-Consejos, accessed July 10, 2014. Secondary sources differed considerably in their estimates (e.g., Sosa González 2009; Taks 2006, 2010).
21 In Spain, the list compiled by the Uruguayan government includes 50 associations. See details at www.mrree.gub.uy/frontend/page?1,inicio,ampliacion-ppa l,O,es,0,PAG;CONC;73;3;D;espana-1848;2;PAG, accessed February 5, 2014.
22 Interview with Ana M. Sosa, Department 20, Office of Linkages and Return, Ministry of Foreign Affairs, Montevideo, April 26, 2012.
23 Interview with Jorge Muiño and Andrés Peláez, Montevideo, April 25, 2012.

24 See www.parlamento.gub.uy/leyes/AccesoTextoLey.asp?Ley=18250&Anchor=, accessed October 5, 2012.

25 The law commits the state to negotiate bilateral agreements with other countries in order to guarantee their equal treatment of nationals in those countries; it lists the main characteristics of the linkage policy mentioned previously and the institutions in charge of its implementation; it also awards tax exemptions to returnees for the import of personal items, tools, and other things.

26 Personal communication with Adela Pellegrino, professor, Universidad de la República, specialist on population and migration issues, Montevideo, April 26, 2012.

27 See declarations issued after the general meetings at www.d20.org.uy/-Encuentros-Mundiales-, accessed October 2, 2012.

28 As of today, voting is compulsory and *in situ* (i.e., expatriates willing to vote have to return to Uruguay to register and cast their votes).

29 Cf. http://elecciones.corteelectoral.gub.uy/20091025/SSPMain.asp, accessed February 9, 2013.

30 Indeed, in early 2014, a special parliamentary commission met to study this issue. The persistence of opposite views among political parties and about upcoming elections appeared as the main obstacles to act promptly. See www.d20.org.uy/IMG/pdf/LA_DIARIA-Carta_al_Presidente—.pdf, accessed July 10, 2014. Also, two social organizations with links to migrant associations and consultation councils (Ronda Cívica por el Voto and Coordinadora por el Voto en el Exterior) submitted a proposal to all political parties to encourage, in the short run, an interpretation of constitutional norms to reaffirm and facilitate voting rights of citizens living abroad and, within 5 years, the formation of a working group to elaborate a new bill and make changes effective by the following presidential elections in 2019. The Frente Amplio endorses these proposals, which are posted in the governments' official site. See www.d20.org.uy/Proyecto-de-ley-y-Comunicado, accessed July 10, 2014.

31 For instance, the Ministries of Foreign Affairs and Housing, together with a major bank, signed an agreement in November 2013 to facilitate returnees' access to mortgages. See www.lr21.com.uy/comunidad/1141427-bhu-plan-ahorro-adquisicion-vivienda-uruguayos-retornados-exterior, accessed July 10, 2014. Recent returnees with at least 3 years of residence abroad can also apply for support to business projects within the Softlandings Uruguay Program—an initiative in which the National Agency for Research and Innovation is involved. See http://softlandingsuruguay.org/en/, accessed July 10, 2014.

32 See www.mrree.gub.uy/frontend/page?1,consular-vinculacion,c-u-a-c,O,es,0, accessed February 9, 2013.

33 Interview with Juan J. Calvo, professor, Population Program, Universidad de la República, and consultant for various international organizations, Montevideo, April 24, 2012.

34 Interview with Mariela Dardanelli, Montevideo, April 25, 2012.

35 Merklen (2007) ably explains the tensions, ruptures, and complex adaptations of Uruguayan exiles in France, as well as the compromises made to integrate them in the receiving society, to justify allegiance and belonging to a country that expelled them, and to make sense of the constant transformation of their individual and national identities. Coraza de los Santos (2003) offers a parallel study of Uruguayan political exiles in Spain.

36 Other arguments were also voiced, and political calculations played a role. Traditional political parties opposed the project, assuming that the emigrant community is mainly formed by political exiles who would eventually vote for left-wing candidates. The number of potential absentee votes—approximately

250,000—is also a source of worry. Although these may not be accurate projections, the role of citizens abroad in the 2004 election results intensified the concerns about the political costs of implementing such a change. Legal, moral, and logistical arguments were also expressed in parliamentary commissions to oppose; questions revolved around how to legally implement secret absentee ballots while preserving transparency and efficiency and how to justify that those who are physically absent decide on the lives of those who will actually endure the consequences of decisions (Moraes Mena 2009:117–118).

37 See congressmen's speeches and the document presented by the Councils for Consultation in the launching of the campaign, cited in Sosa González (2009:50–52, 58).

38 At the last meeting of consultation councils in December 2013, the General Directorate of Consular Affairs and Linkages adopted a new label: *Soy Uruguay* (I am Uruguay) to encourage, in migrants' minds, the passage from the notion of "belonging to" a country or place to "embodying" the nation, a concept that calls for commitment and responsibility in each and every action. See www.mrree.gub.uy/frontend/page?1,dgacv,DGACVAmpliacionVinculacion,O, es,0,PAG;CONC;2013;21;D;soy-uruguay;1;PAG; accessed July 10, 2014.

39 Interview with Juan J. Calvo, Montevideo, April 24, 2012.

40 Interview with Carlos Luján, director, Strategic Analysis Unit, Ministry of Foreign Affairs, Montevideo, April 24, 2012.

41 According to several informants, President Mujica has a serious concern with the long-standing depopulation problem in the countryside and deep sympathy for emigrants' situations. He has often referred to the advantages of immigration and the need for foreign workers. For instance, at the moment of signing cooperation agreements with the government of Peru (January 2011), he invited Peruvians to live and invest in Uruguay, although his references to the "type" of preferred immigrant and female workers were unfortunate and made evident generalized stereotypes and prejudices of the Uruguayan society. He said that Uruguay wanted more than "third-class sailors" who are often hired by foreign fishing companies at a minimum wage or "maids who usually work for rich families and have a reputation of being good, honest, and docile workers." Instead, he urged entrepreneurs to realize the good investment opportunities the country offers. The comments might have been well-intentioned and correctly described the trend in terms of immigrant labor incorporation (OIM 2011:72; Taks 2010:162–163), but the phrases were at odds with a policy based on human rights considerations. See http://elpolvorin.over-blog.es/article-uruguay-mujica-pidio-que-vengan-peruanos-pero-no-cualquiera-65853837.html, accessed February 8, 2013.

42 Interviews with Jorge Muiño and Andrés Peláez, Montevideo, April 25, 2012.

43 Interview with Carlos Luján, Montevideo, April 24, 2012.

44 Personal communication with J. Peralta, Montevideo, April 26, 2012.

45 Interview with Ana M. Sosa, Montevideo, April 26, 2012.

46 Interviews with Andrés Peláez and Jorge Muiño, Montevideo, April 25, 2012.

47 Interviews with Mariela Dardanelli, Montevideo, April 25, 2012, and Juan J. Calvo, Montevideo, April 24, 2012.

48 Interview with Carlos Luján, Montevideo, April 24, 2012.

49 Interview with Juan Artola, director, Regional Office for South America, OIM, Buenos Aires, May 9, 2012.

50 Interview with Juan J. Calvo, Montevideo, April 24, 2012.

51 Personal communication with Adela Pellegrino, Montevideo, April 26, 2012.

52 Interviews with Andrés Peláez and Jorge Muiño, Montevideo, April 25, 2012.

53 Interview with Mariela Dardanelli, Montevideo, April 25, 2012.

54 Personal communication with Adela Pellegrino, Montevideo, April 26, 2012.

55 Some of those attitudes are documented in recent studies. See Ministerio de Desarrollo Social (2012).
56 See, for instance, *La Jornada*, January 20, 2011, and August 26, 2010.

Works Cited

Aguiar, César A. 1982. *Uruguay: País de Emigración*. Montevideo, Uruguay: Ediciones de la Banda Oriental.
Almagro, Luis. 2012. "Migración en Uruguay: Hacia una Política de Estado." Intervención del Ministro de Relaciones Exteriores en el Seminario "Monitoreo Social Sobre las Migraciones en Uruguay." Montevideo, Uruguay: Ministerio de Relaciones Exteriores. 28 de Marzo.
Borraz, Fernando and Susan Pozo. 2007. "Remittances in Uruguay." *Revista de Ciencias Empresariales y Economía*. Año 6. pp. 19–43.
Calvo, Juan José y Pablo Mieres. eds. 2007. *Importante pero Urgente. Políticas de Población en Uruguay*. Montevideo, Uruguay: UNFPA/Rumbos.
Chasquetti, Daniel. 2008. "Uruguay 2007: El Complejo Año de las Reformas." *Revista de Ciencia Política*. 28(1): 385–403.
Comisión Sectorial de Población. 2011, April. *Visión, Objetivos y Lineamientos Estratégicos Para la Implementación de Políticas de Población en Uruguay*. Montevideo: Presidencia de la República Oriental del Uruguay, Oficina de Planeamiento y Presupuesto.
Coraza de los Santos, Enrique. 2003. "Realidades y Visiones del Exilio Uruguayo en España." *América Latina Hoy*. 34, August: 79–102.
Dickinson, Jen and Adrian J. Bailey. 2007. "(Re)membering Diaspora: Uneven Geographies of Indian Dual Citizenship." *Political Geography*. 26:757–774.
Finch, Martin H.J. 1982. *A Political Economy of Uruguay since 1870*. New York: St. Martin's Press.
Gamlen, Alan. 2011. "Creating and Destroying Diaspora Strategies." International Migration Institute, University of Oxford, Working Paper No. 31. April.
Ho, Elaine Lynn-Ee. 2011. "Claiming the Diaspora: Elite Mobility, Sending State Strategies and the Spatialities of Citizenship." *Progress in Human Geography*. 35(6): 757–772.
Itzigsohn, J. 2000. "Immigration and the Boundaries of Citizenship: The Institutions of Immigrants' Political Transnationalism." *International Migration Review*, 34 (4), Winter, 1126–1154.
Ladra, Antonio. 2012. "La Oposición Sumaría más Votos que el Frente Amplio." *Clarín*, September 24.
Merklen, Denis. 2007. "Sufrir Lejos, Quedarse Juntos. El Exilio de los Uruguayos en Francia." *Anuario de Estudios Americanos*. 64(1): 63–86.
Ministerio de Desarrollo Social. 2012. *Caracterización de las Nuevas Corrientes Migratorias en Uruguay. Inmigrantes y Retornados: Acceso a Derechos Económicos, Sociales y Culturales*. Informe final. Montevideo, Uruguay.
Moraes, Natalia et al. 2009. "Estrategias de Vinculación de los Estados Latinoamericanos con sus Diasporas: Un Análisis de las Iniciativas Desarrolladas por Colombia, Perú, Brasil y Uruguay." In *Migración y Participación Política: Estados, Organizaciones y Migrantes Latinoamericanos en Perspective Local-Transnacional*, ed. by Ángeles Escrivá, Anastasia Bermúdez, and

Natalia Moraes. Madrid: Consejo Superior de Investigaciones Científicas. pp. 297–325.

Moraes Mena, Natalia. 2009. "El Voto que el Alma no Pronuncia: Un Análisis de las Movilizaciones y los Discursos Sobre el Derecho al Voto de los Uruguayos en el Exterior." In *Migración y Participación Política: Estados, Organizaciones y Migrantes Latinoamericanos en Perspective Local-Transnacional,* ed. by Ángeles Escrivá, Anastasia Bermúdez, and Natalia Moraes. Madrid: Consejo Superior de Investigaciones Científicas. pp. 103–123.

Moreira, Constanza and Adela Pellegrino. 2001. "Ciudadanía y Migración: Las Fronteras del Uruguay Como Comunidad Política." In *Ciudadanía en Tránsito: Perfiles Para el Debate,* comp. by Laura Gioscia. Montevideo: Instituto de Ciencia Política, Facultad de Ciencias Sociales, Ediciones de la Banda Oriental, Colección Política Viva. pp. 109–140.

Narbono, Pedro. 2011. "La Reforma de la Administración Central del Uruguay: Entre Proyectos Neoweberianos y un Statu Quo Discrecional y Heterogéneo a un Neoliberalismo Subdesarrollado." Informe de Coyuntura no. 10. Montevideo, Uruguay: Instituto de Ciencia Política.

OIM. 2011a, November. *Migrantes Sudamericanos en España: Panorama y Políticas.* Cuadernos Migratorios no. 1. Buenos Aires: Organización Internacional Para las Migraciones.

OIM. 2011b. *Perfil Migratorio de Uruguay 2011.* Buenos Aires: Organización Internacional Para las Migraciones.

Østergaard-Nielsen, Eva. ed. 2003. *International Migration and Sending Countries: Perceptions, Policies, and Transnational Relations.* Houndmills: Palgrave/Macmillan.

Panizza, Francisco. 2002. "Discurso e Instituciones en la Reforma de la Administración Pública Uruguaya." *Revista Uruguaya de Ciencia Política.* 13: 59–93.

Pastorini, Laura. 2007. "No Estamos Todos los que Somos ni Somos Todos los que Estamos. Relaciones Entre los Procesos Migratorios y los de Construcción de Identidad en el Caso de los Migrantes Uruguayos Residentes en México." In *Migración Uruguaya: Un Enfoque Antropológico,* ed. by Beatriz Diconca and Gabriela Campodónico. Montevideo, Uruguay: Universidad de la República/OIM. pp. 37–62.

Pellegrino, Adela. 2001. "Trends in Latin American Skilled Migration: 'Brain Drain' or 'Brain Exchange'?" *International Migration.* 39(5): 111–132.

Pellegrino, Adela. 2002, September. "Skilled Labor Migration from Developing Countries: Study on Argentina and Uruguay." International Migration Papers #58. Geneva: International Labour Office, International Migration Programme.

Pellegrino, Adela and Andrea Vigorito. 2005. "Emigration and Economic Crisis: Recent Evidence from Uruguay." *Migraciones Internacionales.* 3(1): 57–81.

Pellegrino, Adela and Andrea Vigorito. 2009. "La Emigración Calificada Desde América Latina y las Iniciativas Nacionales de Vinculación: Un Análisis del Caso Uruguayo." *Pensamiento Iberoamericano.* 4: 189–215.

Petruccelli, José Luis. 1979. "Consequences of Uruguayan Emigration: Research Note." *International Migration Review.* 13(3), Autumn: 519–526.

Portillo, Álvaro. 2006. "La Política Migratoria del Estado Uruguayo." In *Relaciones Estado-Diáspora: La Perspective de América Latina y el Caribe,* coord. by Carlos González Gutiérrez. México City: Secretaría de Relaciones

Exteriores, Instituto de los Mexicanos en el Exterior, Universidad Autónoma de los Zacatecas, Asociación Nacional de Universidades e Instituciones de Educación Superior, Miguel Ángel Porrúa Librero-Editor. Tomo II. pp. 313–328.

Ragazzi, Francesco. 2009. "Governing Diasporas." *International Political Sociology* 3: 378–397.

Sosa González, Ana María. 2009. "La Política de Re-Vinculación del Estado Uruguayo con su Diáspora." *Tempo e Argumento*, Revista de Pós-Graduação em Historia, Florianópolis, Brasilia. 1(2): 37–63.

Taks, Javier. 2006. "Migraciones Inernacionales en Uruguay: De Pueblo Trasplantado a Diáspora Vinculada." *Revista THEOMAI*. 14, Second Semester: 139–156.

Taks, Javier. 2010. "Antecedentes y Desafíos de las Políticas de Migración en Uruguay." In *Estado Actual y Perspectivas de las Políticas Migratorias en el MERCOSUR,* coord. by Cristina Zurbriggen and Lenin Mondol. Montevideo, Uruguay: FLACSO/Logos. pp. 151–179.

Trigo, Abril. 2003. *Memorias Migrantes. Testimonios y Ensayos Sobrela Diáspora Uruguaya.* Rosario, Argentina: Beatriz Viterbo Editora/Ediciones Trilce.

6 Argentina
Selective and Intermittent Flirting

Introduction

Argentina is the second largest country in South America, after Brazil. It occupies an area of 2,780,400 square kilometers of rich natural resources. Its third position in the ranking of largest and strongest economies is currently challenged (by Colombia), mainly due to Argentina's mounting inflation, weak currency, low growth, and long-standing political problems with repercussions in economic (mis)management. The total population of 41.45 million is unevenly distributed in the territory.[1] It has been estimated that 956,800 Argentines resided abroad in 2010 (2.4% of the total population then).[2] This stock of citizens abroad, on which statistics are elusive, has been relatively constant for the past decade. There were some historic peaks in the outflows, notably during the 1970s, when people escaped political violence and dictatorship, and around the time of the 2001 financial default and dramatic politico-economic crisis.

It is only in the aftermath of such crises that official discourses started to include concrete references to emigrants and attempt to court citizens abroad were launched, particularly to those in Spain. As a result, emigration momentarily acquired preeminence in the domestic and international agenda, and new institutional spheres and interinstitutional collaboration practices were created and transnational links proliferated. That was a remarkable shift for a country that built its identity around the idea of being a receiving nation. However, in contrast to other cases in this book, Argentina's new emigration policy did not follow a constant, incremental path toward further courting.

Therefore, the Argentine case invites us to revisit some assumptions about sending states' involvement in transnational policies and the nature of engagement states are pursuing. Some characteristics of this case question general assumptions: the number of Argentine emigrants is not very large (although it was significant at certain points in time); emigration is not simply motivated by poverty and unemployment; the level of organization of the emigrant community is relatively low, and state efforts to court the diaspora soon stalled. The initiatives implemented by the Argentine government in early 2000s and their evolution suggest some analytical refinements and further comparisons.

This chapter shows that the Argentine state's initiatives have contributed to the development of a transnational space, even though in the last few years outreach efforts receded. In order to understand the motivation, intensity, and impact of the state's initial involvement, we need to look at the following: characteristics of the emigrant community (rather than its size and organizational level); specific political projects (e.g., rebuilding political representation ties, broadening support, and recapturing human capital, rather than nationhood ideas or state dependence on remittances); specific domestic agents like the presidency (rather than political parties) and processes (e.g., historical society–state relations, political instability, human rights issues, economic crises); and bilateral and multilateral agreements, regardless of their level of institutionalization.

To explain the apparent fading of emigration policy, it is necessary to situate it within broader concerns with migration dynamics and the evolution of policymakers' definitions of the problem at hand. Thus, this case suggests that one possible outcome of emigration policy is the redefinition of the problem (which in this case ceased to be considered a problem). This, in turn, introduces an element that is also present in the other cases: the possibility that courting may not lead to engagement; rather, emigration policies may evolve through cycles or fragmented episodes of rapprochement and withdrawal.

Population and Migration Problems: A Brief Historical Overview

Population and migration policies in Argentina have been linked to political and economic needs and ideas. The unification of the territory, the formation of the state, the implementation of different development strategies, the prevalence of certain notions of ethnic and cultural eligibility, and external factors (e.g., international crises, wars, cooperation agreements) have shaped migration policies since the 19th century.[3] Emigration is a relatively new phenomenon in Argentina. The country was historically (and still is) considered a place for immigration. Emigration has received increasing academic and political attention in the last few decades, and especially since the 1990s, when the numbers rose and the characteristics of flows changed. While in the past emigration was considered a temporary problem that was mostly linked to political instability and persecution, in the early 2000s it was seen as a relatively constant and heterogeneous trend related to the deteriorating political and economic situations (Bertoncello 1986; Gurrieri 1982; Lattes and Oteiza 1986; Marshall 1991; Novick 2005).

Since immigration in Argentina was historically seen as a tool for development and was linked to the notion of progress and national wealth, emigration has always been associated with failure to develop and loss of valued human resources. It was usually assumed that emigration was a short-term, temporary phenomenon originated by specific (negative) domestic conjunctures. These are recurrent themes in public officials' discourse and scholarly analyses of emigration in Argentina. Nevertheless, it is difficult to identify a comprehensive and consistent set of norms and policies to account for a global state approach to migration issues. As in other Latin American countries, population and migration policies have never been at the top of the governmental agenda, and this has been more true since the mid-1980s/early 1990s, when neoliberal programs were implemented and states withdrew from planning and regulation of socioeconomic activities (Novick 2005:7). Migration policies in Argentina have also shared a number of negative traits with other countries in the region, such as lack of definition, weak content, excessive rhetoric, and time frame and other inconsistencies (Martínez Pizzarro 2003).

From a long-term historical perspective, the period between 1870 and 1929 was one of massive European immigration, which (together with foreign investment) was promoted by the government as a way of populating the recently unified territory and expanding the export-oriented agricultural model of development. The Depression led to a review of that economic strategy because commodity prices and demand fell abruptly, as did capital inflows. In 1930, Argentina entered a period of political instability characterized by the attempt by dominant political elites to stop the ascendancy and the increasing political power of middle and lower classes. Migration policies became restrictive and European immigration declined. The flows of migrants from Latin American countries increased as of that time. The new development strategy that gradually gained momentum (import substitution industrialization) produced significant domestic migration toward urban centers. The industrialization process that followed created a demand for labor. Therefore, during the first two Peronist governments (1946–1955), population and migration policies were seen as part of a broader development policy and, thus, necessarily subject to planning and management.

The military governments that followed implemented restrictive migration policies, especially toward immigrants coming from neighboring countries. There was also an emphasis on illegal flows and on the potential security implications of unrestrictive immigration. The xenophobic discourse was accentuated as social demands and unrest increased toward the end of the 1960s and the state applied repressive policies. Emigration and exile of political and intellectual cadres increased as political violence escalated. The brief democratically elected administrations in between military rule (1963–1966; 1973–1976) again linked economic development and migration policies when taking some measures to increase, manage, and geographically reorient immigration, reduce emigration, and integrate Latin American immigrants while also promoting immigration from outside the region. The first precedents for policy initiatives toward emigration were in the late 1950s, when governments showed some concern over the exit of scientists and drew up some plans to repatriate them. In 1965, a special commission was created to study the problem.

The lengthy period of military government that took hold in 1976 initiated important changes in the socioeconomic model and intensified persecution and repression. Concerns about the low population growth rate led to favoring immigration, albeit selective, managed, and regulated by a new, broader, and more comprehensive legal framework. As for emigration, there was an attempt to encourage scientists and technicians to remain in the country, as well as to promote migration return. In 1973, emigration was included as part of an overall design of public policies, and the need to repatriate technicians and scientists was acknowledged. The democratic government that followed (1983–1989) formally adopted an open-door migration policy, enacted a general amnesty in 1984, and showed preoccupation with emigration. In 1984, another commission was created within the Ministry of Foreign Affairs to advise the presidency on migration return matters and other issues. The government was particularly concerned over the loss of highly skilled professionals. In 1984, it implemented a plan for the return of Argentine refugees and all others living abroad, as well as a special program to facilitate the return of "gifted Argentines." As part of an attempt to break with the authoritarian and antidemocratic past, the government (and former President Alfonsín, in particular) committed to ending persecutions, respecting human rights, and welcoming exiles (Albarracín 2004:103–108). But, at the same time, it implemented restrictive immigration measures on the basis of the increasingly critical economic situation. Moreover, according to Novick (1997:116), there was no attempt to include the demographic dimension in economic and social planning during this period.

Similar restrictive policies were implemented during the 1990s, because immigration was associated with illegality, rising unemployment and crime rates, displacement of the native labor force, and disrespect for national institutions. Yet by that time, regional integration had advanced and required at least some flexibility in the treatment of immigrants from neighboring countries. A generous amnesty was decreed in 1992, just a year after the signature of the MERCOSUR foundational agreement (i.e., the Treaty of Asunción). By virtue of the preeminence given to market-oriented reforms during this period, there was less emphasis on the state's role and planning than in previous decades. Regarding emigration, in 1991, Law 24,007 was passed to allow Argentines living abroad to vote (Novick and Murias 2005). In addition, increasing concerns translated into institutional developments, such as the creation or expansion of specific offices to address emigrants' demands. The Argentines Abroad Office, within the Ministry of Foreign Affairs, has expanded considerably over the last 20 years in terms of personnel and functions. The International Affairs Office was created within the National Directorate of Migration (Ministry of the Interior) in 1998 to deal with all issues and negotiations that involve foreign state and nonstate actors.[4]

Finally, it is worth noting that the international and regional contexts have been moving migration issues from the strictly domestic sphere to the foreign policy agenda and including them in bilateral and multilateral negotiations. As it is explained in Chapter 3, the idea of a shared responsibility in the causes and consequences of international migration and the need to cooperate started to be part of policymakers' definitions of the problem. Argentina became a leader of this multilateral approach in the past decade. The friendly relations established with European countries since the return to democracy in Argentina—particularly with Spain—provided a propitious environment for collaboration when the migration flows reversed in the first years of the 21st century and the number of Argentines (mostly descendants of Italians and Spaniards) emigrating to Southern Europe increased considerably.

Political and Economic Expats

All sources and all people interviewed for this study agree on the difficulties in accurately assessing the number of Argentines living abroad under different immigration statuses. As it was mentioned in the introduction of this chapter, it is tentatively estimated that they amount to around 1 million today. There are very few and only partial studies on this issue. They point out the following trends: (a) there is a lack of reliable quantitative information; (b) emigration is not a totally new phenomenon: it started in the mid-1950s and has been incremental since then, though with oscillations; (c) numbers increased since the mid-1970s and peaked at the time of the 2001 crisis and immediately afterward;[5] (d) developed countries and particularly Western Europe (mainly Spain and Italy) became the preferred destinations for the last wave of emigrants; (e) domestic factors (namely political and economic crises, together with an underlying questioning of basic cultural and ethical beliefs) are the determinants of the decision to emigrate;[6] (f) members of this last wave of outflows were mostly young (between 25 and 44 years old) and with high educational levels and jobs at the time of leaving, though the socioeconomic profile is more heterogeneous today than in previous waves (i.e., professionals, technicians, as well as other occupations are included); and (g) in contrast to other South American cases where women led outflows, the number of women and men was almost the same.[7]

As for Argentines in Spain, Martínez Pizarro (2003:35) argues that the number almost doubled between 1991 (53,837) and 2001 (103,831), but it is estimated that the figure may be considerably higher today. According to the Ministry of Foreign Affairs of Argentina, the total number in 2005 was somewhere between 380,000 and 500,000, including legal residents who have dual citizenship in Spain or another country within the European Union (and consequently do not appear in the statistics as immigrants) or are under different types of visas (e.g., workers, students) and illegal residents (a figure that is impossible to calculate exactly). From that total, at least 150,000 are believed to have emigrated in the past decade (mostly around the time of the 2001 crisis).[8] Yet, the only official figures refer to those who have residency cards or authorization to stay, and these come from the Ministry of Labour and Social Affairs of Spain (see note 12) or the National Institute of Statistics. The latter counted 231,630 Argentine immigrants (that is, individuals born in Argentina, over 15 years old, who had resided in Spain for a year or more) in 2007.[9] Immigration flows have declined and even reversed in the last few years, mostly affected by the global economic crisis.[10] By 31 December 2012, the number of Argentines holding residency cards was down to 93,696.[11]

In the heyday of the concerns with emigration in Argentina, the regularization process[12] conducted by Spain between February and May 2005 shed some light not only on the magnitude of the flows but also on the incipient development of some transnational processes. As a result of the regularization, the number of immigrants with working permits increased considerably and, as explained in the next section, the Argentine state became increasingly involved in the affairs of the emigrant community to cultivate courting.[13] The profile of the last wave of Argentine emigrants (i.e., young, educated, with relatives or networks in Spain, employed at the time of leaving, and not active in migrants' associations) is closely related to the state motivation to promote transnational links.

As for the development of emigrants' networks and their links with state institutions, it is worth noting the increasing mobilization of a set of associations formed by Argentine expatriates in Spain. These associations (called *casas*, which means houses in Spanish) take various institutional forms and gather members from the local milieu, except for a few groups that have been working only through websites accessible to people in different places. The casas coexist with older associations formed by political exiles in the 1970s. A detailed analysis of associations' roles is provided in Chapter 8. Suffice it to say here that only some of them have maintained regular links with state offices (notably, the Casa in Madrid). In the mid-2000s, the regularization process in Spain created an opportunity to develop an incipient relationship with Argentine consulates. However, lack of experience and knowledge on both sides of the relationship put some limits on collaboration at that time.[14]

From the state side, the Ministry of the Interior made some timid steps in that direction (see next section). The Ministry of Foreign Affairs, through its office of Argentines Abroad, embassies, and consulates, has a long tradition of assistance to individual emigrants (i.e., people who request help to solve specific problems), but has lacked a comprehensive, proengagement approach toward the entire emigrant community and the development of broader links. Even though officials at that ministry are interested in cultivating those relations, they admitted a decade ago that it would take time and some restructuring of their professional training and the consular institution itself in order to pass from an assistance-oriented and technical function to one that is more political in relation to expatriates.[15] As it is explained in the last section of this chapter, Argentine officials still expect the emigrants to organize further and take the lead in defining a collaboration agenda. This is seen today as a prerequisite for the state to respond.

Launching Outreach Efforts

There is consensus around the idea that a new migration policy developed when President Néstor Kirchner took office in 2003 and that it revolved around the idea of migration as a right, in consonance with the government's stance in the defense of human rights in general. Important measures were taken regarding both emigration and immigration, such as a legislation update and the regularization of Latin American immigrants (mainly from Peru, Paraguay, and Bolivia), family reunification, and related issues. Increasing immigration from neighboring countries has lately refocused the agenda on these issues.

However, in the early 2000s, there were some specific initiatives and several new institutional spheres created to address the problem of emigrants. Most of these initiatives were not originated in (nor did they try to answer) emigrants' demands. The government's concern with updating and expanding governing techniques beyond borders paralleled the increasing salience given to these questions by the press at that time (Albarracín 2004:106–107; Novick and Murias 2005:18–19). Yet, both government and media attention to these issues have been intermittent since then.

One of the first measures was the creation of a website to conduct an online census of Argentines in Spain. The idea originated in the Ministry of the Interior, after the minister visited Spain in February 2004. The National Directorate of Migration implemented it between March and September 2004, thus creating a direct communication line between individuals and a state agency. The online census of 13,242 emigrants who answered the questionnaire (from a total of 17,000 people who had registered) shed light on the profile of expatriates,[16] which was then consistent with the trends observed then when looking at potential emigrants (Novick et al. 2005) and a sample of 250 Argentines residing in Madrid (Novara 2005).

Another initiative is the *Raíces* Program (*Raíces* is the Spanish acronym for Network of Argentine Researchers and Scientists Abroad, and it also means *roots*), which was initially implemented by the Secretariat of Science, Technology, and Productive Innovation within the Ministry of Education. Like similar endeavors launched by Uruguay, the program aims to strengthen the scientific and technological capacities of the country by promoting the permanent residency of national researchers in Argentina and collaboration links with Argentine researchers residing abroad. Specific goals include increasing relations between Argentine researchers living at home and abroad; dissemination of information about their work and about working opportunities in Argentina; creation of networks of scientists; and engaging firms, foundations, and NGOs in the program's activities. There are also subsidies to favor the return migration of professionals and knowledge transfer (e.g., through the development of scientific activities during sabbatical years).[17]

In addition, the government increased efforts to provide support and assistance to emigrants on several issues. It tried to facilitate certain procedures, such as being connected to embassies and consulates, voting, renewing IDs, and completing other paperwork. Bilateral agreements were signed with both sending and receiving countries (members of MERCOSUR, Peru, Bolivia, Spain, and Italy) and addressed social security issues and norms on obtaining or validating driving licenses. In particular, the Argentine government was very active during the regularization process of immigrants to Spain in early 2005. The Ministry of Foreign Affairs allocated ad hoc personnel for 3 months to some consulates and created itinerant offices to provide information, help people to fill in the forms, and help them obtain the necessary documents on time (e.g., birth certificate, clean police record). This was an opportunity to establish some contacts with the emigrants' associations, which occasionally demanded information and help.[18]

Those steps were consistent with the spirit of Migration Law 25,781, passed on December 17, 2003, and effective on January 20, 2004. Title IX of that law is devoted to Argentines abroad and establishes that the government might sign treaties with receiving countries in order to guarantee emigrants' access to labor and social security rights and the possibility of sending remittances. It also establishes tax exemptions in cases of returnees who want to send their personal belongings home. Embassies and consulates have to provide information about those exemptions and related matters to expatriates willing to return to Argentina. In addition, the adoption of this law reflects the increasing role played by Congress in drawing up a new and more comprehensive policy approach. The discussions of the bill within the Commission on Population and Human Resources and among legislators, human rights NGOs, experts, and officials from other bureaucratic agencies took 3 years. The law established important and innovative principles and placed the state in the role of guarantor of the right to migrate (as part of general human rights), access to information, equal treatment for foreigners, equal access to social services (education and health), family reunification, international convention norms, and others (Giustiniani 2004; Novick 2005).

The Ministry of Foreign Affairs became increasingly involved in questions concerning emigrants. Its Secretariat of Foreign Relations has included the "protection of Argentines abroad" among its strategic goals, together with the promotion of the regularization of immigrants so that they can become socially and economically integrated.[19] A new bureaucratic unit (called UEXIL) was created within the same ministry to provide support to former political exiles in the process of social reintegration and to coordinate further action with other national, provincial, and local institutions. The Argentines Abroad Office has been growing hand in hand with the increase in emigration flows over the last 20 years: its personnel tripled in a decade, it was upgraded from department to *dirección* in the organizational structure of the ministry, it has engaged in new activities as demands increased, and it has acquired a more prominent role as governments showed interest in migration issues.[20]

In addition, The Center for the Assistance and Help to Immigrants and Emigrants was created in 2003 within the *Defensoría del Pueblo* (Ombudsman) Office of Buenos Aires city to provide legal assistance and general information to migrants and facilitate paperwork for emigrants. Per the request of the Casa Argentina in Barcelona, it signed cooperation agreements with that institution and the Casa Argentina in Madrid.[21] This policy initiative had a very short life, though. After a few months, emigration issues disappeared from the center's agenda, mainly because the kinds of claims emigrants might have do not fall within its institutional (local) jurisdiction.[22] However, the creation of the center reflects the increasing attention and sensitivity of public officials toward this issue at that time. Alejandro Nató, then ombudsman and main promoter of this initiative, declared: "We are far from promoting emigration. However, there is an Argentine province that nobody wants to see and that entails many dismembered families, an uprooting, and serious socio-economic and cultural problems" (Camps, 2003).

Along the same lines, in 2004, Minister of the Interior Aníbal Fernández launched a new initiative named the "Province 25 Program," in reference to the Argentine community living abroad.[23] Although the program requires the collaboration of other ministries (e.g., foreign affairs, labor), it was considered that the Ministry of the Interior would be the "natural" place to manage it because it is the agency that, according to the Law on Ministries and constitutional design, deals with population issues. The rationale behind the initiative was that the state has to help recover or maintain nationhood links with expatriates, especially with those who left around the time of the 2001 crisis and felt extremely disappointed by, and upset with, the country and the political elite—that is, those who felt "expelled" by a socioeconomic model that failed to provide for their needs and aspirations. The 2001 crisis confirmed their sense of frustration, reinforced negative expectations about the future, and accelerated their plans to emigrate. Tentatively estimating that there are around a million Argentines living abroad, emigrants would today represent the fourth largest province in terms of population. Most of them belong to the middle and upper classes and have high levels of education. Therefore, according to the view of the first appointees to that office, the country needed to explore ways to benefit from that human capital, either by establishing collaboration programs (such as those already existing with associations of Argentine scientists in the US and UK) or by providing incentives for return.[24]

The immediate goals of the program had to do with facilitating certain procedures (ID and passport renewals, clean police record certificates, etc.) that tend to be long, expensive, and difficult for expatriates and increasing their participation in national elections. From the point of view of the Ministry of the Interior, the latter seemed to be a key point of this new policy. It was expected that, once adopted and after some modifications to the electoral laws were passed, the program would increase expatriates' electoral participation (which is now optional and extremely low) to at least 100,000 voters by 2007. In the long run, the program sought other goals, too, such as the homogenization of the institutional format of emigrants' associations (which still include a very diverse array of organizations) and the allocation of some seats in the Congress for expatriates' representation. In other words, in policymakers' views, emigrants' political rights were a key component and aim of the program, but today such a goal is dormant (see next section).

Back then, the transnational dimension of courting gained momentum. The friendly relations between Argentina and Spain under Néstor Kirchner's and José Luis Zapatero's administrations facilitated collaboration with Spanish immigration officials and made Argentine emigrants residing in Spain the main addressees of this program. A few formal and informal contacts with emigrants' associations took place to gather information and to find ways to respond to their main concerns.

In addition, although capturing migrants' economic resources has not been a priority, Argentina acknowledged migrants' rights to send remittances, and the 2003 national migration law established tax exemptions for returnees who wanted to bring their personal belongings, tools for productive activities, and vehicles. Efforts to capture or manage remittances have been very limited, probably because figures remain relatively low in comparison to other countries.[25] In late 2008, the possibility of migrants or their families opening bank accounts (called Savings Account Province 25) was announced by the Ministry of the Interior and a major public bank (Province of Buenos Aires Bank), presumably to facilitate remittances and access to credit.[26] The product is still advertised online by the bank.[27] Discussions between private firms and the National Bank about opening lines of credit for Argentines residing abroad who might want to buy new property were held in mid-2000s, with the aim of increasing inflows of capital and stimulating activity in the construction sector.[28] To the best of my knowledge, the project has not materialized. In addition, the Ministry of Foreign Affairs manages a Fund for the Assistance to Co-Nationals, which is used for repatriation of migrants with no economic resources and to provide financial support for those facing medical emergencies (Buira 2006).

Given that the relations between Argentina and Spain are not merely based on sympathy between administrations but also long historical and close ties that include massive migration (from Spain to Argentina in the early 20th century), the Spanish government was initially very receptive to the sending state's moves, as well as to Argentine immigrants' demands, and they were willing to cooperate on several fronts. This certainly changed toward late 2000s, as economic conditions deteriorated in Spain. However, opinions have always differed as to how the "migration card" would play on a negotiating table that in the last decade included many other (and more pressing) issues, especially economic and financial ones. Some of the interviewees (e.g., officials at the Ministry of Foreign Affairs) argued that issue linkage is not possible because migration is not high enough on the bilateral agenda while others (especially officials at the Ministry of Interior) considered that there is a lot at stake for both countries because the Argentine and Spanish emigrant communities are (or are likely to become) increasingly significant in electoral terms; for others, issue linkage is not desirable because migration issues deserve to be evaluated on their own terms and not subject to the give-and-take of other negotiations.

The last one was actually Argentina's position when a trade agreement was negotiated between MERCOSUR and the EU in mid-2004. EU officials suggested the inclusion of an article about migration. The Meeting of Ministers of the Interior of MERCOSUR argued that migration issues were significant enough to be the subject of a comprehensive accord and it was proposed that experts draw up a specific agreement. The proposal also reinforced the position contained in the Santiago Declaration (signed on May 17, 2004) about migration principles, which included the recognition that migrations require a multilateral approach, that policies to establish links with nationals abroad are very important, and that MERCOSUR would request reciprocal (fair and humanitarian) treatment for nationals living in countries outside the bloc. The trade agreement was not signed and negotiations were postponed.[29]

Ups and Downs of State Transnational Initiatives

In contrast to other cases in this volume, the previously discussed initiatives have not followed a linear, progressive path. Some of them have been relatively successful in terms of achieving initial goals, such as the

Raíces Program. Other goals have somehow faded or reached a plateau (e.g., the Province 25 Program). The reasons are to be found largely in changes in the migration dynamics and lack of political push from key actors (i.e., the president, ministers). Given receding migration outflows and the domestic repercussions of the increasing volume of intraregional immigration,[30] the Kirchners' governments (2003–present) refocused the attention toward immigration in the mid-2000s (more so under Mrs. Kirchner's terms, 2007–present), thus concentrating efforts in expanding bureaucratic capacities to process the newcomers' demands and, in particular, the regularization of their legal status. The remarkable expansion and streamlining of the National Directorate of Migration in the past decade illustrates this point well.[31]

This was concurrent with the definition of a new, comprehensive migration policy based on human rights considerations (including the right to migrate) and an inclusive, welcoming approach to immigrants. For those coming from neighboring countries who were historically discriminated and persecuted, this implied a radical shift. Thus, among other things, the Directorate suspended deportations and engaged in 2004 in what was defined as its top priority: the full implementation of the so-called *Programa Nacional de Normalización Documentaria Migratoria*, established by Decree No. 836/04. This program tackled what the government defined as the most pressing problem then: the irregular/illegal status of a considerable number of immigrants who were already in the territory but lacked the necessary documentation to claim legal residency (Domenech 2011).

It is also worth noting that since Mrs. Kirchner took office in 2007, the president's office has not been directly involved in emigration as it was under her husband's administration. This has certainly deprived the earlier initiatives of one of the main political impulses and put them on hold since no other major political figure has carried that flag lately.

It is in the context of such policy redefinition that the evolution of emigration policy has to be understood. On the one hand, the Province 25 Program went from a phase of intense activity and exchanges with migrant associations (particularly those in Spain) between 2007 and 2009 to low-profile, assistance-oriented activities since then. Several meetings with representatives of emigrants were held and a bill to create the Exterior (extraterritorial) District and to grant emigrants parliamentary representation was submitted in 2009.[32] However, the project did not receive enough endorsement in Congress, and the meetings did not lead to the institutionalization of a certain mechanism of dialogue and collaboration like in other countries (e.g., consultation councils).[33] Those bills are not under discussion today. Moreover, migrant associations seem to have lost organizational and mobilization capacity. The unit running this program remained small (with only four appointees today), and the changes in leadership (from a very proactive director, Sara Martínez, to technicians) also contributed to lost momentum.[34] Coordination with other offices (e.g., Ministry of Foreign Affairs, National Administration of Social Security) has been relatively low and mostly informal, largely because there have not been political decisions to set clear priorities, goals, and jurisdictions, and functions. "This policy lacks a North [a guiding goal] and clear definitions from higher ranks."[35] Thus, in practice, the program has turned away from its initial political goals and has lately become totally focused on maintaining communication with and providing services to citizens residing abroad (e.g., processing concrete demands, offering information to potential returnees, facilitating paperwork).[36]

On the other hand, another small unit (with a staff of three appointees) provides similar services: the Department of Argentines Abroad within the Directorate of International and Social Affairs at the National Directorate of Migration. This office was created by Resolution 250/08 in 2008 as part of the general restructuring of the Directorate. It maintains an online mechanism of communication with expats by which it provides information and advises on paperwork and specific demands. As of today, it has received 1,500 inquiries on various topics (e.g., migration return, tax exemptions, tourism, nationality children born abroad). The office is also in charge of providing certificates to those who need records of exit/entry over a certain period of time and for those who return with family members born in another country, including a fast track for those returning through the *Raíces* Program. This unit does not maintain relations with migrant associations. It is engaged with emigrants insomuch as it has negotiated reciprocity agreements with neighboring countries, thus making the norms of the Residency Agreement signed within MERCO-SUR in 2002 (soon after adopted by Argentina but not by other signatories) effective for Argentines residing in those nations. It has not gone beyond that because the chief officials understand that the competency to design an emigration policy lies with the Ministry of Foreign Affairs.[37]

As it was explained in previous sections, this ministry also has an office of Argentines Abroad (within the Directorate of Consular Affairs) that mainly focuses on assistance, too. That is not seen as an area to develop engagement programs. If there were ever intentions to develop diaspora engagement policies, those would be based in another unit: the Directorate of International Migrations within the Ministry of Foreign Affairs. No plans to do so exist yet. Officials in that Directorate argue that because emigrants are "outside the territory of the country" and Argentina cannot act on the sovereign jurisdictions of other countries, it is up receiving states to dictate the main norms affecting those migrants. And "coordination [with other offices] is not the path to take; we do not have an institutionalized arena, although we maintain contacts, and we are often pressed to make urgent decisions."[38] As in the case of Uruguay, references to territorial sovereignty are present in policymakers' mind-sets, and bureaucratic practices have not kept up with increasing needs to coordinate state actions in multidimensional issues such as migration.

As a result, this Directorate's efforts are concentrated in having an impact on the global debate on international migration (e.g., promoting an approach based on human rights and national development considerations and requesting that Argentine nationals are treated in equal conditions as natives in the host countries).[39] Although this office maintains some informal contacts with migrant associations, a deeper relationship is still pending. Also, in contrast to the case of Brazil, there is no intention to shape organizational efforts or to institutionalize the channels and format of communication. In officials' views, migrant mobilization seems to have faded, and geographical dispersion might be an obstacle. Until emigrants are able to show a clearly articulated and constant demand, this office sees no reason to engage further.[40] "We hope that associations go through their own maturity process. Our expectation is that at some point they will submit proposals."[41] Therefore, no expansion of personnel (currently there are six appointees) or resources is expected in the near future. Neither a political nor an electoral debate on emigration is expected either, because migration "is not considered a problem; it has been naturalized and nobody would dare to question state migration policy."[42]

Finally, in consonance with the discourse linking migration and development, the *Raíces* Program (declared "state policy" by Law 26,421 in 2008) is probably the initiative that has achieved more consistency and sustainability over time. The reason is the governmental concern with strengthening national capacities in the realm of knowledge and science. As a result, repatriation of scientists has increased, as has the number of doctoral scholarships and funds to support research projects, in line with other policies to improve human resources and encourage scientific and technological investigation, including the creation of the Ministry of Science, Technology and Productive Innovation in 2007. Today the program has a database of around 4,500 scientists abroad and various mechanisms to engage with those who do not plan to return. Since 2003, it has contributed to the return and reinsertion of 820 scientists and to a decline of brain drain (Presidencia de la Nación 2011:5, 9, 13). In this respect, Argentina joins the group of countries that court highly skilled emigrants as a way of capitalizing on their human resources and networks. Scientists and other professionals are deemed a privileged sector within the emigrant community that is worth engaging with.

Analysis and Conclusions

Coming to terms with an increasingly visible emigration problem, the Argentine state developed an incipient and limited transnational policy in the early 2000s. With respect to timing, Argentina thus exhibits points in common with the other cases discussed in this book. The inclusion of the emigration issue in the domestic and foreign policy agendas, contacts with emigrants' associations, some interinstitutional collaboration, and the increasing relevance of migration questions in bilateral and multilateral negotiations have contributed to creating links between public institutions and the emigrant community. It can be argued that such policies have been taking more time to fully develop than in other cases, especially in Ecuador and Brazil. In the first stages of implementation, lack of experience and information on both sides of the state–diaspora relationship hindered further and faster progress. Another limitation comes from the fact that the state's approach (and, to some extent, emigrants' expectations) have been mainly based on assistance, that is, on facilitating certain solutions rather than building partnerships. But there are other factors at play, too.

The sending state's main motivation to engage with migrants initially derived from emigrants' profiles (rather than the size of that community and economic or political gains) and, as in Ecuador, the need for an emerging governing coalition to build up its identity and support base. This, together with a concern with national development, has led to an emphasis on return of highly qualified expats and/or scientific collaboration as a way of reversing the emigration trend and compensating for the loss of human capital. Although Argentines abroad can be considered a relatively small group (in comparison with other Latin American diasporas), their socioeconomic and educational profiles make them an important source of human capital and a potentially influential group as a constituency abroad, ambassadors/lobbyists in the host countries, or potential returnees.

Yet, fully tapping into the material and symbolic resources of communities overseas and involving them in home politics have not been high on the agenda of current incumbents. This is reflected in the policy tools used and the scope of innovation—two aspects that set this case apart from the others in this book. Political enfranchisement—not a new measure, but a preexisting right—remained confined to extraterritorial voting in presidential elections. The project to award emigrants parliamentary representation has stalled. There has been no attempt to explicitly "name" the entire diaspora or to coin a symbolic label that might contribute to identity formation. Linkage programs have been of limited scope. Thus, courting has not led to strong engagement. Emigration policy seems to have reached a plateau and, from the state side of the relationship, there are no signs of upcoming changes in the near future.

Apparently, the societal side of that relationship is not likely to induce further changes either. Argentines abroad (particularly those in Spain) have proved able to organize, mobilize, and work as an interest group to advance certain demands at specific moments in time. And this was effective in combination with access to public officials in key executive positions, when attainable. But the level of organization varies considerably among associations, and members' participation is very low (see further details in Chapter 8). Thus, the state (rather than bottom-up movements) has been the engine of a relatively weak and intermittent state-led transnationalism.

As in all other cases in the region, the state represents a heterogeneous and complicated actor to drive these initiatives. More than a decade has passed since the last politico-economic crisis in Argentina, and a number of reforms were implemented along the lines of postneoliberal principles. Hence, state capacities stand out in this case, pointing (as in other cases) to bureaucratic practices that are being reformed and still are only partially transformed into efficient working mechanisms. My findings in this respect document the relevance of an analytical focus on the state, specific political projects, and strategic bureaucratic interventions. In particular, state performance in Argentina exhibits the coexistence of changes made under promarket neoliberal reforms in the 1900s with remarkable efforts since 2003 to reassert the state's role in key areas. These efforts have had implications for human mobility because they affected social security schemes, labor markets/working conditions, health, and education, among others areas. It has been argued that these changes are characterized by (a) lack of a comprehensive, strategic vision that could have integrated and given consistency to policy innovations; (b) uneven distribution of technical capacities across sectors, a factor that certainly affects the multidimensional nature of migration issues; (c) scarce areas and efforts devoted to coordination across the state apparatus and levels of government (national, state, local); and (d) the overwhelming role of the executive power on decision making, leaving the pace and direction of state initiatives subject to the personal choice of incumbents on whether and how to lead (Repetto 2014). The oral testimonies herein clearly illustrate the impact of these factors on the passage of Argentine state-led transnationalism from proactive to inertial mode.

Other features of the Argentine case confirm some of the existing arguments in the diaspora policy literature but, at the same time, they suggest the need to further explore and incorporate political factors. As it was explained in Chapter 2, the literature on transnational migration from developing to developed countries has mainly focused on massive emigration and has emphasized structural economic conditions (mainly, the logic of capitalist expansion) and changes in labor markets. There is relatively less information about diasporas mainly composed by highly skilled migrants, their specific networks, and the dynamics of crisis-driven exodus. Argentina is a critical case in that respect. It points out the need to specify and compare the characteristics of different waves of emigrants and to analyze their political behavior in relation to their motivation to emigrate, the impact of crises on perceptions, and historical links with the state and policy elites. This case suggests that the "context of exit" (in Portes's terminology, 2003) matters when it comes to transnational activism—a point I will resume in Chapter 8. Given the critical circumstances that make Argentines emigrate (i.e., most of them had a job, but the fulfilment of expectations in the long run was crucial), many individuals still show a great deal of resentment, anger, and distrust of political institutions and elites. Actually, these are arguably generalized sentiments among Argentines both at home and abroad and part of a long legacy of authoritarian rule that has nurtured a notion of a repressive and unreliable state rather than an approachable state that provides for the common good. Such a record creates a distance between state institutions and elites and society, discourages participation and mobilization, and intensifies the difficulties of establishing fluid and intense relations.

Moreover, earlier literature suggests the need to look at foundational moments in society (e.g., nation-building projects, major reconfigurations of sending states' global system relations). However, Argentina highlights the importance of other (somewhat different) domestic conjunctures and their impact on state capacities and priorities. In developing and unstable countries, a post-crisis context and a nation-reconstruction political project (e.g., the aftermath of the 2001 crisis in Argentina) may well help explain both state responses to increasing emigration and migrants' attitudes. Unfinished democratic consolidation processes and the defense of human rights may also represent alternative national projects that promote the enactment of certain norms and principles at the domestic and transnational levels. As the previous sections explained, the number of emigrants increased at the time of dramatic political and economic crisis, exacerbating the historical trend toward expulsion of citizens due to political and economic problems and failed policies. Emigration became part of the social debt that some democratic governments have felt compelled to address. Thus, courting the diaspora was presented as part of the necessary reparations.

Furthermore, the respect and promotion of human rights in times of democratic consolidation made governments more sensitive to the issue. The Kirchners' administrations have placed the social debt and human rights at the center of their political discourse and of several policy initiatives, including migration policy in general. President Néstor Kirchner, in particular, was the main spokesman of that position. As usual, in a highly centralized presidential system with a strong tendency toward personalism and concentration of decision-making power, the president's stance translated into a rapid advance of several initiatives. As priorities shifted under Mrs. Kirchner's two terms (emigration has not been a top item in her speeches and concerns), the issue faded from the public debate, and those initiatives have lately followed an inertial path. This suggests the importance of specific political contexts (i.e., unstable democracies with serious institutional deficiencies and crises legacies) and specific actors (the executive rather than political parties) in pushing for (or not) and ultimately shaping transnational policymaking.

The distinctive traits of this case also indicate the relevance of cycles or phases of policies vis-à-vis outcomes. This contributes to accounting for the results of sending-state initiatives: if a problem is redefined as a natural fact that does not require immediate action, then policy content and evolution are not likely to progress. If this is compounded by low migrant organizational and mobilization capacity, state–diaspora relations are likely to enter into stalemate. Exploring these propositions in a large number of cases would open up a promising line of research to study the impact of courting diasporas.

Finally, earlier literature on transnationalism has emphasized the society side of the diaspora–state relationship. States were assumed to enter the picture when their sovereignty was at stake and once transnational networks were already in place. International cooperation efforts were deemed significant as long as they attained a significant level of institutionalization, thus affecting the chances of success of transnational coalitions. This study confirms the importance of effective emigrant activism and international cooperation and, yet, stresses the role of governments as agents and key players in multiple (domestic, international, and transnational level) games. It underlines the impact of international norms (modernization, democracy, human rights) that lead to policy convergence and continuity over time and of diverse international arrangements on sending countries' policies, even if the level of institutionalization of those agreements is relatively low, as in the case of MERCOSUR. Past and ongoing negotiations between Argentina and neighboring countries have promoted certain adjustments and changes in policy content and have reinforced states' commitments to certain norms and principles (see details in Chapter 3). Clauses agreed within MERCOSUR (most of them proposed by Argentina) have later been brought to the negotiating table with the EU and Spain and to discussions in global forums. In other words, foreign policy and regional integration have encouraged and reinforced the development of a transnational migration policy and might explain why some pieces of these initiatives have survived, though in an inert form.

Notes

1 See http://data.worldbank.org/country/argentina, accessed July 16, 2014.
2 See http://siteresources.worldbank.org/INTPROSPECTS/Resources/334934–1199807908806/Argentina.pdf.
3 For more details on the trends described in this section, see Kritz and Gurak (1979); chapter 3 in Graham (1999); Lattes and Oteiza (1986:39–49); Novick (1997); and Albarracín (2004).
4 Interview with Adriana Alfonso, chief, International Affairs Office, National Directorate for Migrations, Ministry of the Interior of Argentina, Buenos Aires, December 27, 2005.

5 According to Novick and Murias (2005:33), 222,000 people left Argentina between 2000 and 2002; 104,500 of them left between December 2001 and September 2002. However, the deterioration of living conditions has been a long process that gradually reached larger segments of society, including a relatively wealthy and educated middle class. For more about increasing poverty and changes in the socioeconomic structure that led to the last crisis see, among others, Minujin (1992).

6 As Murias points out (Novick and Murias 2005:42, 76), the motivations to emigrate have recently become more complex and extend beyond economic considerations. The 2001 debacle generated a generalized questioning of the Argentine social, political, cultural, and moral orders, thus exacerbating the disenchantment and anger of vast sectors of the population.

7 These trends are largely consistent with the regional ones in early 2000s. See Martínez Pizarro (2003) and Pellegrino (2003).

8 Interviews with officials at the Argentines Abroad Office, Consular Affairs, Ministry of Foreign Affairs of Argentina, Buenos Aires, December 5 and December 7, 2005. There are no records of these figures. Others interviewed agreed on the estimates. However, these figures are considerably higher than the ones provided by the Casa Argentina in Madrid. Based on the electoral municipal records, the Casa estimated that there were around 275,000 living in Spain by mid-decade; 175,000 had dual (Argentine-Spanish) citizenship, and the rest had dual citizenship in another EU country or are illegal. Interview via e-mail with Enrique Borcel, president, Casa Argentina in Madrid, December 12, 2005.

9 See www.ine.es/jaxi/tabla.do, accessed July 16, 2014.

10 See the most recent detailed figures at www.ine.es/jaxi/menu.do?type=pcaxis&path=/t20/p277/prov/e01/&file=pcaxis, accessed July 16, 2014.

11 See http://extranjeros.empleo.gob.es/es/Estadisticas/operaciones/con-certificado/201212/Residentes_Principales_Resultados_31122012.pdf, accessed July 16, 2014.

12 Amnesties in Spain have taken the form of *regularización*, that is, the process by which an immigrant becomes a "regular" resident—"irregular" being a terminology preferred to "illegal," which is usually associated with those who break the law.

13 In the case of Argentines, the figures have been increasing since the mid-1990s and peaked between 2002 and 2003. Only a small number of Argentines (22,602, that is, 3.3% of the total) opted to regularize their situations in 2005, and 20,271 became legal workers with access to social security benefits— fewer than expected and slightly less than half of those who had initiated the application process. The number was probably low because the regularization did not include autonomous (independent) workers. Also, the difficulties to fulfil all requirements and paperwork worked against the success of this initiative. See http://extranjeros.mtas.es/es/index.html.

14 A survey of 64 potential emigrants conducted in Buenos Aires between December 2003 and February 2004 indicates, among other things, that 53% of them saw state institutions as the main source of information and assistance, though 16% of those who wondered about emigration did not find any institutional help, and 44% of the total did not know what kind of help state institutions should provide (Novick 2005:29–30).

15 Interview with Rubén Buira, minister, Argentines Abroad Office, Consular Affairs, Ministry of Foreign Affairs of Argentina, Buenos Aires, December 7, 2005.

16 Information provided by the National Directorate for Migrations, Ministry of the Interior. Interview with Adriana Alfonso, Buenos Aires, December 27, 2005.

17 See www.raices.secyt.gov.ar/.
18 Interview with José María Venede, minister, Argentines Abroad Office, Consular Affairs, Ministry of Foreign Affairs of Argentina, Buenos Aires, December 5, 2005.
19 See www.mrecic.gov.ar/.
20 Interview with Alejandra Morales, coordinator, Department of Social Assistance, Argentines Abroad Office, Ministry of Foreign Affairs, Buenos Aires, January 3, 2006.
21 See www.defensoria.org.ar/noticias/notas/230.html.
22 Interviews with Pablo Corradini, coordinator, Center for Assistance and Help to Immigrants and Emigrants, and Mario F. Ganora, chief officer, Area of Individual Rights, Discrimination, and Institutional Violence, Defensoría del Pueblo de la Ciudad de Buenos Aires, Buenos Aires, January 3, 2006.
23 Argentina is politically and administratively divided into 23 provinces plus one autonomous district (the capital city).
24 Interview with the first official in charge of the preparatory tasks to launch the program, Darío Díaz, advisor to the secretary for provinces, Ministry of the Interior, Buenos Aires, December 21, 2005.
25 Remittances increased in the 2000s up until the 2008 crisis in the North, and they amounted to $640 million in 2010, which is only 0.17% of the GDP (OIM 2012b:64). In 2012, remittances were down to $573 million (0.1% of the GDP), 35% of which came from Spain. See www.pewhispanic.org/2013/11/14/3-sources-of-remittances-to-latin-america/ and www.pewhispanic.org/2013/11/15/remittances-to-latin-america-recover-but-not-to-mexico/ph-remittances-11–2013–1–03/, both accessed on July 15, 2014.
26 Cf. *La Nación*, November 18, 2008, available at www.lanacion.com.ar/1071380-los-argentinos-que-viven-en-el-exterior-podran-abrir-cuentas-bancarias-en-el-pais, accessed May 31, 2013.
27 See www.bapro.com.ar/provincia_25.asp, accessed May 31, 2013.
28 See www.iprofesional.com/notas/15706-Crditos-a-argentinos-no-residentes-para-comprar-propiedades-en-el-pas, accessed May 31, 2013.
29 Information provided by the National Directorate of Migration, Ministry of the Interior of Argentina. Interview with Adriana Alfonso, Buenos Aires, December 27, 2005.
30 For details on this point, see OIM (2012a).
31 Details on this process, activities undertaken, budget expansion, and the performance of the Directorate can be found at www.migraciones.gov.ar/accesibleingles/?institucional, accessed July 16, 2014.
32 See full text of the bill at http://boletinargentino.blogspot.com/2009/12/argentina-creacion-del-distrito.html, accessed July 16, 2014.
33 On this respect, a bill to create councils of residents abroad and a general council of emigration was sent to Congress in 2004, but it has not been approved yet. See www.diputados.gob.ar/proyectos/proyecto.jsp?id=49684, accessed July 16, 2014.
34 Interview with Osvaldo Verrastro, advisor, Province 25 Program, Buenos Aires, June 3, 2014.
35 Interview with Leticia Casajus, National Director of Regional Policies, Ministry of Interior, Buenos Aires, June 3, 2014.
36 Formally, the program still maintains a focus on emigrants' political rights and links with homeland. See www.mininterior.gov.ar/provincias/p25_mision.php?idName=provincias&idNameSubMenu=provinciasProv25&idNameSubMenuDer=intProvProv25Mision, accessed July 16, 2014.
37 Interview with Luciana Literio, director, Department of Argentines Abroad, National Directorate of Migrations, Buenos Aires, June 12, 2014.

38 Interview with Gabriel Servetto, chief official (ministro de segunda), Directorate of International Migrations, Ministry of Foreign Affairs, Buenos Aires,
June 13, 2014.
39 Interview with Gabriel Servetto, Buenos Aires, June 13, 2014.
40 This view obviously contrasts with migrant associations' arguments about
their demands, such as creation of an extraterritorial district and congressional representation, itinerant consulates, and postal voting, among others
(FEDEAR 2009). See Chapter 8 for more details.
41 Interview with Gabriel Servetto, Buenos Aires, June 13, 2014.
42 Interview with Nora Pérez Vichich, advisor, Directorate of International
Migrations, Ministry of Foreign Affairs, Buenos Aires, June 13, 2014.

Works Cited

Albarracín, Julia. 2004. "Selecting Immigration in Modern Argentina: Economic,
Cultural, International, and Institutional Factors." Ph.D. dissertation, University
of Florida.

Bertoncello, Rodolfo. 1986. "Algunos Antecedentes Sobre la Investigación de la
Emigración de Argentinos." In *Dinámica Migratoria Argentina (1955–1984):
Democratización y Retorno de Expatriados,* coord. by A.E. Lattes and E.
Oteiza. Buenos Aires: Centro Editor de América Latina. pp. 51–60.

Buira, Rubén. 2006. "Políticas de Estado-diáspora en Argentina." In *Relaciones
Estado-Diáspora: La Perspective de América Latina y el Caribe,* coord. by
Carlos González Gutiérrez. Tomo II. México City: Secretaría de Relaciones
Exteriores, Instituto de los Mexicanos en el Exterior, Universidad Autónoma
de los Zacatecas, Asociación Nacional de Universidades e Instituciones de Edu-
cación Superior, Miguel Ángel Porrúa librero-editor. pp. 299–311.

Camps, Sibila. 2003. "Crearon un Centro de Ayuda para Emigrados y para Inmigrantes." *Clarín,* October 28.

Domenech, Eduardo. 2011. "La Nueva Política Migratoria en la Argentina:
Las Paradoja del Programa Patria Grande." In *Migraciones Internacionales
Contemporáneas: Estudios Para el Debate,* coord. by Cynthia Pizarro. Buenos
Aires: Ediciones Ciccus. pp. 119–142.

FEDEAR. 2009. "Cuestiones Prioritarias Para el Colectivo Argentino Residente
en España." Ponencia de la Federación de Asociaciones Argentina de España y
Europa presentada al 2° Encuentro de Argentinos en el Exterior Por la ampli-
ación de la Nación. Cámara de Diputados de la Nación, Salón Auditorio, Ciudad Autónoma de Buenos Aires, 21 de diciembre.

Giustiniani, Rubén. ed. 2004. *Migración: Un Derecho Humano.* Buenos Aires:
Editorial Prometeo.

Graham, Richard. ed. 1999. *The Idea of Race in Latin America, 1870–1940.*
Austin: University of Texas Press.

Gurrieri, Jorge R. 1982. "La Emigración de Argentinos: Una Estimación de su
Volumen." Buenos Aires: Dirección Nacional de Migraciones, mimeo.

Kritz, Mary M. and Douglas T. Gurak. 1979. "International Migration Trends in
Latin America: Research and Data Survey." *International Migration Review.*
13(3): 407–427.

Lattes, Alfredo E. and Enrique Oteiza. coord. 1986. *Dinámica Migratoria Argentina (1955–1984): Democratización y Retorno de Expatriados.* Buenos Aires:
Centro Editor de América Latina.

Martínez Pizarro, Jorge 2003, September. "El Mapa Migratorio de América Latina y el Caribe, las Mujeres y el Género." Series Population and Development, no. 44. Santiago de Chile: CELADE/CEPAL.

Marshall, Adriana. 1991. "Emigración de Argentinos a los Estados Unidos." In *Fronteras Permeables: Migración Laboral y Movimientos de Refugiados en América,* comp. by P.R. Pessar. Buenos Aires: Planeta. pp. 151–164.

Minujin, Alberto. 1992. "En la Rodada." In *Cuesta Abajo. Los Nuevos Pobres: Efectos de la Crisis en la Sociedad Argentina,* ed. by A. Minujin, L. Beccaria, E. Bustelo, M. del C. Feijóo, S. Feldman, A. Gershanik, H. González, J. Halperín, J.L. Farol, M. Murmis, and E. Fanfani. Buenos Aires: UNICEF/Losada. pp. 15–44.

Novara, Diana. 2005. "La Emigración Argentina Actual." In *Casa Argentina de Madrid, Migraciones: Claves del Intercambio Entre Argentina y España.* Buenos Aires: Siglo XXI de Argentina Editores.

Novick, Susana. 1997. "Políticas Migratorias en la Argentina." In *Inmigración y Discriminación. Políticas y Discursos,* ed. by E. Oteiza, S. Novick, and R. Aruj. Buenos Aires: Grupo Editor Universitario.

Novick, Susana. 2005. "Evolución Reciente de la Política Migratoria Argentina." Paper delivered at the XXV International Population Conference, Tours, France, July 18–23.

Novick, Susana, M. Palomares, C. Castiglione, O. Aguirre, D. Cura, and L. Nejamkis. 2005. "Emigración Reciente de Argentinos: La Distancia Entre las Expectativas y las Experiencias." Paper delivered at the XXV Congress of the Latin American Sociology Association (ALAS), Porto Alegre, Brazil, August 22–26.

Novick, Susana and M.G. Murias. 2005, March. "Dos Estudios Sobre la Emigración Reciente en la Argentina." Working Paper 42. Buenos Aires: Instituto de Investigaciones Gino Germani, Facultad de Ciencias Sociales, Universidad de Buenos Aires.

OIM. 2012a, April. "El Impacto de las Migraciones en Argentina." Cuadernos Migratorios no. 2. Buenos Aires: Organización Internacional para las Migraciones.

OIM. 2012b. *Perfil Migratorio de Argentina 2012.* Buenos Aires: Organización Internacional para las Migraciones.

Pellegrino, Adela 2003, March. "La Migración Internacional en América Latina y el Caribe: Tendencias y Perfiles de los Migrantes." Series Population and Development, no. 35. Santiago de Chile: CELADE/CEPAL.

Presidencia de la Nación. 2011. *Programa RAICES. Una Política de Estado.* Buenos Aires: Ministerio de Ciencia, Tecnología e Innovación Productiva, Presidencia de la Nación.

Repetto, Fabián. 2014. "Políticas Sociales: Una Mirada Politico-Institucional a sus Reformas, Desafíos e Impacto." In *El Estado en Acción. Fortalezas y Debilidades de las Políticas Sociales en la Argentina,* comp. by Carlos H. Acuña. Buenos Aires: Siglo Veintiuno Editores. pp. 19–70.

7 Brazil
Courting Without Being Noticed

Introduction

Brazil is the largest country in South America and the fifth largest in the world. It occupies an area of 8,515,767 square kilometers and shares borders with all other South American countries except Chile and Ecuador. Its highly developed and competitive economy was one of the most successful examples of the import-substitution industrialization in the region. Between 2000 and 2012, Brazil's average GDP annual growth rate was over 5%, making it the sixth largest economy in the global ranking today.[1] Brazil has a proactive approach and a high profile in international affairs and in major international organizations; this builds on its long tradition of foreign policy in which the ideas of national development, leadership, and autonomy have been closely intertwined. Its emigrant community is relatively small at 1% to 2% of the total population, which has grown from 195,210,194 people in the last census in 2010 to 200,361,925 in 2013.[2]

Thus, factors like the size of the diaspora, the amount of remittances, and the structural position of the country in the world economy would not necessarily create motivations for the state to engage with emigrants; in addition, state resources and capacities would presumably not be scarce in a country where the state historically had a strong presence and led the process of development. Yet, the Brazilian state has lately developed outreach efforts in a systematic, albeit low profile and low investment, fashion. In comparison with the other cases in this book, Brazil does not stand out as the most innovative or as a trendsetter, but as a country that follows a pragmatic, intense approach to "courting without being noticed." It maintains a gradual and cautious approach, thus far keeping the state–diaspora relationship within the framework of traditional consular activities.

This may be partially explained by the fact that emigration has not acquired enough visibility and/or sustained visibility or has not had the dramatic consequences observed in other cases that make public attention unavoidable. The state's measured approach, though, shows some consistent steps in incorporating emigration in the policy agenda and has points in common with other (more innovative) cases here, such as the linking of the emigration discourse to the pro-inclusion democratizing policies of neopopulist tone. It departs from other cases in the policy-making dynamic and main actors driving the process, as well as in the scope and implications of the new emigration policy that is currently at a crossroad between falling into inertial mode or finding its rightful place in a more comprehensive approach to the entire set of migration issues that call for state attention today. Brazil is also a case that is relatively neglected in the academic literature on emigration policy in English. An integrated explanation of the motivation, timing, and impact of emigration policy is not available. This chapter addresses that gap and also sets the Brazilian case in a regional comparative perspective.

Emigration Trends and How They Are Becoming a Policy Problem

Brazil shares with the rest of the cases here the imprint of being a country of immigration, with its demographic profile initially being shaped by indigenous people, Portuguese colonization, and slave trade—the latter stimulated by the expansion in the production and international trade of two main commodities: sugar and coffee. During the last quarter of the 19th century and until approximately 1930, immigration continued as economic development and industrialization attracted workers. Around 4.4 million immigrants arrived in that period, mainly from Italy, Japan, Portugal, Spain, and Germany (OIM 2010:9). Major external shocks (i.e., the Great Depression, the world wars) disturbed both economic and migration dynamics and, at the same time, encouraged further industrialization through an import-substitution strategy that prompted internal (domestic) labor mobility. Since then, although immigration flows were not as intense as in the past, the national narrative maintain the characterization of Brazil as a country of immigration. Questions of demographic composition and distribution, race (in particular, race mixture and whitening of the population), and inequality have been present in political and policy elites' discourses (Skidmore 1990), but there has not been a clear, specific concern with migration management, let alone with governing citizens residing abroad.

This is a country that is only slowly and reluctantly coming to terms with emigration as a policy problem. As in other Southern Cone countries, long repressive authoritarian regimes led to a wave of political exiles in the 1970s. Migration outflows peaked the following decade, this time more related to economic hardship and the search for better living conditions, to reach a relatively stable volume in the 1990s and onward. Hence, it was toward the end of the 20th century when the word *emigration* and the issue started to be discussed in connection with a specific policy. Former president Fernando Henrique Cardoso (1995–2003) pushed for some initial steps in this regard, suggesting the intention "to flirt," but serious courting only happened in the mid-2000s.

A decade later, there is scarce academic literature on the subject. The existing works in English were previous to the institutionalization of the new policy (e.g., Levitt and de la Dehesa 2003) or focused overwhelmingly on the emigrant community in the US from sociological and anthropological perspectives (e.g., Braga Martes 2011; Marcus 2009; Margolis 2013). Scholarly interest has been growing among the local academic community in the last two decades, but today it is centered more on immigration than emigration. As a result, diaspora issues are not currently as salient in Brazil as in other cases in this book, and scholarly works do not explore these issues in terms of foreign policy, state-led transnational policies, or governance.

When studying the recent emigration flows, one confronts difficulties in access to data. Figures on the volume of outflows are neither extensive nor totally reliable. In the absence of statistics, policymakers have relied on estimates based on the data collected by the Foreign Affairs Ministry through consulates.[3] Such estimates indicate that there were approximately 2.6 million Brazilians abroad in 2005 (Firmeza 2007:188). The Organization for International Migration used the same source to claim that there were 3,045,000 Brazilians abroad in 2008, with 85% of them residing in a few countries: the US (where over a third of the emigrant population is concentrated), Paraguay, Japan, the UK, Portugal, Italy, and Spain. In contrast to other cases in this book, the UK has surpassed Southern European countries as a preferred destination in the last decade (OIM 2010:40). It is also worth noting that these mounting numbers were taken as indicative of a trend at the moment of launching the main components of the emigration policy, thus justifying and pushing for further state involvement.

Given the improvement in socioeconomic conditions in the country, by 2012 the Ministry of Foreign Affairs estimated that the total number of expats was down to 2.5 million (SGEB 2012:20). These numbers led to the assumption that migration outflows had stabilized, and they are still used by policymakers today.[4] At that time, the regional distribution of Brazilians abroad was as follows: 1,102,559 in North America; 752,132 in Europe; 369,040 in South America; 22,037 in Asia; 29,683 in the Middle East; 24,123 in Oceania; 16,091 in Africa; and 6,291 in Central America and the Caribbean, thus amounting to 2,521,576 total (SGEB 2012:23). Main states of origin include Minas Gerais (mostly going to the US, Portugal, and the UK), Espírito Santo, São Paulo, Mato Grosso do Sul, Santa Catarina, Goiás, and Rondônia.

The majority of those who left Brazil in the 1980s were from middle-class urban sectors, except for emigrants moving to border zones (e.g., on the border with Paraguay, where migrants are usually working on agricultural activities, or on the border with French Guiana, which attracts mainly single, unskilled male workers). When looking across destination sites, emigrants' profiles look considerably heterogeneous. For instance, those in the US come from various regions, are predominantly male, and have mid-level education; workers going to Japan usually have family links that date back to Japanese immigration to Brazil in the early 20th century and have a relatively high level of education; and the gender distribution tends to be balanced. Emigrants in neighboring countries differ in their destinations: in Paraguay and Bolivia, they are predominantly young families with low levels of education and income; in Uruguay and Argentina, they tend to be mature, more qualified workers involved in the industrial and service sectors. European destinations ranked high in the preferences of emigrants in the last two decades, especially for the young and highly educated, and for an increasing number of women (OIM 2010:41–43).[5]

As a result of these recent flows, the consulates reported a significant increase in demands, especially in places such as Boston, Milan, and Rome. Those demands created an incentive for diplomats to consult, share experiences, and learn from comparing experiences. This was the case for the consulate in Washington, where a few officials took the lead in gathering information about other cases (including Mexico), organizing meetings to exchange ideas, and seeking the attention of the ambassador and officials at home. Some of the ideas were compiled in a volume published by the Ministry of Foreign Affairs, which paved the way for further innovation.[6] The analysis of trends and outcomes focused on the 1986–2006 period. By then, the author argues, these issues have gained momentum: "In the national context, this question [an incipient emigration policy] in the midst of an evolution process" (Firmeza 2007:16).

In 2006, the tasks of the Joint Parliamentary Commission on Emigration concluded, the Parliamentary Front on Citizenship Without Borders was established, and conversations to form the National Council on Migration were held (see details later). The diagnosis then was that the emigration waves of the 1980s and 1990s were mainly driven by economic causes and facilitated by existing migrant networks that provided key information about job opportunities abroad. In other words, there was no reference to engagement with the diaspora; instead, considerations mainly revolved around assistance to mobile workers in search of better living conditions. Moreover, state efforts did not focus on highly skilled or more resourceful emigrants as a group to engage with because brain drain was not a major concern. Instead, for those involved in the process, the work of the parliamentary commission and the visibility of migrant mobilization (e.g., in Lisbon) was an incentive to act; otherwise, Itamaraty (i.e., the Ministry of Foreign Affairs) would have lost the lead in affairs that typically fall within its competencies.[7] Accordingly, the government took specific measures along concrete paths: provision of information, reform of the consular system, support of emigrants through international law instruments, and integrated action with other units within the state (Grandilone 2009:68–69).

In sum, looking at these antecedents through the lenses of courting, it was not until the mid-1990s, and in the last decade in particular, that specific state attempts to reach out to citizens abroad were made in Brazil. Until then, policies in this realm were limited to the traditional consular approach. The Ministry of Foreign Affairs considered assistance to, and protection of, migrants as part of the provision of consular services. Therefore, it continued with that tradition, largely in the form of reactive steps such as assistance in the case of repatriation and prisoners—a problem relatively more common in the US, where there is a considerable number of Brazilians in irregular status. However, since the mid-1990s, a conceptual change and the attempt to adapt to new demands gained momentum. As it was expressed by one of the officials involved: "the consulates should reach out to the migrant communities instead of just waiting for demands to come" (Firmeza 2007:213). As the next section explains, this is what they actually did.

Main Features of the Emigration Policy

The first steps in addressing emigration were taken in the mid-1990s when the government acknowledged that outflows represented a stable trend that was likely to continue with significant economic and social implications. Thus, under President Cardoso's administration, a consular policy geared toward protection and assistance to emigrants was included among foreign policy priorities as illustrated by the president's and top officials' speeches and the changes in the administrative culture that followed suit. Those changes were premised on the need to shift from reception of demands to outreach, to spread information about consular services and migrant rights, and to engage in an increasingly professional, modern, and democratic forms of assistance (Rego Barros 1996:108).

In 1995, the General Directorate of Consular and Judicial Affairs and Assistance to Brazilians Abroad was created within the sphere of the General Secretariat of the Ministry of Foreign Affairs, thus gaining political salience. Within the Division of Consular Assistance (which was part of this new unit), a Nucleus of Assistance to Brazilians was created the same year to facilitate and expedite urgent consultations. Simultaneously, visits to the main communities abroad to establish direct links were carried out, as were specific actions to assist prisoners and others in need of legal assistance. The consular network was expanded, and the Councils of Citizens were created (29 councils in total by 1997), formed by citizens abroad to act as a channel of communication between the government and emigrants and to contribute to specific actions in the areas of health, counseling, event organization, and so forth. In addition, the network of honorary consulates was expanded to further support the assistance tasks, and teams of officials were sent to destinations with the largest numbers of expats to work as itinerary consulates.

Further institutional developments took place in the following decade. In 2004, the creation of General Undersecretariat of Cooperation and Brazilian Communities Abroad—which substituted the existing unit—was a significant move forward. A breaking point came in 2006, with the creation of General Undersecretariat of Brazilian Communities Abroad (SGEB in its Portuguese acronym) in December by Decree 5979. This new office includes two departments: one called Foreigners and the other called Brazilian Communities Abroad. In addition, in that period, the number of consular offices abroad expanded, as did the network of honorary consulates which supports itinerary missions and other assistance activities (Firmeza 2007:210–215, among others).

Other developments followed suit, illustrating the adaptation of governmental techniques beyond borders and cooperation with other actors. For instance, to address the irregular situation of a good number of Brazilians abroad, the government negotiated agreements with countries of reception in the early 2000s, namely Bolivia, Suriname, Guiana, and Portugal. As it was explained in Chapter 3, around that time Brazil also endorsed negotiations and agreements to regularize the situation of people in the move within MERCOSUR. Brazil also worked in destination localities to expand legal assistance to migrants on criminal and family matters. This was done sometimes in collaboration with nongovernmental organizations—a common modality that resembles the governance practices described in Chapter 8 for other cases. Another opportunity to develop such networks arose in the light of incipient return migration; for returnees, Brazil has implemented a concrete initiative through the *Serviço Brasileiro de Apoio às Micro e Pequenas Empresas* (Sebrae, in its Portuguese acronym) in order to train migrants in Japan and help them develop investment projects (Firmeza 2007:225). This was done in collaboration with the Inter-American Development Bank and migrant associations, attesting again to the new public–private networks that evolved around state-led long-distance policies.

The institutional developments mentioned previously went well beyond the expansion of consular services; they included their modernization, too. For example, in 2004, a project to expedite and simplify routine procedures was launched, including significant technological upgrades. The government also made use of technological means to increase communication with the expats. In 2006, a new website was created (the so-called Consular Portal) to diffuse news, information, and services and to gather questions and comments. The same year, the government took note of the relevance for the community abroad of making a *matricula* consular available (a form of identification that would facilitate bank transactions and other activities, as Mexico implemented for its citizens in the US). Thus, it launched a pilot project and aimed to follow up with full implementation in 2007 (SGEB 2012:115–124).

Furthermore, other developments illustrate the intention to go beyond courting and to support the emigrant communities in crucial areas such as human rights defense, cultural activities, guarantees of fair working conditions, health, education, social security, access to information in all areas of concern, and others. These linkage efforts fall within what the Ministry of Foreign Affairs calls "second generation consular services." Programs that fit into that category include, for instance, the *Plano Comunidade Brasil*, a pilot project launched by the Brazilian consulate in San Francisco in 2005 to broaden the scope of consular activities and to address the emigrant community concerns in the area (e.g., personal attention to irregular migrants, workshops to discuss community claims, organization of cultural events to preserve and enhance links with younger or second generation migrants, monitoring violations of human rights, providing information about health services, etc.). In the cultural realm, the preservation of culture and language were identified as goals. Consequently, most consulates have worked on the distribution of classical literary works and other reading materials and providing access to bilingual courses (especially for children of emigrants). Also, in 2005, the Day of the Brazilian Community Abroad was established, encouraging sponsorship of cultural activities, conferences, and artistic shows (Firmeza 2007:223).

The years between 2007 and 2012 were probably the most intense in terms of defining and institutionalizing emigration policy. In 2007, a major plan (*Plan Director*) to reform the consular service was elaborated.[8] The Integrated Consular System was established the following year, including the website Consular Portal and the adoption of new technologies for consular procedures such as passports, visas, birth/marriage certificates, notary acts, and others. This represented a major cultural and organizational change that replaced traditional routines (paperwork was mostly done in hardcopies until then) and was a general technological upgrade. In November 2009, a Consular Ombudsman Office was created to process suggestions, inquiries, and claims as if it were a mechanism of quality control for the consular services.[9]

Through Decree 7214 of 15 June 2010, former president Luiz Inácio (Lula) da Silva gave the new policy more impetus; the decree established the basic guidelines of an approach to communities of Brazilians abroad, granted the Ministry of Foreign Affairs the role of coordinator of the policy, created the Council of Representatives of Brazilians Abroad, and further institutionalized the consultation meetings—the conferences called *Brasilerios no Mundo*.[10] The same year, two other measures reinforced governmental efforts to improve linkages. On 24 May, President Lula inaugurated an international TV channel at the Empresa Brasileira de Comunicação, from where three special programs addressing some of the diaspora's concerns have been broadcasted; and on November 25, another specific service online was launched, the Portal of Brazilian Communities Abroad, to improve communication with emigrants.

Within the official view, this is all consistent with broader positive changes that are placing the country in a more relevant status at the international level; better socioeconomic conditions create incentives to travel and generate migration flows well beyond the ones driven by economic necessity. Therefore, in the words of former Foreign Affairs Minister Antonio de Aguiar Patriota: "It is not just questions of economic survival but new opportunities that take co-nationals to live in other countries where they already have a stable and meaningful presence, thus requiring permanent attention from the government to protect and support citizens, preserve citizenship, and maintain links with Brazil" (SGEB 2012:3). In sync with other forms of participation explained later, these institutional developments are tied to a democratic process that promises to pay due attention to citizens' demands and represents a "new form of governmental interlocution with the Brazilian civil society abroad" (SGEB 2012:6).

Regarding expats' enfranchisement, Brazil follows general trends in the region. Brazilians abroad have the right to vote for president and vice president if they have previously registered in the closest consulate to their place of residency. However, this neither emerged as part of policy innovation nor became a contested issue. It has been included in electoral regulations since 1965 (Chapter VII of Law 4737 of 15 July 1965).[11] Its implementation was obviously not possible under dictatorship; thus, the exercise of the right became effective for the first time after the return to democracy in 1989.

As in other cases, political participation is still relatively low. The explanations revolve around three main factors: very little information reaches emigrants; those who are in irregular status tend to stay away from any procedures and offices that may require registration; and not all destinations are close to embassies or consulates where polling stations are usually set (de Ribas Guedes 2009). In 2006, there were 86,000 Brazilians abroad registered to vote in presidential elections, but only half of them did so. Back then, there were 292 electoral districts set in 61 embassies and consulates with 240 electronic station polls. In 2010, numbers almost tripled: over 200,000 people registered, with 589 station polls set in 119 embassies. However, only 60% of those who were registered actually cast a vote (SGEB 2012:43).

According to the Superior Electoral Court, registration has increased lately. In the last (2014) presidential election, 354,154 Brazilians abroad were registered. A few destinations gathered most of them: New York, Miami, Boston, Nagoya, Lisbon, and London.[12] However, only 141,501 voted on 5 October 2014, and most voted in favor of the opposition candidates. Aécio Neves from the Brazilian Social Democratic Party (PSDB)

won 49.51% of the votes abroad; Marina Silva, from the Brazilian Socialist Party (PSB), obtained 26.01%; and the incumbent Dilma Rousseff
of the Workers' Party (PT) won 18.35%.[13] Officials at the Ministry of
Foreign Affairs admit that such low turnout rates discourage the implementation of further changes; opening more polling stations is a work
in progress, and it often faces resistance from both consulates and the
Superior Electoral Court.[14]

Nevertheless, some bills were sent to Congress to broaden the scope
of voting rights beyond the presidency and to amend the National Constitution regarding representation (see details in de Ribas Guedes 2009).
At present, Brazilians abroad do not enjoy any formal representation in
Parliament. Senator Cristovam Buarque submitted a proposal in 2005 to
create a special, extraterritorial jurisdiction (PEC 05/05). The Joint Parliamentary Commission supported the project but recommended a previous
broad debate within Congress and society at large. From the perspective
of Itamaraty officials, this is not an urgent or desirable goal. Although
they argue that the guiding force is today migrant empowerment, they do
not see political representation as a means. Granting parliamentary seats
would run "counter our [current] bottom-up strategy." It would be better
for migrant leaders "to stay focused on their projects at the grassroots
level, learning; otherwise, an appointment (and what comes with it, such
as a good salary, trips, and power) may change them."[15]

In the realm of symbolic initiatives, the Brazilian state has done relatively little. Its actions mainly focus on diplomatic interventions on
behalf of migrants, defending their rights and showing sensitivity to their
claims (Padilla 2011:21). Only recently has the term *diaspora* become
accepted in policy circles (Feldman-Bianco 2011:238). It is also worth
noting that discursive mechanisms are not a centerpiece of courting in
this case. There has not been an attempt to coin any special label to name
the diaspora. There is no deliberate emphasis on inclusion of emigrants
in the nation. Brazil names its citizens abroad and specific institutions
(e.g., Ministry of Foreign Affairs specialized office, annual meetings with
migrant representatives) as *Brazilians no Mundo* or *Brazilians no Exterior.* The former actually conveys a global approach to a dispersed population. In the words of the former director of the consular Department
of Brazilians Abroad (Ministry of Foreign Affairs), this a specificity of
this emigrant community: "Like Brazil has become a global player and
a global trader, a Brazilian appears as a 'global migrant' if we take into
account that there is a significant number of Brazilians in all regions of
the world today" (Gradilone 2009:49). Other officials' explanations for
this choice are that emigrants do not constitute a homogeneous and
distinct diasporic group, and they are highly dispersed, not very organized, and relatively well integrated in host societies. There would be no
echo for a special label because emigration does not resonate with the
rest of society.[16]

Further to the intention to strengthen linkages already mentioned, the use of itinerary consulates and new technologies has allowed the implementation of a number of linkage initiatives. The SGEB has collaborated with local governments, nongovernmental organizations, and the media in host societies to carry out information campaigns about services that might help with returnees and resettlement. The SGEB has also encouraged regular consultation online within the existing network of consulates to improve implementation of all changes in the main sites of destination. Consulates also make use of social media, running a special page on Facebook. The compilation of guidelines for citizens abroad (known as *Manual de Servicio Consular y Juridico*), made public on 2 August 2010, is also available online, together with practical legal advice and a leaflet for consular and other services (SGEB 2012). Remittances and investments may also be considered a particular type of linkage. In this realm, state actions are incipient, mainly led by local authorities from the states or municipalities where massive outflows originated (e.g., Governador Valadares, in the state of Minas Gerais) to capture and/or channel those resources (Padilla 2011:21).

As a result of this whole array of initiatives, today the Ministry of Foreign Affairs makes a distinction between its classic consular activities (typically addressed to individuals or institutions) and general actions that target the entire emigrant community, have a distinctive political and/or diplomatic character, and often require negotiations with other nation-states. Yet, in practice, the distinction is not so clear-cut. Some projects fall in a grey area (and are usually labelled as second-generation consular activities) because they involve not only assistance, protection, and processing of documentation but also education, health, work, social security, and other issues, and sometimes preservation of the Brazilian culture and of nationality bonds, too (SGEB 2012:19). Because they are in a grey area, these may be included within negotiations with other governments on broader migration and consular topics, while relations with the diaspora in particular are considered political in nature and fall within the Division of Brazilian Communities Abroad.

Explaining State-Led Initiatives: The Intrastate Dynamics

As soon as political elites took note of the emigration phenomenon and increasing consular demands, they responded by setting in motion a number of institutional and procedural changes. This was a pragmatic and technical response led by the Ministry of Foreign Affairs. Given that the new policy had to be mostly implemented abroad, it was assumed that it had to be carried out by this ministry because foreign relations are within its "natural" competencies (Grandilone 2009). But it has not been the only ministry involved, let alone the sole driver of policy innovation.

As a result, policymaking dynamics have gone beyond responsiveness and assistance.

On the one hand, official political discourses draw on human rights considerations and democratic practices to emphasize state responsiveness to citizens' rights and claims. In particular, top officials at the Ministry of Justice have lately underlined those ideas[17] and the need to address all migration issues together, in an integrated fashion. This is certainly in sync with a regional current trend. Yet, Brazil differs from other cases in this book in some respects. The role of the executive was crucial when institutional reforms were implemented. In particular, former President Cardoso requested a report on emigration when he was Minister of Foreign Affairs; he fostered changes in consular services later; and once he was in office, he initiated a tepid rhetorical shift when he argued that "we need you" (the emigrants) and he issued an invitation to return and/ or engage with home affairs (cited in Green 2008:423). Later on, former President Lula was the voice of the new approach. During his presidential campaign, he issued a "letter to Brazilians who live far from home." He then promised to create the conditions for the creation of organizations of representation, to address emigrants' needs, to negotiate bilateral agreements with receiving countries in defense of migrant rights, and to facilitate their making a contribution to places of origin.[18] His visits to some communities abroad were illustrative of his intention to bring emigration up in the foreign relations agenda and his commitment to deepen institutional changes and dialogue with the emigrant community (Padilla 2011).

Nevertheless, presidential involvement has not been a constant (e.g., President Rouseff has hardly referred to these issues), and it might not be as necessary as in other cases because diaspora issues are channeled at a sustained and regular pace through consular offices. As explained previously, the Ministry of Foreign Affairs has conducted most of the launching and implementation of outreach measures. The specialized units include the Division of Brazilian Communities that hosts the undersecretariat of Brazilian Communities Abroad, which is the main liaison office for activities with the diaspora. But these units' actions intersect with other state agencies with competences on migration issues. For instance, the Ministry of Justice has been increasingly involved in designing a new approach to migration in the last few years. It typically oversees questions of residency, transit, and mobility. It has special units addressing foreigners' issues (*Departmento de Estrangeiros*) and the problem that is the focus of attention today: refugees (CONARE). The view from that area of the state is that presidential involvement is not what drives policy because "ministries, which are in touch with daily problems, are the ones that push for changes: [impetus] goes from them up."[19]

On the other hand, according to Law 10,683 of 28 May 2003, migration is also within the sphere of the Minister of Labor and Employment, where the National Council of Immigration sits. The council works as another focal point of activities and initiatives that cut across several state offices because it gathers representatives from various state agencies, private companies (in their capacities as employers), and workers. It also includes a representative of Itamaraty. It is in charge of guiding, coordinating, and overseeing immigration issues. It is under discussion whether it should be hosted in another ministry or under the presidency. Nevertheless, at present, and until a new migration law is passed, it plays a crucial role for two reasons: (1) the existing law delegates to this office competencies to actually "legislate" in cases of normative lacunas and to resolve specific situations, and (2) the council is also the one that convokes all sectors to have a dialogue and provides the arena for discussions on how to address immigration-related issues. Thus, it has gained considerable leverage over policymaking.[20]

From a comparative perspective, this tripartite structure is relatively unusual; the existence of a collegiate unit in the policymaking process (the council) is also unique to this case. All public officials interviewed agreed off the record that coordination is scarce and tensions exist, mainly between the Council and the Ministry of Justice, and this is usually reflected in a competition to lead and in the type of concerns and priorities (e.g., human rights versus security considerations; refugees versus highly skilled immigrants).

Thus, although emigrant issues have been largely encapsulated in Itamaraty, some recent developments suggest that a more comprehensive approach to all migration flows is in the making and might have consequences on policymaking, especially in terms of coordination across state units and competencies. The question of concentrating decision-making power in a single, autonomous, overarching unit has been discussed, but no agreement was reached, and it is a point not included in the proposed bill under consideration. At present, foreign affairs officials do not see any need for further coordination and/or institutional changes regarding emigration. These are not considered to be pressing or timely enough to encourage further migrant political engagement.[21]

Moreover, congressional involvement has been relatively more intense than in other cases, although lack of engagement of political parties with migration and lack of expedience have rendered Congress as one of the main breaks to policy innovation. Migration issues fall within its commissions on human rights and external relations. Itamaraty often invites legislators to provide information and sends parliamentary missions abroad to reach out to expats, but, as it was explained previously, it is reluctant to share leadership on these matters. Legislators have occasionally advocated for emigrants' rights, collaborated with migrant associations, and visited communities abroad, thus involving themselves in what Padilla (2011:16) calls a "parliamentary diplomacy" that paved the way for courting.

The work of the Joint Parliamentary Commission for the Investigation of Emigration in 2005–2006 was a significant step in gathering information about emigration and designing a policy response. On the basis of that work, Senator Valdir Raupp (PMDB-RO) submitted a bill to create the special secretariat for the support of Brazilians abroad. Some members of that commission attempted to go beyond their specific tasks and promoted the creation of the parliamentary front called Citizenship without Borders in 2005, hoping that this would give further support to emigrant-related initiatives (Firmeza 2007:235).

Yet, this happened in the context of low resonance of migration in political competition and debates. Political parties do not have specific proposals in their programs. Only the PT (Workers' Party) developed some links with migrant organizations abroad. These topics do not enter into the electoral agenda either.[22] At the same time, the lack of parliamentary consensus and delays in updating migration legislation in general, and passing the project to grant emigrants political representation in Congress in particular, represent major obstacles to policy innovation today.

Social Activism Meets State Initiatives

In the last few years, interactions between government representatives and migrant leaders have happened in the context of conferences or meetings convoked to discuss problems and suggestions. To some extent, these conversations have been setting and shaping the state–diaspora agenda, adding one more layer of institutionalization to the new policy. Although these meetings are usually convoked by the Ministry of Foreign Affairs, public officials from other units and legislators are also invited. Such consultation also builds upon forums organized by the emigrants themselves in several destinations, leading to important documents that summarize their concerns and expectations. This illustrates that consultation and migrant participation in this case have always had a broader scope than in other countries—a point further reinforced by last year's developments (see next section). It also demonstrates that in this case, state-led initiatives at times converged with peaks of social activism.

The *Casa de Brasil de Lisboa*, a migrant association created in 1992 by Brasilians in Lisbon played a crucial role in articulating migrant demands with policymakers' initiatives. Some of its leaders had fluid contacts with members of the PT, including former president Lula. They fostered mobilization and support to the party, as well as links with other associations of immigrants of all nationalities to defend their rights (Feldman-Bianco 2011). Their claims were amplified by collaborations with religious institutions and nongovernmental organizations that also became agenda-setters and sponsors of major events, propositive documents, and publications (Milesi and Fantazini 2009). This activism gave the Casa visibility and access to policy circles in both Portugal and Brazil.

Immediately after the Brazilian government took the initial steps toward addressing diaspora issues in late 1990s, this association participated in meetings with scholars, activists, and policymakers in both countries to discuss such issues in Lisbon in 1997 and 2002. Both meetings encouraged investigation of emigrants' living conditions and needs. The 2002 gathering was particularly relevant because a document was issued with a number of proposals for action; it is known as the Carta de Lisboa. That same year, presidential candidate Lula made public his letter to "Brazilians who live far from home," and in his first presidential trip abroad, he visited the Casa.

Fieldman-Bianco (2011) argues that the role of the Casa de Lisboa contributed to broader transnational activism, thus paving the way for a common agenda. Similar meetings were organized in other top destinations, also giving place to important documents that informed the new emigration policy: the 2005 Carta de Boston and the 2007 Carta de Brussels (see details in Milesi and Fantazini 2009). The meeting in Brussels included representatives of Brazilians living in 11 European countries who envisioned forming a network or federation. This group spearheaded another meeting in Barcelona in 2009, where the terms of dialogue and the potential for engagement with the Brazilian government were discussed. Migrant claims and proposals were gathered then in the Carta de Barcelona. Their representatives, as well as those of the Casa de Lisboa, had an active participation in the general gatherings (also known as conferences) convoked by the Ministry of Foreign Affairs with all emigrant communities in the following years.

The state made a considerable effort to structure these events that progressively provided an arena for courting. According to the assessment made by the SGEB, a series of gatherings helped to shape the state–diaspora relationship. The First Conference of *Brasileiros no Mundo* (Brazilians in the World) took place on 17–18 July 2008 and included panels organized by geographic areas of emigrants' residency and topics (e.g., international migration and state actions in that area, scientific cooperation, etc.). The idea of creating a Provisory Council of Representatives of Brazilians Abroad emerged then. This council was created during the second conference, held in Rio de Janeiro on 14–16 October 2009. A concrete working plan that gathered the diaspora's claims was drawn then.[23] The third conference was also held in Rio de Janeiro on 2–3 December 2010. It acquired particular visibility because of President Lula's attendance (accompanied by other high-ranking public officials), which set the council's activities in motion for the first time. The council was formed with 16 representatives of emigrant communities in four regions of the world; members were elected through a consultation mechanism via the Internet. After 2 years of tenure, they gathered with public officials again to elaborate a plan for the following 2 years.

As in other cases, frequent and fluid contacts between a few migrant leaders and public officials in key destinations are what makes a difference. It is in those sites, and mainly through informal ties, that visits from top political figures (such as presidential candidates, presidents in office, ministers) gain visibility and, at the same time, allow emigrants to gain temporary exposure. This introduces a degree of volatility to migrant agency inasmuch as it is contingent on a few individuals' initiatives.

Overall, the convergence of state outreach and social activism has been a fertile ground for keeping state–diaspora relations moving forward. However, on the society side of the state–diaspora relationship, we observe similarities with other cases, namely incipient and varied forms of organization and difficulties of emigrant groups in forming well-structured and effective associations. This is why public officials suggest that community claims emerged "through spasms, in the form of manifestos such as the Carta de Lisbon in 2001 and the Letter of Boston in 2005" (Firmeza 2007:237). It is not clear, though, to what extent the government is willing and able to invest in building organizational capacities and empowering emigrants. It has relied, for instance, on nongovernmental organizations and churches to provide assistance (in a similar fashion to the public–private policy networks described in Chapter 8 for other cases) because they provide physical space and volunteers, thus requiring little public expense.[24]

Other initiatives cast doubt on whether empowerment might be a goal at all. Encouraging the formation of citizens' councils was controversial. The first ones were created in the 1990s in parallel with the initiatives discussed previously. Citizens' councils worked as informal forums of discussion; they were presumably nonpolitical representations that acted as channels of communication between migrants and consulates. The emphasis was on dialogue, not on empowering these councils or other goals. It was assumed that the councils would help distribute information among the emigrant communities. Their activities tended to focus on different issues that vary across destinations. As in other cases, the level of participation has been low in all receiving countries, and leaders were not elected by the migrants but appointed by consuls. Therefore, councils were far from being an articulated and effective form of representation. Almost a decade ago, officials argued: "In general, the councils do not have autonomy, they remain attached to consulates, still in sync with the design of the State Secretariat that created them in the 1990s and gave them only orientation and advising functions" (Firmeza 2007:227).

In other words, diaspora organization shows the fragility and volatility that have been noted in the cases of other South American communities. But the shape of councils has been changing and evolving from the initial ones just mentioned (created in the 1990s) to the formation of Councils of Citizenship in 2011. The main difference is that the latter are formed by elected members. Their work revolves around priority issues such as culture, education, legal matters, and so forth. They act in collaboration with the SGBE. By 2012, there were around 60 of Councils of Citizenship around the world (SGBE 2012:38).

Consequently, viewed from the point of view of state courting, the Brazilian case stands out as an intense state effort to organize the diaspora, graduating and structuring to what extent and how migrant leaders participate in policymaking (as Mexico did for a while) rather than simply supporting migrant organizational efforts. Going beyond that would probably require an integrated approach to other actors, too. The role of civil society in forging regular interactions and collaboration is acknowledged to some extent, as is the increasing activity of churches in assisting migrants. A notable example is NGOs' concern with human trafficking. Thus, in 2006, the state secretariat enlisted consulates to gather information about foreign NGOs working on emigrant issues. Yet, officials argue: "In spite of sporadic contacts carried out in Brazil and abroad, Itamaraty has not developed a comprehensive and systematic policy to interactions with civil society regarding policies towards emigrant communities" (Firmeza 2007:228).

The Tasks That Lie Ahead

During Dilma Roussef's administration (2011–present), three main initiatives moved the general migration agenda: (1) the creation of a special commission to study a new proposed migration bill, (2) the adoption of a humanitarian approach to the reception of Haitians,[25] and (3) a broad consultation mechanism that was set in motion. Overall, these steps point to a shift in attention and actions from emigration to immigration. The last initiative, in particular, reinforces a distinctive characteristic of the policymaking process: it extends to the entire set of migration issues the modality of the so-called conferences.[26] The practice is consistent with new forms of social participation that have intensified since 2003 (see next section). To some extent, it is also a response to social criticism toward nondemocratic management of migration issues in general and insufficient state involvement, especially coming from nongovernmental and religious organizations concerned with the defense of human rights.[27] In line with the transnational processes explained in Chapter 3, the International Organization for Migrations echoed these claims, provided the arena for the discussion (which included the input from a dozen emigrant associations), and made recommendations for migrant integration and inclusion (Projeto OIM-DEEST 2013).

In the light of social claims, gaps in knowledge, and lack of visibility of migration issues, the government organized the First Conference on Migration (also known as COMIGRAR) in 2014. The underlying goal was to bring up an issue in the governmental agenda and/or public debate. Inevitably, since the initial steps to launch a conference involve identifying and convoking interlocutors, any conference would have an impact on the state–society relationship in that policy area. COMI-GRAR was spearheaded by the Ministry of Justice (the equivalent to the Ministry of Interior in neighboring countries) with the collaboration of the Ministry of Foreign Affairs and of Public Works and Employment, and it was held in São Paulo on 31 May 2014. It was designed as a consultation mechanism, with participation of individuals and institutions on numerous panels. Brazilians abroad were also invited, and the Ministry of Foreign Affairs had a roundtable on their specific issues. Top officials at the Ministry of Justice framed the initiative in human rights-related considerations, arguing that this procedure would contribute to upholding migrant rights, increase awareness of their relevance across areas of the state apparatus, broaden and improve services to migrants, identify demands, and discuss preventive measures to avoid violation of rights, among other things.[28] Moreover, the conference was presented as a breaking point in migration policymaking inasmuch as it promised to "naturalize the issue in the public policy agenda at all levels of government, as well as migrants' presence, and to disseminate in society the relevance of migrations for the present and future of the country" (Secretaria Nacional de Justiça 2014:4).

The rationale is illustrative of the ideational basis of the initiative. Such an attempt, it is argued in the same document, implies a critical revision of the historical approach to migration that in the past was instrumental and utilitarian and included violation of rights, racist stances, and security-oriented considerations. The new approach proposes to go beyond the idea of treating migrants as simply addressees of state concerns and interventions. It also aims at ending with the invisibility of the topic and the barriers to access to services for migrants, and encouraging individual and collective participation in policymaking. The debate within the conference revolved around five main areas: equal treatment and access to service and rights; social, economic, and productive insertion of migrants; cultural citizenship and diversity; violations to migrant rights and prevention measures; and social participation and transparency.

The impact of this event on future developments is largely uncertain. Specialists who participated had mixed feelings about the final product. Doubts revolved around the representativeness of individuals and groups convoked due to the relatively short time for preparation and lax norms on who could participate and set the agenda and how, as well as whether and how participants' claims would be effectively incorporated into policies. The timing of the meeting (i.e., right before national elections, which usually increase uncertainty and tend to lead to officials' turnover) also cast doubts on the continuity and sustainability of an emerging consensus, if there is one.[29] When I asked the organizers whether there would be more future conferences, they eluded the answer, suggesting that this was pending further discussions and news about changes in appointments after the elections.

By all accounts, lack of progress on the legislation update is standing in the way of a comprehensive and effective approach to all migration problems, not just emigration. The current *Lei do Estrangeiro* (Law 6,815 of 1980, regulated a year later by Law 6,964) still reflects the military government's concerns with security. Its restrictive character tends toward criminalization of immigrants and bureaucratic obstacles to their integration. It is at odds with the rights-centered approach and concerns with migrants' roles in labor markets of late democratic governments. A reform bill (Law Project 5,655) contemplating all pressing population problems, migration flows (including transit and naturalization norms, among other things), and human right considerations was sent to Congress in 2009. It also included the transformation of the National Council of Immigration into a National Council of Migration, reflecting an attempt to adopt a comprehensive approach that included the issues concerning Brazilians abroad (OIM 2010). The project has been discussed and revised several times, but it has never been passed. At the moment of this writing, a new project is under consideration by a commission of experts; a draft has circulated among all migration-related state institutions that contributed suggestions. The Ministry of Labor and Employment, for instance, made explicit the existence of ambiguities and differences in policy orientation across units. The Ministry of Justice is expected to circulate a final revised version of the project to all other parties before it is sent to consideration of the Parliament (OBMigra 2014:34–49).

Analysis and Conclusions

In contrast to other cases, the Brazilian state exhibits a form of transnational intervention that is very specific or "surgical," identifying and tackling particular problems as they arise. Although courting was a proactive top-down initiative, this case shows a selective approach to concrete problems in each destination, as well as an adaptation of programs to what each group within the diaspora seems to demand and is able to mobilize for. That was the case for the initiatives on migrant working conditions, health, and education, and it is particularly the case for the Brazilians in Japan, where the Brazilian government negotiated bilateral agreements in various areas, such as social security. Yet, it is an approach that also stands out for having a comprehensive scope in terms of geographic outreach: the reference to Brazilians *no mundo* (in the world) reflects the awareness of a diaspora dispersed across the globe and the attempt to include all destination sites in outreach efforts.

In addition, despite the fact that emigration is not perceived as an urgent, pressing problem today, there has been an explicit acknowledgment of the links between the diplomatic and consular agendas, as well as the potential tensions or damage that migration questions may cause to bilateral relations and/or to the image and credibility of the country in international affairs (Rego Barros 1996:109–110). The new emigration policy then reflected the awareness that these agendas cannot function properly if they are addressed independently (and if officials continue to be trained in separate tracks). Therefore, foreign policy and Itamaraty's administrative culture were deliberately adapted to recognize the political dimension of some consular problems and the need to engage with emigrants beyond assistance. This contributed to making policy innovation consistent and persistent over time.

Moreover, the way policy changes came to fruition indicates that this is a case in which the bottom-up and the top-down activism at times converged in a mutually reinforcing dynamic. On the one hand, the state acted quickly on increasing demands. On the other hand, civil society abroad mobilized intensely for a few years; more important, it issued some documents that informed policy and indirectly required further governmental commitment with an agenda that was discussed and agreed on.

As in other cases in this book, the redefinition of state functions stands out as crucial to understanding the modality of policy innovation. The reform of the consular service happened in parallel to a comprehensive plan of state reform launched under Cardoso's administration. Instead of having neoliberal overtones, this reform was framed in social-democratic or socioliberal proposals that, rather than radically withdrawing the state, aimed at "rebuilding" and giving it more capacity to govern and to facilitate the conditions for the national economy to become more competitive. It pursued two main goals: fiscal adjustment and modernization of public services to address citizens' needs in a professional and efficient manner (Bresser Pereira 1998:5–6, 20). It included changes in three main dimensions: institutional, cultural, and procedural, inspired by democratic ideals and the need to adopt a managerial strategy to public administration (in contrast to the bureaucratic and patrimonial model adopted in the 1930s).[30] As in Uruguay, the reform of the state built upon an entrenched tradition of state intervention and preserved for the state strategic areas of action. In Brazil, it also maintained the role of the state as guarantor of social rights while engaging nonstate actors in the delivery of services, namely welfare assistance, thus creating the conditions for public–private partnerships (Bresser Pereira 1998:6–7).

This reformist attempt faced initial resistance to change in administrative and political fronts, as acknowledged by former minister Bresser Pereira, who designed the plan and implement it (Bresser Pereira 1998, 2001). It gathered some support later, especially for its fiscal adjustment goals. But the institutional changes proposed looked like a threat to the distribution of power within the state bureaucracy and its control over the outcomes of the transformation. The reformist attempt did not overcome resistance to changes that required a shift from old rules to performance-based results. Public officials' cooperation was only partial, and the reform was finally abandoned after 5 years (Cunha Resende 2002).

Nevertheless, it was a milestone in the debate about the crisis of the state and it paved the way to other changes. The underlying approach supported the modernization and expansion of consular activities described in previous sections. It was entirely consistent with the rationale given for addressing emigrants' demands in a more efficient way and engaging nongovernmental organizations and religious institutions in migrant assistance. The postneoliberal approach that followed under Lula's administration added citizens' rights and democratic considerations, thus embedding emigration policy into a sociopolitical agenda rather than a purely instrumental strategy.

As for the involvement of social actors, the dialogue and consultation processes have become intensive both at home and abroad. Migrant associational life and political mobilization have contributed to this outcome, although the general levels of organization and participation of emigrants are still too low to drive the process. The state is reaching out, but in a gradual and measured fashion. The combination of these two factors makes it difficult to make long-distance engagement more intense in the short run.

At home, the COMIGRAR conference carried out last year is in line with participatory practices that have increased since the return to democracy and, particularly, in the last few years. As Avritzer (2007) explains, the presence of civil society in public policymaking has broadened in Brazil; there are increasing institutional channels for participation and new forms of representation that do not fit neatly into the top-down traditional dynamic and do not have fixed territorial boundaries. Article 14 of the 1988 Constitution has further supported these developments by establishing the possibility of setting in motion legislative processes via popular initiative. Since the 1980s, although old political practices persist (e.g., clientelism) and political elites reluctantly accept social input, civil society has increasingly engaged in diverse forms of associational life, claiming increasing autonomy from the state and redefining the notions of both public services and community participation. Positive synergies have developed, for instance, through the implementation of a participatory budgets, policy councils, and urban plans managed at the local level (Avritzer 2008). The same author argues that this new civil associationism implies a departure from homogeneous forms of collective action and does not necessarily seek an integration into the state as in the past. At the local level, it also includes schemes of power sharing in institutions that may be formed by the state but where state officials sit together with civil society representatives (Avritzer 1997, 2008). At the national level, though, conferences generate doubts because their scope may become too broad, participation is uneven (thus casting doubts on representativeness), and their effects on agenda setting and policymaking tend to vary considerably across policy areas (Avritzer and Leite de Souza 2013). Because COMIGRAR was the first one on migration, there is little evidence to compare and to assess whether this might have repercussions on migrant mobilization at long distances (e.g., migrants residing in Europe).

These insights are particularly relevant because, although courting was initiated and largely shaped by the state, broader societal and democratization processes are impinging on migration policymaking in general, and they might potentially make it more pluralistic and more permeable to nonstate actors' input than in other cases. If emigration eventually becomes part of a broader agenda, there are antecedents in institutions and practices to pave the way for greater diaspora participation in policymaking.

The evidence here is also supportive of other works that emphasize the multiplicity of actors that intervene in foreign policy today and the increasing salience of human rights issues and considerations in foreign policy actions, especially under Lula's two terms (e.g., Giaccaglia 2010; Milani 2012; Projeto OIM-DEEST 2013). These works also suggest that Brazilian foreign policy is closely intertwined with domestic political processes and is increasingly affected by several state agencies. Therefore, the traditional isolation or concentration of decision making solely in Itamaraty cannot be taken for granted any longer.

This chapter further documents that fact and suggests that, in the absence of an emigration crisis, Brazil is thus far a case of "courting without being noticed" inasmuch as policy innovation follows a technical, low profile approach. At present, there are no plans to expand or modify the mandate and competences of the SGEB, let alone in the context of budget restrictions. And there is no intention "to make noise" around emigration or to allocate more resources; instead, the focus is on daily tasks of responding to specific needs, offering assistance, improving services, broadening dialogue, and creating links.[31] In short, only an emigration crisis or radical innovation policies regarding all migration issues seem to be the (unlikely) reasons to move from courting to further engagement.

Notes

1 See http://data.worldbank.org/country/brazil, accessed March 11, 2015.
2 See http://data.worldbank.org/indicator/SP.POP.TOTL, accessed March 11, 2015.
3 As each consulate follows its own preferred mechanism to collect this data, accuracy and consistency cannot be assumed. In addition, the procedure does not capture those in irregular situations or those who decide not to register. Only data for the case of Brazilians in Japan tends to be more reliable because most of these emigrants are registered with the host country and appear in the statistics produced by the Japanese government. This is a significant community that the Ministry of Foreign Affairs monitors regularly.
4 Interview with Sergio Franca Danese, general undersecretariat of Brazilian Communities Abroad, Ministry of Foreign Affairs, Brasilia, May 27, 2014.
5 On recent Brazilian migration to Southern Europe, see Magalhães Fernandes and Rangel Rigotti (2009).
6 Interview with Maria Luiza Ribeiro Lopes da Silva, Brasileiros No Exterior, Ministry of Foreign Affairs, Brasilia, May 27, 2014.

 7 Interview with Maria Luiza Ribeiro Lopes da Silva, Brasilia, May 27, 2014.
 8 This plan was elaborated in consultation with consulates abroad who gathered information and suggestions discussed in the First Conference of Brazilians Abroad.
 9 It receives around 1,000 requests a year (SGEB 2012:55).
10 See www.planalto.gov.br/ccivil_03/_ato2007–2010/2010/decreto/d7214.htm, accessed May 14, 2014.
11 See www.planalto.gov.br/ccivil_03/leis/L4737.htm, accessed March 13, 2015.
12 See http://english.tse.jus.br/noticias-tse-en/2014/Agosto/tse-authorizes-electoral-sections-abroad-outside-embassies, accessed March 28, 2015.
13 See http://agenciabrasil.ebc.com.br/en/internacional/noticia/2014–10/brazilian-voter-turnout-abroad-63, accessed March 28, 2015.
14 Interview with Maria Luiza Ribeiro Lopes da Silva, Brasilia, May 27, 2014.
15 Interview with Maria Luiza Ribeiro Lopes da Silva, Brasilia, May 27, 2014.
16 Interview with Maria Luiza Ribeiro Lopes da Silva, Brasilia, May 27, 2014.
17 This is partially explained by officials' background: some of them had previous working experience in legal matters and defense of human rights during the transition from authoritarian rule to democracy.
18 See http://lulaforpresident.tripod.com/carta.htm, accessed May 14, 2014.
19 Interview with Paulo Abreu, secretary of justice, Ministry of Justice, Brasilia, May 27, 2014.
20 Interview with Paulo Sergio de Almeida, president, National Council of Immigration, Brasilia, May 29, 2014.
21 Interview with Maria Luiza Ribeiro Lopes da Silva, Brasilia, May 27, 2014.
22 Interview with Marcia Spangel, Senate, Brasilia, May 28, 2014.
23 It is worth noting that delegates from the Mexican government participated in the 2009 event. This illustrates the kind of incipient bilateral cooperation that these issues have encouraged in the region.
24 Interview with Maria Luiza Ribeiro Lopes da Silva, Brasilia, May 27, 2014.
25 For details on the policy challenges raised by increasing Haitian immigration to Brazil, see OIM (2014). For a historical account of Brazil's approach to refugee protection, see Fischel de Andrade (2015).
26 Conferences are structured processes of consultation put in motion by the government to "listen" to various social actors. They help identify problems, stakeholders, diagnoses, and solutions. They have been practiced since 1930 in various policy areas such as health, education, environment, gender, and others. They make take different forms, from the discussion of a specific plan or program to be implemented to just an open consultation to capture the main demands of a sector of the population. For a detailed analysis of the characteristics, actors involved, and effectiveness, see Avritzer and Leite de Souza (2013).
27 Interview with Rosita Milesi, Instituto de Migraciones y Derechos Humanos, Brasilia, May 29, 2014.
28 Interview with João Guilherme Granja, director of the immigration department, Ministry of Justice, Brasilia, May 27, 2014.
29 Personal communication with Leonardo Cavalcanti, Observatorio Migrações, University of Brasilia, Brasilia, May 28 and July 14, 2014, and interviews with Rosita Milesi, Instituto de Migraciones y Derechos Humanos, Brazil, May 29, 2014, and Marcia Spangel, Senate, Brazil, May 28, 2014.
30 For a historical account of the state apparatus design and previous reforms, see Bresser Pereira (2001).
31 Interviews with Sergio Franca Danese, head of the undersecretariat of Brazilian Communities Abroad, Ministry of Foreign Affairs, Brasilia, May 27, 2014, and Rodrigo do Amaral Souza, director, Department of Immigration and Legal Affairs, Ministry of Foreign Affairs, Brasilia, May 28, 2014.

Works Cited

Avritzer, Leonardo. 1997. "Um Desenho Institucional Para o Novo Associativismo." *Lua Nova: Revista de Cultura e Política.* 39: 149–174.

Avritzer, Leonardo. 2007. "Sociedade Civil, Instituições Participativas e Representação: Da Autorização à Legitimadade da Ação." *DADOS.* 50(3): 443–464.

Avritzer, Leonardo. 2008. "Instituições Participativas e Desenho Institucional: Algumas Consideracões Sobre a Variação da Participação no Brasil Democrático." *Opinião Pública.* 14(1): 43–64.

Avritzer, Leonardo and Clóvis Henrique Leite de Souza. orgs. 2013. *Conferencias Nacionais. Atores, Dinâmicas Participativas e Efetividade.* Brasilia: IPEA.

Barros, Sebastião do Rego. 1996–1997. "O Itamaraty e os Brasileiros no Exterior." *Revista Política Externa.* 5(3), 106–114.

Braga Martes, Ana Cristina. 2011. *New Immigrants, New Land: A Study of Brazilians in Massachusetts.* Gainesville: University of Florida Press.

Bresser Pereira, Luiz Carlos. 1998. "Uma Reforma Gerencial da Administração Pública no Brasil." *Revista do Serviço Público.* 49(1): 5–42.

Bresser Pereira, Luiz Carlos. 2001. "Do Estado Patrimonial ao Gerencial." In *Brasil: Um Século de Transformações,* org. by Pinheiro Wilheim e Sachs. São Paulo: Companhia das Letras. pp. 222–259.

Ciaccaglia, Clarisa. 2010. "La Influencia de los Actores Domésticos en la Política Exterior Brasileña Durante el Gobierno de Lula da Silva." *CONfines.* 6(12), 95–121.

da Cunha Resende, Flávio. 2002. "Por que Reformas Administrativas Falham?" *Revista Brasileira de Ciências Sociais.* 17(50): 123–143.

Feldman-Bianco, Bela. 2011. "Caminos de Ciudadanía: Emigración, Movilizaciones Sociales y Políticas del Estado Brasilero." In *La Construcción Social del Sujeto Migrante en América Latina. Prácticas, Representaciones y Categorías,* comp. by Bela Feldman-Bianco, Liliana Rivera Sánchez, Carolina Stefoni, and Marta Inés Villa Martínez. Quito, Ecuador: FLACO, CLACSO, and Universida Alberto Hurtado. pp. 237–282.

Fischel de Andrade, José H. 2015. "Refugee protection in Brazil (1921–2014): An Analytical Narrative of Changing Policies." In *A Liberal Tide? Immigration and Asylum Law and Policy in Latin America,* ed. by David James Cantor, Luisa Feline Freier, and Jean-Pierre Gauci. London: Institute of Latin American Studies, School of Advanced Study, University of London.

Firmeza, George Torquato. 2007. *Brasileiros no Exterior.* Brasilia: Fundação Alexandre de Gusmão, Ministério das Relações Exteriores.

Gradilone, Eduardo. 2009. "Uma Política Governamental para as Comunidades Brasileiras no Exterior." In *I Conferência sobre as Comunidades Brasileiras no Exterior. Brasileiros no Mundo.* Rio de Janeiro, 17–18 July 2008. Brasilia: Fundação Alexandre de Gusmão, Ministério das Relações Exteriores. pp. 47–80.

Green, Paul. 2008. "Family and Nation: Brazilian National Ideology as Contested Transnational Practice in Japan." *Global Networks.* 8(4): 418–435.

Levitt, Peggy and Rafael de la Dehesa. 2003. "Transnational Migration and the Redefinition of the State: Variations and Explanations." *Ethnic and Racial Studies.* 26(4): 587–611.

Magalhães Fernandes, Duval and José Irineu Rangel Rigotti. 2009. "Os Brasileiros na Europa: Notas Introdutórias." In *I Conferência sobre as Comunidades Brasileiras no Exterior. Brasileiros no Mundo.* Rio de Janeiro, 17–18

July 2008. Brasilia: Fundação Alexandre de Gusmão, Ministério das Relações Exteriores. pp. 399–446.

Marcus, Alan. 2009. "(Re)creating Places and Spaces in Two Countries: Brazilian Transnational Migration Processes." *Journal of Cultural Geography.* 26(2): 173–198.

Margolis, Maxine. 2013. *Goodbye, Brazil: Émigrés from the Land of Soccer and Samba.* Madison: The University of Wisconsin Press.

Milani, Carlos R.S. 2012. "Atores e Agendas no Campo da Política Externa Brasileira de Direitos Humanos." In *Política Externa Brasileira. As Práticas da Política e a Política das Práticas,* org. by Leticia Pinheiro and Carlos R.S. Milani. Rio de Janeiro: FGV Editora. pp. 33–70.

Milesi, Rosita and Orlando Fantazini. 2009. "Cidadãs e Cidadãos Brasileiros no Exterior—O Documento de Lisboa, a Carta de Boston e Documentos de Bruxelas." In *I Conferência sobre as Comunidades Brasileiras no Exterior. Brasileiros no Mundo.* Rio de Janeiro, 17–18 July 2008. Brasilia: Fundação Alexandre de Gusmão, Ministério das Relações Exteriores. pp. 317–332.

OBMigra. 2014. *Ações do Conselho Nacional de Imigração (CNIg). Políticas Públicas para Migração 2014.* Brasilia: Observatório das Migrações Internacionais. Available at http://portal.mte.gov.br/obmigra/home.htm.

OIM. 2010, September. *Perfil Migratório do Brasil 2009.* Geneva: Organização Internacional para as Migrações.

OIM. 2014. "La Migración Haitiana Hacia Brasil: Características, Oportunidades y Desafíos." Cuadernos Migratorios no. 6. Buenos Aires: Oficina Regional para América del Sur, Organización Internacional para las Migraciones.

Padilla, Beatriz. 2011. "Engagement Policies and Practices: Expanding the Citizenship of the Brazilian Diaspora." *International Migration.* 49(3): 10–29.

Projeto OIM-DEEST-SNJ. 2013. *Colóquio sobre Direitos Humanos na Política Migratória Brasileira.* Brasilia: Organização Internacional para as Migrações.

de Ribas Guedes, Carlos Eduardo. 2009. "A Eleição de Representantes do Brasil no Exterior para o Congresso Nacional." In *I Conferência Sobre as Comunidades Brasileiras no Exterior. Brasileiros no Mundo.* Rio de Janeiro, 17–18 July 2008. Brasilia: Fundação Alexandre de Gusmão, Ministério das Relações Exteriores. pp. 105–146.

Secretaria Nacional de Justiça. 2014, May. *Texto Base, COMIGRAR, 1ª Conferência Nacional sobre Migrações e Refúgio.* São Paulo: Ministério da Justiça.

SGEB. 2012. *Diplomacia Consular 2007–2012.* Brasilia: Fundação Alexandre de Gusmão, Ministério das Relações Exteriores.

Skidmore, Thomas E. 1990. "Racial Ideas and Social Policy in Brazil, 1870–1940." In *The Idea of Race in Latin America, 1870–1940,* ed. by Richard Graham. Austin: University of Texas Press. pp. 7–37.

8   Ecuadorians and Argentines in Spain and Italy

The Political Activation of Emigrants

Introduction

As it was explained in the preceding chapters, a significant emigration wave from South America took place in the late 1990s and early 2000s (especially from Ecuador, Bolivia, Peru, Argentina, and Colombia), and it was largely encouraged by dramatic economic and politico-institutional crises. An increasing number of Ecuadorians and Argentines emigrants preferred Europe over the US this time, in particular, Madrid, Barcelona, Milan, and Genoa. Chapters 4 and 6 explain in detail how sending countries have been recently courting these emigrant groups. The purpose of this chapter is to assess the results of those outreach attempts from the point of view of the addressees and in reference to migrant political engagement. Interestingly enough, assessing those results has not been on the agendas of the nation-states involved. Thus, I explore the following question: to what extent, and how, does sending-state courting encourage migrant organizational efforts and political transnational activities?

The question situates the study of state-led transnational initiatives in a dialogue with the work of international relation scholars concerned with the articulation between global and local practices. In particular, I engage with their work by addressing a gap in the migrant transnationalism literature: long distances (Lyons and Mandaville 2010, among others). I do so by looking at the implementation of emigration policies at the local level and how sending states, in collaboration with other public and private actors, may activate their diasporas politically. In other words, I explore migrant organizational dynamics in the light of sending states' attempts to reach out to emigrants and mobilize them with political purposes—a factor neglected by comparative studies on the determinants of individual and collective migrant transnational engagement across localities in Southern Europe (e.g., Morales and Pilati 2013; Bauböck and Faist 2010:267–294).

I focus on cases where sending and destination countries are not in geographic proximity to tease the question of political transnationalism across long distances and, in contrast to studies on migrant associational life that emphasize the impact of institutions and policies in the host society (e.g., citizenship regimes, immigrant integration policies)[1] or the relative amount of (ethnic) social capital of different immigrant groups,[2] I explore whether, how, and with what results sending states might expand or constrain the range of opportunities for migrants' organization and transnational political engagement.

Rather than generalizations, this chapter offers a situational and synchronic answer to this question based on the cases of Ecuadorians and Argentines in their top destinations in Southern Europe, Madrid and Milan, where migrant associational activities have taken different forms across communities and destination sites. Although migrant political engagement may take various forms and be channeled through diverse means, associations are usually the loci of migrant activities and the main interlocutors of governments. They are directly involved in policymaking, thus making them key actors in shaping the diasporas' political roles. In the case of Ecuadorians[3] and Argentines[4] in Southern Europe, migrant associations expanded in the last decade and embody today a form of representation (probably the most visible one) of the newcomers in host societies and, to a lesser extent, back home, too. Given long distances, fragmentation, and inexperience, associations' transnational and political engagement cannot be taken for granted.

The analysis contributes to our understanding of emigration policies as a form of transnational governance inasmuch as it brings new evidence about the actors and processes that shape migrant political transnationalism. In particular, this chapter sheds light on (a) a relatively unexplored case in the literature of emigration policies, Argentina, for which literature on associational life is nonexistent in English; (b) the concrete results and limits of such initiatives across destination sites and in a long-distance transnational context; (c) specific (often unintended) migrant responses to state policies; and (d) the characteristics of emerging public–private transnational policy networks that mold migrant political engagements.

The findings lead me to argue that Ecuadorian and Argentine state policies have been relatively effective in tapping into migrants' symbolic and emotional attachments to homeland (which might help activate them politically), but they have obtained meagre results in terms of grounding that attachment in strong organizations, persistent transnational engagement, and partnership links. Both sending states reached out to emigrants using a similar combination of policy instruments: rhetorical changes, institutional developments, enfranchisement, and linkage programs. The scope, intensity, and results of outreach efforts differ not only across countries but also across localities, suggesting the need to explore factors that may facilitate or hinder state initiatives, namely migrants' profiles and perceptions of state institutions, spatial distance, and the types of private–public policy networks at destinations.

The following two sections provide some background information about general associational trends in both cases. They are followed by a section that focuses on the specific results of sending states' outreach efforts presented along the lines of the four policy instruments mentioned previously, including comparative references to the other cases in this book when appropriate. The conclusions summarize the findings, elaborate on the comparisons, and suggest some venues for future research.

Are Ecuadorians More Gregarious Than Others?

Social activism in Ecuador paved the way for state initiatives. Local informants often resort to a gregarious, participative cultural disposition or ethnic features to explain it: "Everybody is always eager to participate in Ecuador; we all have something to say about public affairs. There is perhaps too much dialogue," argued a seasoned diplomat.[5] Similar statements appeared in my interviews with migrant leaders abroad, together with references to long-standing, unbreakable attachments to homeland ("We brought a participatory culture; most of us had experience leading associations at home."[6] "Our culture is rich and encourages communication. We, Ecuadorians, get organized to communicate among ourselves and with those at home. We cannot be apart from family"[7]). Ties to home, family, and ethnic roots justify maintaining dual engagements. As documented by Kyle (2000), these features, as well as transnational practices, have characterized older and recent emigration waves in Ecuador.

The Correa administration tapped into such activism. All sorts of nongovernmental associations, religious and human rights groups, advocacy organizations, and policy-oriented scholars demanded a centralized, state policy in the early 2000s. These institutions grew as the devastating consequences of emigration became evident, largely to address the multiple needs of families dismembered because of migration (see details in Chapter 4). The government adopted some of their ideas—in particular, the emphasis on human rights—and even recruited some of their best cadres. Ironically, by taking over their flags and initiative capacity, the state increased fragmentation and representativeness problems. Civil society organizations perceive that their participation decreased as state activism increased: "We use to be called to dialogue tables, asked for suggestions; now they call us sometimes but do not take our ideas seriously . . . . Everybody claims to represent migrants. You wonder who really does."[8]

At destination, two main migrant associations stand out in Spain: Rumiñahui Association created in 1997 and based in Madrid, and Llactacaru Association, founded in 2001 in Barcelona. Both have offices in Ecuador and Spain, and they are the largest and most active associations. It is worth noting their transnational reach and political involvement. Llactacaru was founded in the midst of the denouncement of exploitation and marginality suffered by many migrants, fueled by the death of 12 Ecuadorian illegal migrants in a work-related accident. Since its creation, increasing visibility and political leverage were two of the main goals, and another was providing services to migrants and their families back home. Llactacaru often engages with public offices (at the local and national levels), nongovernmental organizations, and international forums, though such activism is led by a few members and mainly through informal channels, and the agendas of sister institutions are independent of each other (Ndjoli Fernández 2006). Rumiñahui in Madrid, with delegations in other Spanish cities, works closely with Ecuadorian public officials and is part of regional federations; with a staff of 12 people, it is involved in a large number of social and political projects, including mobilizing migrants to vote in elections. Some of its members aim at running as candidates, too.[9]

There is also a large number of diverse associations in Spain[10] whose activities revolve around national identity ties and culture, ethnic heritage, recreation and sports, and social activities. Ecuadorians have also been very active in forming federations and centralizing their claim-making efforts to advance their interests in a coordinated fashion. FENADEE, for instance, gathers 52 associations within Spain and claims to represent around 50,000 Ecuadorian immigrants. They consider their activism to be mainly political, related to migrants' exercise of social and political rights, and independent of party affiliation.[11]

In contrast, Italy is perceived as a less friendly context for associational life than Spain for a number of reasons: restrictive national policies, less cultural affinity, different language, lack of open physical spaces for social gatherings in cities like Milan, complicated bureaucratic processes that look incomprehensible to migrants, difficulties for integration, and lack of support for organizational efforts.[12] Ecuadorians in Milan tend to feel discriminated and find it difficult to integrate,[13] though they perceive some responsiveness from the local government lately (e.g., encouragement to participate in migrant training programs).

The main reason for Ecuadorians to select this destination is the existence of a labor market niche, especially for female migrants (namely care service for the elderly and children). These jobs, which keep migrants mainly confined to the household, provide refuge and facilitate the transition for those in irregular status. In addition, there is a long historical record of two-way migration flows between the coastal region of Ecuador and the coast of Liguria and established migrant networks with most cultural and social associations established in Genoa, Milan, and Turin (Avilés Salgado 2005). There are fewer and more dispersed migrant associations than in Spain, though: between 60 and 75 in the whole country; estimates are not exact because creation, re-foundation, and disappearance are frequent. Membership is low and institutional activism is intermittent.[14] Lack of leadership seems to be a recurrent problem.

Associations with social or recreational goals (e.g., sportive leagues) tend to be more engaging and sustainable in the long term. Politicians' outreach efforts are seen as opportunistic, and migrants resort to consulates and, until recently, to SENAMI (National Secretariat of the Migrant) offices in search of help with return plans, job searches, or medical and psychological problems.[15]

Invisible Argentines in the Land of Ancestors

Regarding Argentines, secondary sources and key informants are scarce. References to ethnicity in migrant narratives relate to the host countries rather than the homeland, to European rather than indigenous ancestry. The intention to break ties with the homeland (including home politics) and to blend with the receiving society seem to delineate an individualistic "strategy of invisibility."[16] Emigration historically received low attention in governmental agendas until outflows peaked in the early 2000s. Lack of political attention may be partially explained by the fact that the implications of emigration are less visible in Argentina than in Ecuador, given the small size of the emigrant group and the amount of remittances. However, the profile of recent emigrants makes them an attractive constituency for neopopulist incumbents who have unsuccessfully courted middle-class sectors and identify themselves with the 1970s generation of political exiles and human rights advocates.[17] A good number of emigrants hold dual citizenship, thus making it difficult to trace them because they may not appear as immigrants in the statistics of the host country.[18]

Argentines in Spain formed associations called *casas* (houses) with various institutional forms, including a few that work only online. Their activities are mainly social and cultural, not explicitly political, though they provide immigrants with legal information and help in the process of settling down (e.g., legal advising, a place to share experiences and find some emotional support, job and real estate orientation). The antecedents of several of these institutions are to be found in the previous wave of political exiles and their activism in the defense of human rights issues. The Casa Argentina in Madrid is probably the association with the highest level of internal organizational development because of its size (membership has oscillated between 700 and 900 migrants), numerous activities, and relatively long history. It is also the one that is most often in contact (formally and informally) with the embassy and consulate to organize cultural events and other collaborations. It was refounded in 2002, largely as a response to the new situation created by unprecedented Argentine immigration in Spain, but members' activism remains low (only around 50 pay dues regularly; at most, around 100 attend most events). Other associations were created around the same time by private initiatives, but they have more sporadic and more formal contacts with public officials. Membership in some of them is driven by professions (e.g., psychologists, dentists), making them "mini associations." Former members of the Madrid Casa split in late 2007 to form the *Observatorio Hispano-Argentino,* which gathers around 50 members and focuses on cultural diffusion.[19]

The Madrid Casa was active and successful in demanding some help from the home government when immigrant regularization took place in 2005. Lately, it has focused on cultural and artistic events, and its transnational involvement has been limited to supporting specific development projects in Argentina (e.g., building a school, a school cafeteria). "Politics is out of the conversations in the meetings, largely because the last wave of emigrants went through too many disappointments, first in Argentina and more recently in Spain," argues its former president.[20] The Casa participates in a regional federation, but regional involvement is still very much a work in progress. "The main obstacle to coordinate national and regional strategies is to find common interests among communities in various countries"; each immigrant group tends to mobilize around particular claims, though a federation was created in 2008 (FEDEAR), gathering around 40 associations within Europe. Its leader recognizes the advantage of cooperation since supranational regional institutions are more responsive than national governments, and they have more resources.[21]

Groups outside the capital cities, where there are no consulates, find it more difficult to have access to consular protection and services; they argue that distance represents a cost and has been a serious obstacle in their participation in elections. For most of the associations created in the 2000s, relations with state institutions are sporadic and dependent on formal invitations. In all of them, members' participation is very low, and the associations' functions revolve around providing legal information and other support (psychological advice, placement and real state orientation, etc.) to help Argentine immigrants settle down and integrate into Spanish society. They were active during the regularization process, and they are prone to mobilizing whenever a governmental delegation visits Spain. They have links with other NGOs in Argentina, too, in order to participate in humanitarian and solidarity campaigns. In that sense, it may be argued that they have developed transnational activities and they work as supporting networks that facilitate the migration process. Social and cultural activities serve to preserve links with the home country and provide an environment to share experiences and find some emotional support.[22]

There is very little information about Argentines in Italy, let alone rigorous and systematic academic studies of their organizational and political lives. In the Milan area, and Lombardy in general, the Argentine consulate is in touch with very few migrant associations (mostly devoted to cultural and recreational events), and no attempt has been made to create a formal channel of communication with them. Argentines mostly resort to this office for consular services such as driving license validation, renewal of passports, and nationality documents for their children born in Italy.[23] Migrants tend to rely on family or professional networks and, like those in Spain, to integrate quickly through the labor market (Goldberg 2006:126). The reception context in Lombardy seems to be less friendly, though: migrant narratives attest to hardships, bureaucratic nightmares, and integration problems.[24] In fact, local experts would argue that Milan has been somewhat hostile to all immigrants due to a long tenure of right-wing governments that ended in 2011 (in contrast to Genoa, where left-wing administrations have been more accommodating to immigrants from various countries).[25] Hence, migration dynamics are mostly shaped by labor markets and today tend to favor low-skilled immigrants who can perform domestic services. Argentine immigrants holding dual citizenship are less visible and less subject to negative stereotyping, and they have good chances of finding jobs or moving to other countries within the Schengen area.[26]

Assessing the Results of Sending States' Outreach Efforts

The evidence provided in Chapters 4 and 6 shows that Ecuador and Argentina have used similar policy instruments to court their citizens living abroad. From the broad spectrum of measures already discussed in the preceding chapters, I resume here the consideration of only four mechanisms by which sending states can potentially intervene to politically activate diasporas: (1) the use of a friendly rhetoric to (re)name the diaspora, (2) the creation or upgrading of institutions to address migrant issues, (3) political enfranchisement, and (4) the implementation of programs to establish or reinforce links with expatriates.

Rhetoric

Latin American sending states broke off with past silence and neglect and assigned new labels to emigrants. Rhetoric was a significant component of courting. In Ecuador, some terms or phrases were coined to symbolize the main thrust of the new policy. Rhetoric was also instrumentally used to build up the identity of the party/coalition in government vis-à-vis past administrations or competing political forces that not only neglected migrants but were also responsible for the dramatic crises that triggered emigration. Correa labelled emigration as a "national tragedy" in his 2007 inaugural speech, and he promised that his term would be the "migrants' government." His migration discourse emphasized the inclusion of those who are physically absent, reaffirming the idea that *patria* (fatherland) is "made by all of us" and that migration is an option, not an escape valve. Some slogans have been used by the president, SENAMI, and other migration-related institutions toward citizens abroad and potential returnees: "we are rebuilding the house so that you can return," "we are all migrants," and "welcome home."

Capitalizing on social discontent, both Kirchner and Correa enticed emigrants to participate in the reconstruction of the nation, promising "reparatory" measures and appealing to traumatic social memories and patriotism. However, Argentine governments did not coin a label. They only created a program (Program 25) to symbolically embrace the extra-territorial jurisdiction. Political discourses emphasized path-breaking pluralist, inclusive, and human rights policy considerations. Yet, since the very beginning, officials implicitly acknowledged deficits in terms of supporting associational life: the Director of Consular Affairs (within the Ministry of Foreign Affairs) argued that the government prefers the phrase "Argentines abroad" over "diaspora" because the latter carries connotations regarding migrants' organization, institutionalized links, and other qualifications that the Argentine case does not meet (Buira 2006:299).

Overall, as a governance technique, the intended impact of rhetorical changes is to foster a new view of emigration, one that moves away from the loss of human and other resources toward an image of a borderless nation and of individual migrants as contributors to, and stakeholders in, the process of national development. The shift redefines the contours of the nation and the identities of emigrants, giving a positive connotation to their journeys and strengthening ties with the homeland, and makes them subjects of policies and a specific constituency with rights and obligations. This friendly rhetoric seems to be necessary to recognize migrants as legitimate interlocutors but not sufficient to engage them politically. The emphasis on migrants' contributions is consistent with a neoliberal approach to development that places the burden and responsibility on individuals' shoulders. But South American neopopulist governments have framed their initiatives in a postneoliberal discourse that emphasizes the state's renewed role and links among social policies, equity, and development. Such ambiguity certainly impinges on emigrants' responses, which take note of the contradiction between rhetoric and resource allocation (or between promises and commitment).

For instance, Argentines in Madrid resent the government's request for collaboration because, in fact, the government calls them when needed but it neither deploys any resources nor has a clear, comprehensive plan to develop and institutionalize links with expats.[27] This reflects the view of the few migrants who actively participate in associations. There is no record of whether state outreach efforts actually reach out to ordinary migrants or those who are not involved in associational life. A similar pattern is observed in Milan, where the local Italian government collaborates with the Argentine embassy to support cultural events, but migrants do not receive specific, direct support from Argentine authorities; linkages were not pursued and some initiatives, such as the programs explained later, have never been implemented in that destination.[28]

Ecuador has apparently been more effective in terms of appealing to emotional attachments and making emigrants feel like part of a political project that cares for them. For a few years, SENAMI offices abroad conveyed a message of inclusion and the promise of delivering benefits through its programs, thus boosting expectations. An Ecuadorian migrant residing in Milan (not member of any association but a regular visitor of SENAMI offices) summarized generalized comments: "Correa's administration gave migrants their faith back."[29] For him, in particular, state responsiveness encourages expectations of being able to complete the (always planned and recurrently postponed) trip back home. This clearly contrasts with the testimonies of Argentines who do not have high expectations of changes at home. A 24-year-old immigrant living in Spain, for instance, talks of his emigration journey as an escape from a sinking ship. Despite the hardships, he argues: "Here in Spain, one can be fine notwithstanding the crisis. That is, earnings are low but we know where the horizon is and when things will start to improve. In Argentina, you never see the horizon."[30]

From a comparative perspective, more research is needed to assess the concrete impact of particular labels. For instance, as it was explained in Chapter 5, Uruguay's choice of *Patria Peregrina* (peregrine nation) was not effective; it did not resonate with migrants' experiences, and the government has lately encouraged the use of the expression *Soy Uruguay* (I am Uruguay) to convey the idea that emigrants do not just "belong" to a country but "embody" the nation and, thus, they have responsibility for its fate. Brazil still refers to emigrants as "Brazilians in the World," equating their experience to the country's global projection, and Mexico often refers to the *México de afuera* (Mexico of the outside), leaving engagement and membership subject to real and figurative borders.

Institutions

Governments of sending countries have created or upgraded institutions to function as formal channels for communication, assistance, and migrant claiming-making. Argentina followed a traditional approach: in the early 2000s, the Secretariat of Foreign Relations (Ministry of Foreign Affairs) included protection of Argentines abroad among its strategic goals, a special unit was created to support political exiles' integration, and the Argentines Abroad Office was enlarged and upgraded to Directorate. Nonetheless, in a few years, emigration was partially resituated in another bureaucratic body, showing that governmental attention refocused toward immigration. The most significant bureaucratic expansion in the late 2000s occurred at the National Directorate of Migration (Ministry of Interior) which is now involved in all national and regional dimensions of migration; its functions came to encompass emigration policy proposals and linkage programs.

In contrast, Ecuador is the only case in Latin America in which a secretariat (SENAMI) with ministerial status was created (in 2007), reported directly to the president and, until recently, superseded previous similar offices in the Ministry of Foreign Affairs. For some years, this secretariat played an active role in the diffusion of the new policy, assisting migrants and their families, fomenting ties with homeland, and encouraging voluntary return. Since its creation, SENAMI constantly expanded its personnel and facilities, opened offices in major destinations, and launched a considerable number of programs and itinerary activities. As I noted in Chapter 4, a new bureaucratic reshuffling of uncertain consequences has occurred recently. Also, other institutional developments are in the making. The incipient involvement of Ecuadorian local (city) governments in providing services to migrants, implementing concrete legislation and programs, and participating in co-development projects promises to expand the scope of state action and probably its effectiveness.[31] Decentralization has been a creative state response to the needs and claims of dismembered transnational families. It indirectly encouraged transnational practices and linkage mechanisms at origin and destination. This was the initial idea behind the creation of the SENAMI: while consular offices would still be in charge of foreign policy and international relations, "we needed an office to address the issues of the transnational families and work simultaneously at home and abroad as a nexus."[32] Now that SENAMI's activities are being absorbed by consulate offices, it remains to be seen if such a nexus persists or remains simply dependent on private (migrant) initiatives.

These issues, which have potential repercussions in terms of political mobilization of both migrants and their families back home, have never appeared in the discussion of emigration policy in Argentina. According to public officials' testimonies, the current approach of focusing on online information and request processing seems to keep at least a channel of communication alive, although it is contingent on individual efforts and concrete demands (see details in Chapter 6). There is no evidence that this might lead to comprehensive and regular engagement with the emigrant community.

Moreover, as we learn from the Mexican case, institutional developments may also allow for the implementation of programs that facilitate migrant integration in the host society while encouraging engagement with the country of origin. The South American experience is patchy, though. Ecuador has partially tackled that task through SENAMI offices abroad (see later under linkages). Argentina has not attempted to do so. Brazil has strengthened consular offices to provide more assistance (SGEB 2012), though the driving force is not migrant integration. There is an incipient move in Uruguay to follow the Mexican lead in the case of its emigrants in the US.

For the two cases analyzed here, new or upgraded offices have mainly extended the arm of the state to communicate with, gather information about, and potentially regulate the activities of migrants, including organizational efforts. In Ecuador, public officials consider the use of direct mail exchanges (postal and/or online) "a helpful tool to articulate Ecuadorian emigrants in the hope that they become an *Ecuadorian public opinion* that may act in themes of common interest in a coordinated fashion" and "an additional tool to inform and persuade the emigrant and to generate actions in their benefit, while at the same time produce influential actions in the domestic and foreign policymaking in Ecuador and even in the domestic and foreign policymaking of the countries of residency" (Fornell 2005:223–224).

In other words, dual engagements are part of the policy goals. The overall effects of these institutional developments are mixed, though. Despite generating increasing communication and an incipient, largely informal state–diaspora relationship, these institutions underwent internal changes that undermine the sustainability of policy results. In addition, these efforts were not able to overcome migrant distrust and discontent with state institutions.

While Ecuadorian migrants value the access to orientation and assistance, they look at governmental initiatives with skepticism. "Migrants tend to confide on priests and look for help in parishes rather than in associations or consulates. Politicians, and even the associations, are discredited."[33] Argentine emigrants tend to be even more reluctant to resorting to state institutions. Opinion surveys indicate that they see migrant associations, Internet fora, and even public institutions of the host country as more helpful than Argentine government institutions (Novick and Murias 2005:47–78). Other studies suggest that this attitude is related to emigrants' profile: being in a relatively better-off position, Argentines do not resort to nongovernmental organizations or churches for social welfare services as Ecuadorians and other collectivities do upon arrival; at most, they may approach institutions later, only if they need advising on specific matters (González Martínez 2009:214). They tend to rely on family, professional networks, and ties with locals rather than co-nationals or public offices. These networks seem to be particularly critical in giving them access to the labor market, though ties remain relatively distant and informal compared with those of other immigrant groups in Spain (Aparicio and Tornos 2004). Testimonies are almost unanimous: "Adaptation was immediate." Cultural affinity with the host societies helps considerably, facilitating relations with natives: "The first year I was in touch only with Argentines, but that change[d] over time to the point that I do not have Argentine friends here [in Spain] now."[34] Therefore, regardless of political intentions and policy shifts, the Argentine state seems to have relatively less room than other countries of origin to be effective in reaching out to its emigrants through associations or public offices.

Political Rights

Sending states have also used political enfranchising as a mobilization tool. The 1998 reform of the Constitution in Ecuador awarded migrants political representation in Congress and made extraterritorial votes possible in national elections; this was in effect in 2006 for the first time. Likewise, Law 24,007 of 1991 allows Argentine citizens residing abroad to vote in national elections at consular offices, provided that they are previously registered in the so-called registry of voters residing abroad. The initiative was launched in mid-1980s during the democratic transition as a symbolic move toward political exiles that left during the dictatorship and supported democratization from afar. It became effective for the first time in the mid-term legislative elections of 1993. Political representation in Congress has been discussed but not implemented yet. In addition, in both countries, dual/multiple citizenship is legal. In Ecuador, this right was incorporated in the 1998 constitutional reform. The Argentine Constitution does not permit it, but it allows citizenship retention, and the practice is also regulated through several bilateral agreements. Rights are suspended for the time the individual resides in the adopted country and can be regained if the person moves back home (Escobar 2007).

Enfranchisement is certainly a promising area to trigger migrant mobilization if pursued in combination with other outreach mechanisms. It evokes nationalist sentiments, cherished notions of belonging, and a sense of obligation toward homeland. Capturing migrant votes may be elusive, but not impossible. For instance, the first time Ecuadorians abroad voted (in 2006), results were somewhat disappointing for the governing coalition: turnout was low and Correa lost both rounds abroad. Sixty-one percent of those registered did not vote in the first round of the 2006 presidential elections, and 23% of those who did counted as null votes (a higher percentage than the one obtained by any candidate); these numbers changed to 42% and 12%, respectively, in the second round (SJRM/ILDIS-FES 2007:19–25). Problems were attributed to generalized lack of information, as well as a tendency to vote for relatively known candidates rather than their programs. Since then, SENAMI was very active in encouraging electoral participation. The result was at first modest, mostly reflected in a slight increase in the number of people registered and actually casting votes (Koller 2010:67–69), and hardly attributable to the state mobilization strategy alone. For the 2013 election, though, Correa obtained an overwhelming triumph among citizens abroad: 82.25% of the total votes in Europe, Asia, and Oceania; 65.98% in North America; and 70.94% in Latin America and Africa.[35]

However, whether this is an indication of the incipient formation of a captive constituency is an open question. Some studies cast doubt on the political content of voting. Disenchantment with home politics persists among Ecuadorian emigrants, leading some analysts to argue: "Despite the unprecedented efforts of their homeland government to build a vigorous external constituency, expatriates' reactions seem diverse, emotionally mixed and irreducible to (hence, of limited relevance for) the realm of party politics" (Boccagni and Ramírez 2013:746). And the practice of voting among Ecuadorians abroad (including those in Southern Europe) seems to be an opportunity to reproduce a vague notion of attachment to the nation and to fulfil a sense of civic duty based on an ambivalent sentiment of nostalgia and patriotism, rather than as a strict act of political support (Boccagni 2011).

Unfortunately, there are no studies to extend the comparison to the Argentine case. Regarding turnout, it seems that when outreach is scarce and policies are less institutionalized, results are meagre: external voter registration and voting among Argentines have always been low, political parties make no outreach efforts, and the logistics of long distances are deemed obstacles (Novick 2007: 362; Tullio 2010:87). Improvement mechanisms were under discussion. In 2007, groups of Argentine emigrants mobilized to encourage political participation and demand more governmental attention, with very limited success. At present, public officials at the Ministry of Foreign Affairs consider that emigrant demand (i.e., willingness to register and vote) is not high enough as to justify the addition of more polling stations.[36] In this particular case, the problem is compounded by the fact that political parties have not cultivated long-term links with the diaspora like the PT in Brazil, the Frente Amplio in Uruguay, or the Institutional Revolutionary Party (PRI) in Mexico, and they have not engaged in international campaigns. Current governmental officials welcome the lack of politicization, claiming that migration has been naturalized (i.e., it ceased to be considered a problem).[37]

Nonetheless, in all cases in this book, gathering expats' political support proves to be a challenge. Even in Mexico, where long distance is not an obstacle and electoral campaigns across the border are a usual practice, migrant transnational engagements cannot be taken for granted (see details in Chapter 9). Moreover, for all cases, it remains to be explored whether electoral turnout among expats is also linked to the generalized sense of uneasiness about home politics. This challenge is particularly acute in the case of Argentina. Some testimonies speak of lack of hope and a pervasive sadness about the country's future, to some extent accentuated by long distances: "The news I read or hear—in the radio; that [listening to the radio], I have not managed to change—made me feel very sad. But it is not anger any longer, it is uneasiness. Sometimes I think that Borges's saying on the Peronists—'they are neither good nor bad, just inveterate'—might be extended to all Argentines including, to begin with, myself. But no doubt everything looks more difficult from afar."[38]

As for dual citizenship, the evidence is not conclusive. We learn from the case of Mexico that the legislation update in 1996 to allow citizenship retention increased the naturalization rate of Mexicans in the US and, indirectly, encouraged their integration in the host society (Escobar 2007). However, for South American emigrant communities, there is no evidence of whether the dual citizenship status impinges on migrant transnational engagements. The formal dimension of it has certainly had some unintended effects: holding dual citizenship has facilitated legal South–North migration in times of dramatic economic and political crisis, indirectly shaping the volume and direction of flows in the Latin America–Southern Europe corridor. It might also facilitate circular or regular cross-regional migration (i.e., movements back and forth between origin and destination), but there is no reliable measurement of this outcome. Because economic conditions have deteriorated in Southern Europe lately, South American immigrants have used European citizenship instrumentally and moved within the Schengen area (and more recently to other countries, too) in search of better labor conditions or more friendly integration environments. Their being registered as nationals of European countries makes it more difficult for sending countries to trace them and maintain regular links, especially in the cases of those who aspire to be treated by Europeans as co-nationals, such as Argentines.

Linkage Programs

Sending states directly targeted migrant transnational involvement through linkage policies, including programs to support migrant organizational efforts. With different intensities, all cases in this book have developed specific programs to link with highly skilled emigrants. The two countries that are the focus of this chapter have also used new technologies to increase the visibility of new institutions, expand links with emigrants, and compile information about them (e.g., websites with links to their services and programs, news and discussion forums, a registry where migrants can enter their personal data, online interactive consultation systems).

Efforts in this area have been particularly intense in the case of Ecuador through SENAMI's communication campaigns, website, and itinerant delegations. In collaboration with embassies, the secretariat sponsored cultural events and the celebration of national festivities abroad. It has also been very active in supporting migrants' organizational efforts and providing leadership training. The Organizational Strengthening and Construction of Social Networks Program (FORES, in its Spanish acronym) used to gather migrants in workshops and training sessions to enhance their skills in accounting, planning, and management of projects. SENAMI in Madrid implemented this program with three associations in particular: Rumiñahui, Fenadee, and Aplore, helping the associations develop projects and new leadership; the assumption was that strengthening a few would reduce fragmentation.[39] In 2010, SENAMI in Milan was involved in teaching migrant associations how to prepare and submit applications to the local Italian government for social projects, thus working as a bridge between migrants and Italian authorities and helping them navigate the local bureaucracies.[40] Targeting special groups is also part of the strategy. For example, SENAMI in Milan hosted the First Meeting of Ecuadorian Human Talent Residing Abroad in 2010 to build a network of entrepreneurs, professionals, artists, and students living in Italy and to encourage synergies and collaboration around diverse projects.

Argentina implemented a mechanism to carry out an online census in 2004, which was presented as a direct line of communication between emigrants and the home state; the intention was not only to register migrants but also to gather information about their socioeconomic and educational profiles. Consular offices offer citizens residing abroad the possibility of registering with them in order to receive information and facilitate the access to consular services. Argentina also created the *Raíces* Program to link researchers and scientists abroad, promoting their return or their collaboration in the development of scientific and technological advances through the formation of networks and research projects. In comparison to other initiatives, this program proved more resilient and successful.[41] The Province 25 Program was launched in 2004 at the Ministry of Interior to reconstruct links with expatriates with a focus on the political dimension of linkages, assuming that Argentines abroad would represent the fourth largest province in terms of population. It still has the main goals of guaranteeing the exercise of political rights, increasing political participation in elections, and fostering a project to award migrants political representation in Congress,[42] but it has mainly become a source of information and assistance to migrants (see details in Chapter 6).

The Argentine government has organized three annual meetings with emigrants between 2008 and 2010 to discuss their needs, claims, and suggestions. Contacts between program officers and migrants in Spain are frequent and fluid, though they have not acquired a formal character yet. They have waxed and waned and seem to have lost momentum lately. Initially, lack of experience and politics on both sides of the relationship set some limits to collaboration. At present, there is no attempt to go beyond consular assistance and develop a broad, consistent approach across sites, let alone to invest in strengthening organizational capacities. As documented in Chapter 6, today government officials consider that migrant associational and mobilization capacities have declined, depriving migrants of a unifying voice and agenda; the approach then is to wait and see if organizational efforts acquire a more clearly defined and mature form on their own.

In the two cases considered here, the potential of linkage policies lies in the type and sustainability of the links created. This indicates the need to explore the modality of implementation and the complex network of public and private actors involved in it. The first element that comes up on migrant narratives is that political manipulation of programs and exchange of favors are not uncommon. Linkage efforts tend to reach only few individuals or groups: those who are more frequently in touch with local consular authorities, or association leaders, distinguished figures, or those who are more valuable to incumbents' political projects. This is, indeed, a common feature for all cases, and it often creates tensions (e.g., in both Uruguay and Brazil, questions of representativeness have been an obstacle to building up effective consultation mechanisms and partnerships).

Informants confirmed off the record that there is a give-and-take game between running candidates and parties and migrant associations during electoral campaigns. Attempts to co-op migrant leadership, picking and choosing interlocutors, and clientelism are common practices that travel from the domestic to the transnational realm, undermining the genuine goals and representativeness of migrant organizations. For instance, one of the founders and a key leader of an Ecuadorian association argues that political elites' paternalistic approaches have been major obstacles to the recognition of migrants as subjects, that is, as relevant and autonomous actors who do not depend either on political parties or nongovernmental organizations and "who should not be merely seen as purveyors of resources." He acknowledged, though, that the new policy encouraged the growth of migrant organizations and revived migrants' hopes. Leaders of both Rumiñahui and Llactacaru agreed on the lack of coordination among associations and constant (internal and interassociation) struggles to acquire or maintain representativeness. They resent the top-down character of policymaking, an assistance-oriented approach, lack of responsiveness to migrant proposals, politicization, extensive clientelism, waste of resources, and lack of inclusion of migrant associations in decision making.[43]

In addition, sending-state policies are, to some extent, contingent on the cooperation of state and nonstate actors in the receiving context. In Spain, Ecuadorian associational life was encouraged by both SENAMI's actions and the financial support offered by local authorities, but to opposite ends. The Spanish government also created the State Forum for Migrations (Ministry of Labor) to serve as a consultation arena formed by migrant organizations, nongovernmental organizations, representatives of other ministries, and municipalities. Given the high fragmentation of the association's camp, the forum serves as an implicit mechanism to choose legitimate interlocutors.[44] The norms set by Spanish local authorities are lax in terms of membership and organizational structure, thus facilitating the creation of small associations with a handful of members. This contributes to fragmentation and representativeness problems—just the opposite of what SENAMI sought to accomplish through linkage programs.[45]

Another example is co-development projects, which are usually encouraged by receiving countries to control (and eventually reduce) immigration under the assumption that development would decrease incentives to move. As Cortés Maisonave (2011) ably explains, the Spanish government has involved various stakeholders in concrete projects, including the sending state (Ecuador), local governments at both ends, nongovernmental organizations, and migrant organizations (e.g., Rumiñahui Association). Co-development has been a means for migrant associations to gain visibility, resources, and legitimacy, though in an asymmetrical relation of power vis-à-vis the other actors and adopting the normative discourse proposed by the North (e.g., the standards regulating who has the right to move where and how, good/bad use of remittances). At the same time, this policy tool allows both states to portray their cooperation as a success and to emphasize the participatory, inclusive character of these endeavors. While institutional strengthening of migrant associations may happen, the overall results are debatable. Nobody discusses who is really being empowered by this emerging form of transnational governance.

In contrast, associational life in Italy is less intense for both groups, and sending-state cooperation with host governments is less frequent than in Spain. Different diagnoses and approaches collide. Local governments in Milan gave priority to individual integration through housing support, language courses, or job training (consistent with the definition of immigration as a problem and concerns with criminality), and they relied on an informal network of religious institutions, unions, and other nongovernmental organizations for broader social support. A few local initiatives to incorporate migrant representation in advisory councils have been inconsistent. The emphasis of nonstate actors in helping the poor and vulnerable has given place to clientelistic and dependent ties, including patronizing relations between Italian activists and immigrants (Camozzi 2011:481–482). Neither has encouraged migrant associations' empowerment and autonomy.

In the resulting public–private network, CARITAS plays a key role. It gathers most requests from migrants seeking general orientation, legal advice, job opportunities, shelter, and so on. In Milan, CARITAS works closely, though informally, with churches, foundations, consulates, unions, local authorities, and others to address multiple claims daily, especially from migrants in situations of extreme vulnerability. While Argentines resort to CARITAS's services only for specific purposes and in lower numbers, Ecuadorians are more likely to need social welfare services (around 30% of immigrants of Latin origin who resort to CARITAS are Ecuadorian).[46]

Yet, nongovernmental organizations are more than purveyors of social services. They fill the gaps created by the lack of immigrant integration policies, weak migrant associations, and poor consular services. CARITAS also collaborates with private foundations (e.g., Fondazione

ISMU, Iniziative e Studi sulla Multietnicità) to monitor the evolution of migration trends, compile statistics annually, and publish some of the most updated sources of information. As an experienced broker in the allocation of resources and professional services and a locus of institutional informal collaboration, it competes with sending states in assisting migrants. Together with local parishes, it cultivates relations of trust with migrants, and officers enjoy more credibility than public officials.

Migrant ties to this network are closely related to relative vulnerability. Some studies indicate that Argentine immigrants are better equipped, in terms of cultural and social capital, to integrate faster (especially through the labor market) and they have a more assertive and proactive attitude built on the pride of having a European background and coming from a relatively rich country where social mobility used to be attainable. This helps explain their refusal to define their own condition as equal to other immigrants and their reluctance to seek assistance. On the contrary, Ecuadorians confront more discriminatory situations, have to accept precarious jobs, and have few contacts outside of their kin networks. Some of their attitudes reinforce their unequal position: they exhibit a submissive attitude toward inequality and social hierarchies and cultivate relations mainly with co-nationals that reinforce ethnic networks (Actis 2009; Garzón Guillén 2006). Therefore, Ecuadorians are relatively more likely than Argentines to create ethnic associations to claim basic rights and to be in touch with public or private institutions.

Regarding the transnational character of the linkages, it is still limited and suggests the need to incorporate geographic distance in the analysis. Migrant narratives confirm that long distance is still an impediment to simultaneous and/or intense transnational engagement: trips are not very frequent; technological devices help to stay in touch with relatives but, due to the urgencies of daily life, communications do not necessarily involve a regular update on events at home, let alone political discussions;[47] families and other relations tend to deteriorate; although family reunion is generally a goal, distance and estrangement often result in separation or divorce; and gatherings with co-nationals are sought as instances of recreation or cultivation of religious and cultural practices rather than political participation. For these reasons, the transnational practices of South Americans residing in Southern Europe have been deemed relatively weak in comparison to other cases (Queirolo Palmas and Ambrosini 2007). Studies on Ecuadorians in Italy, in particular, confirm that transnational involvement is low—more so when it comes to group endeavors like sending collective remittances—and their low engagement with the homeland (including their participation in national elections) is the result of ambivalent attitudes that are shaped not necessarily by political motivations but by a mix of patriotism, nostalgia, and negative attitudes about the institutions and/or politics that prompted their departure (Boccagni 2011, 2013).

Analysis and Conclusions

The evidence in this chapter demonstrates that sending-state courting is an attempt to mobilize citizens abroad and engage them politically. These policies redefine the emigration problem with regard to recasting migrants' identities and constituting them into distinctive constituencies with new rights and responsibilities. Outreach initiatives indirectly encourage the development of transnational spaces and practices and can potentially affect not only migrants' engagement with the home country but also their integration in the host society. In particular, in the aftermath of dramatic crises, Ecuador and Argentina aimed at involving migrants in reconstruction and national development projects while supporting associational efforts and opening some opportunities for the accumulation of social capital and the exercise of political rights. However, the results are mixed and vary across cases and destination sites. A number of factors within, above, and below states help explain these outcomes and have analytical implications.

First, although similar policy instruments were used, the scope, intensity, and level of institutionalization of emigration policies differ across countries. The Ecuadorian state has been more consistent than the Argentine one in linking discursive and institutional initiatives and sustaining them over time and across localities, including programs that contribute to building up associations' capacities. The Argentine state has attempted to reach out almost exclusively to emigrants in Spain and, intermittently, did not match rhetoric with resources and did not develop special programs to support migrant organizational efforts. As it was explained in Chapters 4 and 6, domestic politics and intrastate politics largely account for these differences: interbureaucratic struggles and culture, lack of policy coordination and design, and institutional weaknesses have undermined policy consistency. This indicates the need to dig deeper into domestic factors, including intrastate politics and the nature of some specific political projects, to understand the viability and potential impact of state-led transnational initiatives.

Second, such initiatives may also be constrained or facilitated by two factors related to the emigrant community that combine in a complex way: profiles and perceptions of state institutions. While Argentines' human and social capital may equip them relatively better to seize mobilization opportunities, they are less likely to engage in associational life, political transnationalism, and relations with nongovernmental organizations. They need institutions less than other migrants for their integration, making it more difficult for the state to trace and engage them. In contrast, Ecuadorians in vulnerable situations and with fewer resources are more likely to associate with co-nationals, rely on political and social actors' support, and mobilize to claim basic rights. This amplifies the echo of patriotic calls and the range of potential state intervention.

Yet, both communities exhibit a problematic tie with their home states, largely shaped by experiences that prompted emigration. Memories of an authoritarian past, state repression, and economic collapse have left a mark on citizens who exhibit distrust, fear, and disappointment in state institutions—more so in the case of Argentines than Ecuadorians. This introduces an element of ambiguity in migrants' responses and poses limits to sustained and articulated transnational political involvement. Again, incorporating domestic home politics and framing state actions within them sheds light on facets of migrant organizational dynamics that are not captured by studies focusing on contexts of reception (e.g., citizenship regimes, immigrant integration policies) or the relative amount of (ethnic) social capital alone.

Third, emigration policies necessarily have to be negotiated and implemented in collaboration with receiving countries. The viability and effects of measures to protect, engage, and enfranchise migrants partly depend on norms and contextual conditions in the host societies. In some localities, states also rely heavily on the collaboration of local governments and nongovernmental organizations. This encourages the development of a transnational network of public–private relations within which migrant political organization and mobilization take place. Therefore, the study of this form of collaboration that includes and exceeds traditional bilateral cooperation between nation-states is relevant to understanding how migrant association life is being shaped and how global trends are adapted to the local level of politics. It requires a partial shift of the analytical focus away from receiving countries alone and toward new forms of public–private partnership and multilevel transnational governance.

Finally, the modality of policy implementation (rather than policy goals or content) resulted in a sporadic and "sentimental" (rather than sustained and well-articulated) political mobilization of both diasporas, which still confront serious organizational problems and are far from working as strong influential groups at home or as ethnic lobbies in receiving countries. Both sending states reached out to migrant organizations, though in limited, paternalistic ways; they used an assistance-oriented approach which discouraged migrant protagonism. By taking over associations' unifying flags, the Ecuadorian state contributed to divisions and demobilization. An ambiguous, contradictory political discourse in Argentina, together with low migrant propensity toward associational life, maintained organizational efforts at a relatively dormant level. In both cases, migrant organizations oscillate between collaboration with and criticism of the government. Some officials tend to underestimate criticisms or consider them just a necessary part of the competition among associations to redefine their profiles and acquire representativeness; they attribute claims for inclusion to associations' appetites for state resources (including political appointments).[48] Regardless of associations' stances then, holding the lead and managing the resources and institutional channels allowed Ecuadorian public officials to argue that "we advance with or without them."[49] In sum, despite governments' intentions and emphases on migrants' rights, migrant empowerment (and, consequently, articulated transnational political mobilization) is still far from sight in both cases.

Further empirical research in other localities is necessary to extend comparisons. Surveys of migrant opinions would also enrich this study and allow some tentative generalizations. This might also allow researchers to specify the impact of concrete policy instruments and their combined impact. For instance, the use of rhetoric and symbolic measures varies considerably across cases, but we do not have reliable measures of how, when, and where diaspora labels are effective. We need to know more about whether the creation of a special label is relevant and what labels work better in terms of engaging migrants politically. Regarding migrant electoral participation, we observe that efforts focus on facilitating the act of voting and improving logistics, but we know little of whether a combination of state outreach efforts might also create (perhaps less tangible) incentives for migrants to actually register and vote.

Finally, from an analytical point of view, these conclusions also suggest further questions about the redefinition of state–society relations involved in emigration policies and the nature of emerging forms of governance. Are Latin American states simply reproducing old domestic contradictions at the transnational level? Are they merely duplicating domestic forms of inclusion/exclusion beyond borders? How, concretely, might the public–private policy networks described here transform the nature of migrant transnationalism? Are neopopulist regimes able to reconcile the tensions and contradictions of their development projects to live up to the promises of their sociopolitical agendas and foster the empowerment of social actors, including migrants? These questions invite not only further empirical research, but also open-ended dialogues among the fields of international relations, comparative politics, and migration studies.

Notes

1 See, for instance, Bloemraad (2005) and Morales et al. (2009).
2 See the special issue of *Journal of Ethnic and Migration Studies* of May 2004.
3 There were 391,202 Ecuadorians with residency cards or registration certificates in Spain as of March 31, 2013. Numbers peaked in the early 2000s, going from 12,933 in 1999 to 84,699 in 2001 and to 221,549 in 2004, and they remained high even after the crisis: 440,304 in 2009 and 390,365 as of December 31, 2012. The decrease in numbers makes Ecuadorians the third largest immigrant community today, while they had been the second among all immigrant communities (behind Morocco) for more than a decade and the first among Latin American immigrant groups. The ranking of destination sites has remained the same over the years, with Madrid and Barcelona

at the top. See http://extranjeros.empleo.gob.es/es/Estadisticas/, accessed August 14, 2013. Ecuadorians in Italy have been the largest (and second largest in some years) among Central and South American immigrant groups for a decade, growing from 33,506 to 91,635 individuals between 2003 and 2010 (the last year for which disaggregated numbers are available). In the Northwest region, they have been at the top of that ranking since the mid-2000s, with numbers going from 23,972 in 2003 to 64,031 in 2009, and in the Milano municipality in particular, they have been the second largest Latin American immigrant group, with numbers going from 4,157 in 2003 to 12,878 in 2009. See www.demo.istat.it, accessed August 14, 2013.

 4 There were 16,290 Argentines in Spain in 1999 with residency cards or registration certificates; numbers went up to 20,412 in 2001; 56,193 in 2004 (pushing Argentines up to the fourth rank among the largest immigrant Latin American communities); 103,171 in 2009; and 93,696 as of December 31, 2012. Barcelona and Madrid have been the preferred destinations. See http://extranjeros.empleo.gob.es/es/Estadisticas/, accessed August 14, 2013. The total number is higher, estimated at around 500,000 individuals in the mid-2000s, though statistical problems persist depending on whether the estimates include legal residents who have dual citizenship in Spain or another country within the European Union (and consequently do not appear in the statistics as immigrants), are under different types of visas (e.g., workers, students), or are illegal residents. According to Actis and Esteban (2009), the total number of Argentine-born people registered in Spain (including all categories) went from 84,872 in 2000 to 293,227 in 2008, with the most significant increments recorded in the first 4 years of the decade. Regarding Argentines in Italy, estimates are complex, too. Given that statistics do not capture illegal immigrants, those holding dual citizenship, and those using Italy as a transit site, figures do not reflect a dramatic increase in the number of Argentine immigrants to Italy in the last decade. There were 13,174 in 2003 at the national level; 13,907 in 2005; 11,338 in 2009; and 11,239 in 2010 (2003 and 2010 are the most relevant years for which statistics are disaggregated by nationality of origin). In the Northwest area, they decreased from 3,931 in 2003 to 3,702 in 2010 (with a peak of 4,345 in 2005), and increased from 418 to 543 in the municipality of Milano in the same period (i.e., 2003–2010). See www.demo.istat.it, accessed August 14, 2013.

 5 Interview with Carlos López Damm, Quito, May 13, 2009.
 6 Interview with Vladimir Paspuel, Madrid, June 4, 2010.
 7 Interviews with Oscar Imbaquingo, Madrid, June 8, 2010.
 8 Interview with Pablo de la Vega, Quito, May 14, 2009.
 9 Interview with Vladimir Paspuel, Madrid, June 4, 2010.
10 According to Aparicio Gómez and Tornos Cubillo (2010:58), there are 89 Ecuadorian associations in only five territories surveyed (Andalucía, Madrid, Comunidad Valenciana, Murcia, and Barcelona).
11 E-mail interview with Santiago Morales, Spain, July 14, 2010.
12 Boccagni (2013:201) argues that Ecuadorian associations in Northern Italy form and dissolve frequently. Given their focus on local issues and immigrants' urgent daily needs, their transnational involvement is limited.
13 Ecuadorian women, in particular, feel intimidated and demoralized because Italian manners look unusual and rude to them. SENAMI officials often noted that female migrants in precarious working situations and emotional distress tend to develop serious health conditions. Interview with Verónica Montesinos, Milan, May 26, 2011.
14 Local scholars in Genoa (another major destination for Ecuadorians) attribute low and conflictive associational life among the last wave of immigrants

to their region of origin (i.e., the coast), where there has historically been less associational tradition than in the highlands. Personal communication with Francesca Lagomarsino and Emanuela Abbatecola, Genoa, May 27, 2011.

15 Interviews with Verónica Montesinos, Milan, May 26, 2011, and José Galvez, Milan, May 31, 2011.

16 I owe the term to Francisco Cuberos Gallardo, who studied immigrant associations in Seville. Personal communication, Mälmo, August 27, 2013.

17 See Chapter 6 for antecedents and detailed information on emigration trends and emigrants' profiles.

18 Toward the end of the 1990s, Italian consulates in Argentina processed around 800 applications daily; after the 2001 crisis, numbers increased. In 2002, Italian citizenship was awarded to 43,000 Argentine-born individuals; in 2003, the number peaked at 75,000, and it went down to 44,500 in 2004. In Spanish consulates, applications went from around 5,000 in 1997 to 10,000 in 2001; between 2002 and 2005, 72,440 Argentine-born individuals were awarded Spanish citizenship. See González Martínez (2009:200–201).

19 Interviews with Matías Garrido, Madrid, June 7, 2010, and Enrique Borcel, Madrid, June 8, 2010.

20 Interview with Bibiana Degli Esposti, Madrid, June 16, 2010.

21 Phone interview with Oscar Strada, Spain, June 10, 2010.

22 Interviews via e-mail with Vanessa Vannay, secretary, Casa de Argentinos en Salamanca, December 15, 2005; Julio César Donoso, president, Asociación de Inmigrantes Argentinos en Valencia, December 13, 2005; and Valeria A. Andiazabal, co-founding member and website manager, PatriaMadre.com, December 15, 2005.

23 Interview with Natalia Dupuy, Argentine Consulate, Milan, May 30, 2011.

24 See *La Nación*, July 1, 2002, available at www.lanacion.com.ar/410052-tres-historias-de-argentinos-que-eligieron-irse-a-trabajar-a-italia, accessed April 14, 2015.

25 Most immigrant associations in Milan are characterized as "community leisure associations" that are more focused on inward-looking activities (e.g., helping group members or organizing celebrations) than on links with the home country. Lack of resources and experience generate distrust of public institutions. Thus, their role in policymaking remains marginal (for details, see Caponio 2005). Also, the high fragmentation and relatively young character of immigrant associations create representativeness problems and preclude associations from seizing political opportunities nationally and transnationally (Camozzi 2011; Caselli 2010).

26 Personal communication with Maurizio Ambrosini, Milan, May 23, 2011.

27 Interview with Bibiana Deli Esposti, Madrid, June 16, 2010.

28 Interview with Natalia Dupuy, Milan, June 30, 2011.

29 Interview with Abraham Serrano, Milan, May 26, 2011.

30 Online testimony, Alejandro Rolandi, available at https://argentinossiempre shay.wordpress.com/2009/11/29/expatriados-en-barcelona/, accessed April 14, 2015.

31 Interview with Gardenia Chávez, Quito, May 9, 2009.

32 Interview with Susana López, Quito, May 19, 2009.

33 Interview with Pedro Di Iorio, Caritas, Milan, May 25, 2011.

34 Online testimony, Mauricio Faenza, 33-year old economist, available at https://argentinossiempreshay.wordpress.com/2010/04/07/una-cosa-lleva-a-la-otra/, accessed April 14, 2015.

35 See http://resultados.cne.gob.ec/Results.html?RaceID=1&UnitID=26&IsPS=0&LangID=0, accessed May 28, 2013.

36 Interview with Gabriel Servetto, Directorate of International Migrations, Ministry of Foreign Affairs, Buenos Aires, June 13, 2014.
37 Interview with Nora Pérez Vichich, Directorate of International Migrations, Ministry of Foreign Affairs, Buenos Aires, June 13, 2014.
38 Online testimony, Magdalena Salgado Fantuzzi, 31-year-old, available at https://argentinossiempreshay.wordpress.com/2009/11/30/elegir-cada-dia-el-lugar/, accessed April 14, 2015.
39 Interview with Oscar Jara, SENAMI, Madrid, June 11, 2010.
40 Interview with José Gálvez, SENAMI, Milan, May 31, 2011.
41 It has continued to expand, promoting exchanges and knowledge transfer and diffusing information about scientists abroad, including job opportunities, seed grants, liaisons with firms, and support for returnees. Through 2010, 600 researchers were repatriated (Ginieniewicz and Castiglione 2010:139).
42 See www.mininterior.gov.ar/provincias/p25_mision, accessed May 21, 2013.
43 Interviews with Patricio Carrillo, Quito, May 13, 2009, and Gloria Jiménez and Luis Sánchez, Quito, May 15, 2009.
44 Interview with Vladimir Paspuel, Madrid, June 4, 2010.
45 Interviews with Oscar Jara, Madrid, June 11, 2010, and Oscar Imbaquingo, Madrid, June 8, 2010.
46 Interview with Pedro Di Iorio, Milan, May 30, 2011.
47 The few surveys available on this point indicate that Latin American immigrants in Spain communicate frequently with relatives at home by phone or Internet, but they travel to their country of origin much less often than other immigrant groups due to the cost of long distance airfares and, in some cases, irregular migrant situation; only half of them send remittances, a practice more normal and involving higher amounts among Ecuadorians than Argentines (Actis 2009).
48 Interview with Arturo Cabrera Hidalgo, Quito, May 11, 2009.
49 Interview with Lorena Altamirano, Quito, May 12, 2009.

Works Cited

Actis, Walter. 2009. "Immigrantes Latinoamericanos en España: Una Visión de Conjunto." *Migraçoes*. 5: 63–86.
Aparicio Gómez, Rosa and Andrés Tornos Cubillo. 2010. "Las Asociaciones de Inmigrantes en España. Una Vision de Conjunto." Documentos del Observatorio Permanente de la Inmigración no. 26. Madrid: Ministerio de Trabajo e Inmigración.
Avilés Salgado, León Pablo. 2005. "Reseña Histórica Sobre la Emigración Ecuatoriana a Italia: Situación Actual y Perspectivas." In *Emigración y Política Exterior en Ecuador*, ed. by Javier Ponce Leiva. Quito: Ediciones AYBA-YALA/FLACSO. pp. 123–146.
Bauböck, Rainer and Thomas Faist. eds. 2010. *Diaspora and Transnationalism: Concepts, Theories and Methods*. Amsterdam: IMISCOE Research/Amsterdam University Press.
Bloemraad, Irene. 2005. "The Limits of Tocqueville: How Government Facilitates Organisational Capacity in Newcomer Communities." *Journal of Ethnic and Migration Studies*. 31(5): 865–887.
Boccagni, Paolo. 2013. "Whom Should We Help First? Transnational Helping Practices in Ecuadorian Migration." *International Migration*. 51(2): 191–208.

Boccagni, Paolo. 2011. "Reminiscences, Patriotism, Participation: Approaching External Voting in Ecuadorian Immigration to Italy." *International Migration.* 49(3): 76–98.

Boccagni, Paolo and Jacques Ramírez. 2013. "Building Democracy or Reproducing 'Ecuadoreanness'? A Transnational Exploration of Ecuadorean Migrants' External Voting. *Journal of Latin American Studies.* 45(4): 721–750.

Buira, Rubén. 2006. "Políticas de Estado-Diáspora en Argentina." In *Relaciones Estado-Diáspora: La Perspective de América Latina y el Caribe,* coord. by C. González Gutiérrez. México: Miguel Ángel Porrúa Editor. pp. 299–311.

Camozzi, Ilenya. 2011. "Migrants' Associations and Their Attempts to Gain Recognition: The Case of Milan." *Studies in Ethnicity and Nationalism.* 11(3): 468–491.

Caselli, Marco. 2010. "Integration, Participation, Identity: Immigrant Associations in the Province of Milan." *International Migration.* 48(2): 58–78.

Caponio, Tiziana. 2005. "Policy Networks and Immigrants' Associations in Italy: The Cases of Milan, Bologna and Naples." *Journal of Ethnic and Migration Studies.* 31(5): 931–950.

Cortés Maisonave, Almudena. 2011. "The Transnational Governance of Ecuadorian Migration through Co-Development." *International Migration.* 49(3): 30–51.

Escobar, Cristina. 2007. "Extraterritorial Political Rights and Dual Citizenship in Latin America." *Latin American Research Review.* 42(3): 43–75.

Fornell, Agustín. 2005. "Acción del Ministerio de Relaciones Exteriores en Temas Migratorios: El Correo Directo Como Herramienta de Gestión Diplomática a Favor de los Emigrantes." In *Emigración y Política Exterior en Ecuador,* ed. by Javier Ponce Leiva. Quito: Ediciones AYBA-YALA/FLACSO. pp. 223–250.

Garzón Guillén, Luis. 2006. "Trayectorias e Integración de la Inmigración Argentina y Ecuatoriana en Barcelona y Milano." Doctoral thesis. Universitat Autònoma de Barcelona.

Ginieniewicz, Jorge and Celeste Castiglione. 2011. "State Response to Transnational Asset Accumulation: The Case of Argentina." *Bullet of Latin American Research.* 30(2): 133–147.

Goldberg, Alejandro. 2006. "Nuevos Migrantes Argentinos en Barcelona: Una Indagación Etnográfica Alrededor de los Procesos de Integración e Inserción Sociolaboral." *Revista Alternativas.* 14: 113–139.

González Martínez, Elda. 2009. "Redes Sociales y Emigración: El Caso de los Marplatenses." *Revista de Indias.* LXIX(245): 199–224.

Koller, Sylvie. 2009–2010. "Équateur: La Politique des Droits." *Problèmes d'Amérique Latine.* 75: 61–73.

Kyle, David. 2000. *Transnational Peasants: Migrations, Networks, and Ethnicity in Andean Ecuador.* Baltimore, MD: The Johns Hopkins University Press.

Lyons, Terrence and Peter Mandaville. 2010. "Think Locally, Act Globally: Toward a Transnational Comparative Politics." *International Political Sociology.* 4(2): 124–141.

Morales, Laura, Amparo González, and Laia Jorba. 2009. "Políticas de Incorporación y Asociacionismo de la Población de Origen Inmigrante a Nivel Local." In *Inmigración en España: Claroscuros de las Políticas y Gobernabilidad,* coord. by R. Zapata. Madrid: Ariel. pp. 113–138.

Morales, Laura and Katia Pilati. 2013. "The Political Transnationalism of Ecuadorians in Barcelona, Madrid, and Milan: The Role of Individual Resources,

Organizational Engagement and the Political Context." *Global Networks.* 14(1): 80–102. DOI: 10.1111/glob.12018.

Ndjoli Fernández, Alejandra. 2006. "Migración, Transnacionalismo y Movilización Social. Un Estudio de Caso: Las Asociaciones Ecuador-Llactacaru." Universidad de Sevilla. Available at http://hal.archives-ouvertes.fr/docs/00/10/30/68/PDF/Ndjoli_1_.pdf.

Novick, Susana and M.G. Murias. 2005. "Dos Estudios Sobre la Emigración Reciente en la Argentina." Working Paper 42. Buenos Aires: Instituto de Investigaciones Gino Germani.

Novick, Susana. 2007. "Políticas y Actores Sociales Frente a la Emigración de Argentinos." In *Sur-Norte. Estudios Sobre la Emigración Reciente de Argentinos,* ed. by S. Novick. Buenos Aires: Catálogos. pp. 297–362.

Queirolo Palmas, Luca and Maurizio Ambrosini. 2007. "Lecciones de la Immigración Latina a Europa e Italia." In *Nuevas Migraciones Latinoamericanas a Europa: Balances y Desafíos.* ed. by I. Yépez del Castillo and G. Herrera. Quito: FLACSO/OBREAL. pp. 95–112.

SGEB 2012. *Diplomacia Consular 2007–2012.* Brasilia: Fundação Alexandre de Gusmão, Ministério das Relações Exteriores.

SJRM/ILDIS-FES. 2007. "El Proceso Electoral de los Ecuatorianos en el Exterior: Reflexiones para un Debate Sobre la Participación en Contextos de Migración." Quito: Servicio Jesuita a Refugiados y Migrantes, Ecuador, Instituto Latinoamericano de Investigaciones Sociales, Friedrich Ebert Stiftung. November.

Tullio, Alejandro. 2010. "Dos Aspectos del Ejercicio Extraterritorial de los Derechos Politicos." *Seguridad y Ciudadanía. Revista del Ministerio del Interior.* 3: 79–96.

9 Mexico

Model or Outlier?

The experience of South American countries in the realm of courting diasporas builds upon and contrasts neatly with that of Mexico. This is one of the best-known cases in the literature on diaspora engagement policies, and one that exhibits the most far-reaching and institutionalized set of programs to liaise with emigrants. Its trajectory has been explained in several detailed studies. For this reason, this chapter does not attempt to rewrite those narratives. Rather, it presents a brief account of the case to highlight specific points. However, most studies do not include an updated account that incorporates the latest policy developments, especially since the PRI (Institutional Revolutionary Party in its Spanish acronym) returned to power in December 2012. It is too early to have detailed academic publications on that period. Thus, this chapter gathers some relevant information to start filling that gap.

It has been suggested that Mexico might have worked as a model for other countries to emulate. However, this case has not been compared to South American countries because some specificities placed it too far apart from regional trends, making it look like an outlier. I did not find conclusive evidence on these points, but I did find that Mexico is lately becoming closer than ever to South American countries in terms of migration discourse and the interplay of domestic and international processes. Its long historical record of courting the diaspora exhibits the cyclical nature of its engagement with Mexicans in the US, a pattern that South American countries have just started to follow. I also found that assumptions about geographic proximity as a factor that facilitates transnational political practices are overestimated. Thus, the incorporation of Mexico in this book allows us to expand not only the comparison but also on our understanding of explanatory factors in national and regional contexts.

A Long Historical Record of Courting

As several sources document, relations between the Mexican state and Mexicans in the US territory can be traced back at least to the mid-19th century, although those relations have intensified, expanded, and institutionalized significantly since early 1990s. Until then, according to Smith

(2003b), state interest in emigrants had followed a pattern of waxing and waning that was largely shaped by political and economic events. Délano (2006) argues that, in general terms and until the 1980s, the Mexican state simply provided consular protection, benefited from emigration as an escape valve that alleviated economic and political problems, and maintained a low profile in relations with the emigrant community, avoiding interference with US domestic politics that might have jeopardized the bilateral agenda; governments' rhetoric for domestic consumption, though, emphasized the importance of promoting return, strengthening links with the diaspora, and dissuading further emigration. Fitzgerald (2006) agrees on the lack of a consistent policy toward emigrants. He argues that policy shifts occurred due to external events (e.g., the Great Depression, World Wars I and II), political events in Mexico, and the impact of other related policies, such as state efforts to regulate labor markets, stimulate agricultural development, or reinforce nationalism vis-à-vis the US. Yet, while several authors characterize the overall state approach during the 20th century as *laissez-faire* and relatively neglectful (Goldring 2002:65; Rosenblum 2006; Smith 2003b), Fitzgerald (2006) argues that for over a century, the Mexican state has implemented a number of concrete measures to control emigration and, in particular, to manage the volume, duration, composition, and geographic origin of the emigrant flows. Durand (2004) concurs on the existence of contradictory policies that nevertheless aimed at administering, balancing, and alternatively dissuading or encouraging emigration. Goldring (2002) underlines the increasing politicization of relations between migrants and the Mexican state since the 1990s.

Notwithstanding subtle nuances in those interpretations, there are clear historical records of early attempts to protect, organize, and/or control expatriates, including the protection of Mexicans in the lost territories after 1848, the engagement with those who massively exited at the time of the 1910–1920 Revolution and the creation of linkage and other commissions to extend protection and assistance, the encouragement of repatriation in the 1930s, and the negotiation of temporary labor migration agreements (namely the Bracero Program) between 1942 and 1964, always assuming that emigration was temporary. Nevertheless, as the size of the emigrant community was growing, Mexicans in the US became firmly settled and created all sorts of organizations to defend their rights, preserve cultural traditions, and provide collective support, sometimes acting in collaboration with the consulates, which keep expanding in number and in the scope of their activities. Thus, the development of kin networks and the evolution and consolidation of migrant associations also shaped the state–diaspora relationship (see details in Cano and Délano 2007), but as governments' efforts to reach out to nationals abroad varied, collaboration waxed (e.g., 1920s–1930s) and waned (e.g., during the Bracero program).

State interest in the emigrant community was revived in the early 1970s and consulates resumed an active role in protecting migrants' rights and fostering their organizational efforts. Yet, failing to negotiate a renewal of the guest worker program with the US, Mexico turned to the so-called "policy of no policy" for the following two decades, that is, the deliberate position of not taking action regarding the bilateral migration problem. Some support to specific migrant organizations continued (e.g., the Chicano movement, members of the business community) and educational and cultural programs developed, though. However, those links did not constitute a formal linkage policy yet, and public officials denied any attempt to support the formation of a pro-Mexican lobby in the US (Ayón 2006:126). By the end of the 1980s, some facts made it evident that inaction was a costly option: the 1986 US Immigration Reform and Control Act (IRCA) not only allowed for the legalization of over 2 million immigrants but also encouraged longer and permanent stays and family reunion. Mexicans in the US acquired political and economic relevance as a constituency and sources of remittances;[1] their organizations and networks expanded; their demands for consular assistance increased; and the 1988 elections showed that many of them resented the PRI politics (Institutional Revolutionary Party, the dominant political party for most of the 20th century) and its neglect for nationals abroad (Durand 2004).

In addition, links with the emigrant community were reinforced throughout this period by visits, meetings, and programs initiated not only by federal but also by state- and local-level authorities. The role of state governments in linkage policies has increased considerably in the last two decades, though the degree of activism and commitment varies across states.[2] The intensity of local-level linkages clearly sets Mexico apart from other cases. Working in collaboration with hometown associations and federations of migrant clubs, state and local governments have been providing services that facilitate immigrant integration and channeling remittances toward communities of origin; they also implement a good number of programs aimed at supporting organizations and offering services to migrants in the areas of education, health, labor, security, and social welfare (see details in Délano 2010; Vel Freyer 2007). It is worth noting that the increasingly complex character of policymaking, the participation of nonstate actors in some of these programs (e.g., the Inter-American Development Bank, private banks, and money transfer companies), and the decentralization strategy required intense coordination and collaboration among different levels of government and offices within the state apparatus—a requirement that was not always attained.

These partnerships are most evident in the realm of economic links. The Mexican experience illustrates well that states have learned to partner with other actors to indirectly capture more benefits from

emigrants. The reduction of costs in money transfers, the encouragement of more competition in that market, and the incorporation of
new technologies have increased the volume of remittances. According to the leader of the World Bank remittances team, the reduction
of money transfer fees worldwide passed from around 15% in a $300
transaction in late 1990s to less than 10% today, while the cost of
sending the same amount to Mexico declined from 9.5% to just over
2% in the same period.[3] Since a good number of migrants do not use
banks because they lack the necessary information and/or identification documents, states have also been proactive in offering financial
education programs and negotiating for flexibility of norms regarding
identification with host states and banks. Mexico, for instance, conducted intensive negotiations to make *matrículas consulares* (consular
identification cards) accepted by banks and local authorities in the US,
an initiative that the Brazilian government also pursued in mid-2000s.
This move has been seen as an adaptation of policy tools to changing
circumstances (i.e., 9/11 and the freezing of bilateral migration talks).
As Waldinger (2009:23–25) explains, Mexico made use of a porous
American political system to reach out to its citizens abroad, using its
consular network to negotiate with public and nongovernmental institutions the recognition of cards, thus facilitating migrants' identification and their transactions.

In addition, in the case of Mexico, the state acted through different
jurisdictions (federal, state, municipal) to engage migrants in diverse
development projects, giving local authorities more autonomy and
resources at times and conflating migrant programs with national initiatives to alleviate poverty at other times, thus reaching out and withdrawing from engagement alternatively, depending on domestic politics
and specific circumstances. As Iskander (2010) ably explains, these
"conversations" between the state and the emigrant community were
often tense, and not all projects translated into development gains. The
experience of the state of Zacatecas with a remittance-based matching-
funds program is probably the best example, and it is well documented.
Although there is no single overall figure that can capture the material
impact of this program over the years, its evolution (from 1:1 to 2:1
to 3:1)[4] and replication in other states is illustrative of the nontangible
results and implications of these policies, namely giving visibility, organizational incentives, and bargaining power to migrants and pushing
the state to not only respond innovatively to constituencies abroad but
also to engage those social actors in policymaking (see, among others,
Iskander 2010:236–273).

Overall, these developments contributed to an incipient awareness of
the need to develop a consistent, long-term policy of engagement with the
diaspora. Domestic political and economic changes in the late 1980s and
1990s paved the way for the emergence of a new approach.

Institutionalization of Long-Standing
Ties With Mexicans in the US

Indeed, the decade of 1990 is considered a breaking point in the evolution of state–diaspora relations in Mexico. Although migration was not included in negotiations for the North American Free Trade Agreement (NAFTA), the Salinas administration (1988–1994) took a proactive stance toward Mexicans in the US, giving priority to consular assistance, encouraging and supporting migrants' organizational efforts, and strengthening ties with business groups, hometown associations, and other organizations. A number of programs were launched and/or expanded in the areas of education, tourism, health, sports, and culture, including the Paisano Program to facilitate migration return and the 3:1 Community Investment Program to channel remittances toward productive activities in the sending localities (González Gutiérrez 2006). One of the implicit goals of state initiatives in the 1990s was to strengthen the lobby capacity of Mexicans in the US and eventually to rely on that to advance the country's interests in bilateral negotiations. This approach implied a recognition of the permanent character of emigration and a significant departure from the previous position of not developing political activities north of the border for fear of US interference in Mexican domestic politics (Cano and Délano 2007:28–29; Délano 2006). This is a stage of engagement that South American countries have not yet cultivated.

Significant institutional developments run parallel to these programs: the Program for Mexican Communities Abroad was created within the Ministry of Foreign Affairs in 1990, and it aimed to provide an official and specialized channel of communication with nationals abroad and further reinforce the linkage activities of consulates. The National Institute of Migration was created in 1993. Measures to protect emigrants were reinforced as violence along the border with the US and anti-immigrant campaigns intensified. Under the Zedillo (1994–2000) and Fox (2000–2006) administrations, Mexico pushed for increasing cooperation with the US on migration issues through bilateral working groups, parliamentary commissions, and coordination of border control mechanisms (Délano 2006). In terms of migrants' rights, 1996 was a crucial year: a constitutional amendment allowed dual nationality or citizenship retention (i.e., those who naturalize in the US would not lose their Mexican nationality), and Congress passed a law later allowing extraterritorial voting rights—two measures that symbolically embrace expatriates as part of the nation and enfranchise them as members of the political community. However, voting rights became effective for the first time 10 years later, in the 2006 presidential elections.

The symbolic incorporation of Mexicans abroad was reinforced in the following years and was reflected in political discourses. Former

President Vicente Fox (elected in 2000) reached out to emigrants during his electoral campaign and acknowledged their multiple contributions to the country. Once in office, he made efforts to place migration issues high on the agenda of negotiations with the US; he sent a weekly message by radio and television to migrants; and he created the Presidential Office for Mexicans Abroad to act as a direct channel of communication between the presidency and nationals abroad. At the rhetoric level, Fox addressed Mexicans in the US as members of the Mexican nation and heroes, in a clear contrast with past pejorative characterizations and accusations of being traitors to the national cause (Kunz 2008:12–13). This change had both symbolic and material effects: it redefined the identities of emigrants, giving a positive connotation to their journeys and strengthening ties with the homeland; at the same time, this constitutes them as subjects of policies and as a specific constituency.

Moreover, in August 2002, Fox announced a new institutional structure aimed at addressing migrant issues in a comprehensive and coordinated fashion: The National Council for Mexican Communities Abroad, formed by the president and members of 11 state secretariats and in charge of designing and coordinating policies across ministries; and the Institute of Mexicans Abroad (IME, in its Spanish acronym), created the following year within the Foreign Affairs Secretariat of the Ministry of Foreign Affairs, which was in charge of policy implementation in close collaboration with the 50 consular offices existing in North America. The Program for Mexican Communities Abroad and the Presidential Office for Mexicans Abroad merged into the IME, which became not only a focus of initiatives related to emigration policies but has also involved nationals abroad in policymaking through the participation of their elected representatives in the third pillar of this institutional structure: the Consultative Council of the IME. This council meets regularly and makes recommendations on all sorts of migration-related topics based on the preliminary work of its commissions. The IME has focused its work on services to the emigrant community through programs in the areas of education, health, economics, and culture,[5] and on providing information and facilitating contacts among migrant leaders (González Gutiérrez 2006).

Ayón (2006:135) suggests that the meetings, the specialized information sessions organized by the IME (which gathered up to 1,200 participants by 2005), and the periodic renewal of the council members have become a sort of training school for migrant leaders. Through its activities, the IME has helped to consolidate a transnational space in which leaders of the emigrant community engage with home politics. Carlos González Gutiérrez, the first executive director of the IME, informally known as the architect of Mexico's diaspora engagement policy, underlines the institute's contribution to empowering migrant leadership and creating opportunities for migrant political participation both in the US and in Mexico (cited in Délano 2011:202, 221). In sum, the IME represents an institutionalized channel for migrants' claims, a formal mechanism of communication between the government and the organized emigrant community, a potential tool to mobilize resources both in Mexico and the US, and the embodiment of how strong the state–diaspora relationship has become.

Nonetheless, doubts persist about the sustainability of these policies in the long run and whether these notable changes reflect a clear, consensual, and consistent policy toward emigration. On the one hand, the Calderón administration (2006–2012) continued the policies initiated by previous governments. Although migration did not stand out in the public discourse during his term, Mexico increased consular protection and mobilized in support of Mexicans in the US facing anti-immigration campaigns (mainly the 2010 Arizona Law). The administration of Enrique Peña Nieto (inaugurated in December 2012) has given signs of continuity and a low profile in this policy realm, too, although it is probably too early to assess policy implications. All officials interviewed for this study agreed on the need to expand and deepen the programs aimed at a better integration of Mexicans in the US. The transition team worked hard on preparing the guidelines on migration to be submitted to the president-elect,[6] and the head of the team (later appointed as director of the IME) promised to relaunch and restructure the IME, revise and make existing programs more efficient, and work for migrants' political rights while avoiding any intervention in the debate on US immigration reform that could be interpreted as a "disrespectful and inconvenient interference in US domestic affairs."[7] But his term lasted only 1 year, and those plans are still in the making.

On the other hand, the overall policy shift initiated in the late 1980s seems to still be a work in progress. Délano (2011) indicates that Mexico is still very cautious in reaching out to Mexicans in the US because of concerns about negatively affecting other areas of the bilateral relationship; she also documents negative reactions and opposition to government initiatives, the lack of references to the IME's activities in key official documents in the past, and the limited understanding of migration issues beyond a specialized bureaucracy at the Ministry of Foreign Affairs.

A recent sign in the direction of a comprehensive understanding of the migration problem is the incorporation of emigration concerns in the National Development Plan 2013–2018, which describes the goals and strategies set by the Peña Nieto administration, sets a guiding and facilitating role for the state in development, and calls on individuals' responsibility to attain prosperity. The plan acknowledges the need to address all dimensions of the migration phenomenon; this would include protecting emigrants' rights and interests as part of a responsible foreign policy; strengthening economic, political, and cultural links with Mexicans abroad; facilitating all flows of human mobility that might contribute to development; and guaranteeing refugees' rights.[8]

Finally, in terms of migrant dual engagements, this case illustrates that norms allowing the retention of nationality may go beyond the intended goal of maintaining formal links between emigrants and their country of origin. Escobar (2007) shows that the 1996 retention-of-citizenship law accelerated the process of naturalization of Mexicans in the US, allowing them to gain and defend their rights as they became more integrated in the host society. The Mexican state portrayed this change as an extension of its protection to citizens abroad at the time of anti-immigration measures in the US, but it also pursued other political goals, such as neutralizing opposition to the PRI and counterbalancing the influence of the PRD (Party of the Democratic Revolution, in its Spanish acronym) among the emigrant community; it also indirectly achieved long-term goals: the more integrated immigrants are, the more likely they are to engage in politics in the receiving country and to work as a lobby group for Mexican interests, and the more likely they are to keep remittances flowing.

With respect to political engagement in home politics, as in all other cases, the level of participation of emigrants is low. According to the Federal Electoral Institute, 40,714 epistolary votes were received in 2012, which represents an increase of 24.8% over the 32,632 received in the 2006 elections.[9] But, this is still significantly low considering that the 2012 US Census reported 33.7 million Hispanics of Mexican origin (of which 11.4 million were born in Mexico).[10] The institute attributes the increase to its efficient campaign through social networks, Internet mechanisms, and better logistics. Yet, lack of information, logistical problems, and an extremely convoluted registration process are usually cited as obstacles to higher electoral participation, and these still persist. Lafleur (2011:488) argues that, in fact, these problems are intended results: enfranchising emigrants was possible once political parties agreed in 2004 on certain restrictions that would minimize the potential adverse impact of migrants' votes. The consequent 2005 legislation established that they would only vote on presidential elections, and only by mail; political parties were forbidden to campaign abroad; and only emigrants holding a voting identity card (which could be obtained only in Mexico then) could register to vote. Nonetheless, the fact that almost 1 million migrants have the card and only 40% voted casts doubts on the real reasons for low participation; some public officials argue that a good number of migrants are not even interested in home politics.[11]

The last presidential campaign offered evidence of the possibilities as well as the limits of engagement. The PRI, in particular, tried to reverse emigrants' long-standing distrust. Instead of simply relying on migrant transnational networks and practices, the party purposely enhanced contacts between emigrants and their families at home, making sure that communication happened. For instance, during the last electoral campaign, politicians visited a resident abroad, took pictures with him/her, and volunteered to deliver the picture and a note to his/her mother or other close relative in Mexico. They did so rigorously, thus making sure to transmit not only the PRI message for elections but also its commitment to deliver and its being a trustworthy political party. In other words, knowing that family communications do not always occur and do not always include political conversations, politicians "made transnationalism happen."[12] This was different than the strategy followed by the National Action Party (PAN) when campaigning for Fox years ago; they distributed cards that migrants had to mail to their families or offered free phone cards for migrants to call home. Within the new strategy, rather working for emigrants' votes, the PRI worked on emigrants influencing their relatives' choices. Instead of assuming transnational outcomes, this time the PRI worked on generating them and achieved significant success. It focused on migrants from the states and specific districts that have traditionally sent the largest migration outflows. Although the PRI still occupies the third place in terms of absentee voters' preferences, electoral results show an improved performance: the PRI went from 1,360 votes in 2006 (4.1% of the total epistolary votes received) to 5,956 (or 15.62%) in 2012; if votes received are classified by state of origin, the PRI did well in the targeted states. It obtained 169 votes in Jalisco in 2006 and 692 in 2012; 71 and 365, respectively, in Guanajuato; 121 and 423, respectively, in Michoacán; and 98 and 641, respectively, in Mexico State, where Peña Nieto was governor and this strategy was designed.[13] Within the Mexico State, around 60 municipalities were particularly targeted, and the PRI improved its performance dramatically: it received 1,333,012 votes in 2006 (running in alliance with the Green Party) and 2,228,719 votes in 2012.[14]

Recent legislation has also broadened emigrants' rights and facilitated procedures: on 30 May 2014, Congress approved a politico-electoral reform that goes into effect in 2015. It allows the extension of extraterritorial voting rights beyond the candidates for the presidency to include senators, governors, and mayor of the federal district. Epistolary votes may be submitted to consulates and embassies, which eliminates citizens' costs of mailing votes to Mexico. Alternatively, voters may request to vote electronically. Citizens abroad can also obtain the necessary identification card from consulates (a form of registration for voters that previously was issued only in Mexico).[15]

Latest Developments: Withering Engagement?

Migration problems in Mexico have recently acquired new dimensions and characteristics that might require a comprehensive, new approach. Transit migration (especially of Central and South Americans on their way to the US) and, to a lesser extent, immigration from neighboring and other countries are two issues that have required increasing attention lately. These two issues confronted the Calderón administration with the challenge of securing borders in the context of mounting violence due to human and drug trafficking at border zones while increasing detention facilities and deportation mechanisms. At the same time, the 2011 migration law aims at protecting migrants' human rights, too, regardless of their status, as well as facilitating international human mobility, return, and reintegration. Yet, this new law was regulated only in November 2012, making it difficult to assess the impact of its implementation. Also, although emigration to the US has receded since 2010, it is likely to continue and involve—as it has in the last few years—a more diverse population in terms of community of origin, educational and occupational levels, and socioeconomic backgrounds. The prospects of an imminent immigration policy reform in the US may also bring significant changes, namely the legalization of over 11 million immigrants of Mexican origin (Alba 2013).

Top Mexican officials at IME and the president's office interviewed for this study at the time of the Peña Nieto inauguration admitted that the "proactive consular activity" is likely to continue, but there are limits to what the IME can do, and the national debate has recently shifted from the diaspora in the North to internal migration, transit flows, Southern border controls, and security policies to stop criminal activities linked to human mobility.[16] The creation of the Unit of Migration Policy in late 2012 within the Secretariat of the Interior (in Spanish, *Secretaría de Gobernación*) illustrates the increasing awareness to adopt an integrated approach at the top of the decision-making state structure. Facing the new trends mentioned, the Mexican state also has to work with an increasingly diverse diaspora, reproducing programs and supporting organizational efforts in new destinations and, perhaps more importantly, promoting migrants' empowerment.[17] The latter is the policy that might help migrants to become more involved in local public affairs and relevant actors in the host country. But it has to be grounded in a comprehensive, integrative view of all dimensions of the migration problem.[18]

In addition, since Peña Nieto has been in office, there have been some signs of a stalemate in policy evolution, which suggests a new cycle of partial state withdrawal from engagement. For instance, the ambitious plans of the transition team above did not materialize, and the leader of the team, appointed director of the IME at the time of inauguration, resigned in a few months to take a diplomatic position abroad. Some of his advisors who had drafted the plan are now appointed at the National Institute of Migration. They argue that the intention to adopt a comprehensive approach to immigration, emigration, return, and transit has not materialized yet and that the attention of the federal government is focused today on illegal transit migration. "Overall, migration policy in Mexico is in conflict [to reconcile] schemes to facilitate [human mobility], national security, and unrestricted respect for migrants' human rights."[19]

Public officials concur with academic specialists that the policy toward emigrants has lost momentum. While it is still on the agenda of the federal government, it is now subsumed within the integral plan the current administration adopted in 2014, known as the Special Program of Migration 2014–2018.[20] This document gathers some of the ideas in the National Development Plan mentioned previously. In the realm of ideas, it is a significant step in setting basic principles: it proposes the adoption of an integrated, long-term view of migration problems and the defense of migrant rights. The actual implementation of those ideas is still an open question. From a comparative point of view, I note the relevance of this document: by underlining the importance of legal human mobility, human rights considerations, and a positive view of migration, it places the Mexican political discourse closer than ever to the South American approach.

Furthermore, although the IME maintains a number of programs—and, comparatively, it exceeds by far any other state institution in the region in terms of interactions and services to citizens abroad—it has played a low profile role in the last two years. Linkage programs have expanded, such as the one involving highly skilled emigrants (known as *Red de Talentos*, Talent Network), and the so-called Global Network of Mexicans, which works around specific projects linking emigrants in all regions of the world.[21] This is compounded by the socioeconomic diversity and relative mobilization capacities of different sectors within the emigrant community and the fact that there are several generations of Mexicans in the US—all factors that make generalizations about the Mexican diaspora inconclusive.[22] Broad consultation processes continued in October and November of 2013 (the so-called *Foros de Consulta Pública*) with the participation of over 700 people and around 1,200 proposals for the elaboration of a migration plan for 2014–2018, but this was interpreted as little effort to convoke citizens abroad through institutionalized channels.[23] In other words, the existing programs have continued to run through a vast consular service, but state political outreach has become more selective.

The role of bilateral relations with the US continues to be a nuanced one. Some sources indicate that the launching of the Deferred Action for Childhood Arrivals (DACA) by the Obama administration in August 2012 prompted an expansion of Mexico's consular services and the revival of links with migrant leaders, especially those from a young generation. In addition, border zones have been the focus of attention: in the last two years, consultation forums worked more intensively at the local and regional levels than through the national Consultation Council of the IME.[24] Overall, the record of the last few years would support Kunz's argument (2011:285) that the partnership discourse adopted since the 1990s "has contributed to reframe migration governance as a technical management issue and thereby to depoliticize migration cooperation in the Mexico-US context."

Two issues stand out today as indicative of whether policy innovation may be necessary and may occur. On the one hand, the IME seems to lack

institutional status and power to play an autonomous role in the management of a multifaceted policy toward the diaspora that cuts across social,
economic, and security areas, among others. The possibilities of institutional upgrade or creation are worth monitoring. On the other hand, the
Consultation Council of the IME is now working under new rules: instead
of members elected by consulates' jurisdiction, it is now composed of members who have submitted projects of relevance for their communities and
have been selected by consulate officials in consultation with members of
the community. This certainly changes the dynamics of migrant representation and potential empowering. In the view of some public officials, this
is the result of a passage from an experimental phase in the 1990s (in which
the state was trying to decipher emigrants' demands), to a phase focused on
two groups (established migrant leaders and the most vulnerable migrants)
in the 2000s, to a new phase today in which the state implements differen-
tiated programs mainly for three groups: the most vulnerable; legal, relatively established migrants; and highly qualified expats. In other words, the
Mexican state acknowledges that most emigrants are not likely to return
or circulate frequently (a possibility that is even less likely under current
US restrictive policies) and, therefore, it has to encourage the circulation of
knowledge and expansion of links with the diaspora.[25]

In sum, further research is necessary to assess where Mexico's emigration policy may be heading in the next few years. If there is no policy
innovation and the signs of withering engagement persist, this may imply
that Mexico's trajectory is in an inertial mode now, although it relies on
extensive and relatively strong and institutionalized ties built over decades
of state–society courting. At the level of discourse, Mexico is joining the
rest of the region in its emphasis on human rights, the state's role, and
development considerations. More recently, Mexico has also become
more similar to South American states like Brazil in the sense of moving
toward a comprehensive approach to all migration issues and implementing "surgical" interventions in specific questions of relevance for the diaspora. Most important, if we were to observe these trends over time and in
a larger number of cases, it might be plausible to theorize that, in the long
term, diaspora engagement policies are only sustainable through cycles of
sporadic and intense strategic engagement and partial withdrawal.

Notes

1 As of 2010, Mexico was the third top remittance-receiving country with
   $22.6 billion. See World Bank 2011, p.13.
2 Vila Freyer (2007) identifies active states in which the executive branch leads
   linkage efforts, federal assistance programs are implemented, and specific
   initiatives are also pursued (e.g., Jalisco, Yucatán); reactive states that mostly
   act to respond to migrants' demands (Zacatecas, Veracruz); states that almost
   exclusively follow federal policies (Puebla, Mexico); and states where linkage
   activities are practically null (Morelos, Chiapas).

3 See *New York Times,* April 28, 2013, p. 22.
4 For details on types of projects, increases in the funds provided by migrants and governments, and results, see Soto Priante (2006).
5 For full details, see the IME's website at www.ime.gob.mx/.
6 The transition team was then working on two documents: one focused on border controls, linking migration to the problem of national security; and the other focused on international migration, defining emigrants as a vulnerable group, and framing the topic within social and foreign policies. The second document includes some of Peña Nieto's statements during the campaign promising to disincentive emigration, work to promote and protect migrants' human rights, lower the cost of remittances, implement programs for a "dignified return," provide social security benefits to migrants and their families, support migrant organizations working on the US immigration reform, seek dialogue on migration with the US government, encourage migrant political participation, improve mechanisms of extraterritorial voting, intensify links with migrant organizations and their involvement in policymaking, and allocate more financial and human resources to consulates. Both documents made policy recommendations based on a diagnosis of problems and challenges and the identification of best practices in countries from all regions of the world. Interviews with Fernando Ali Urbina Avendaño and David Blake, deputy coordinators, Migration Affairs, Transition Team, President-Elect Peña Nieto, Mexico, D.F., October 12, 2012.
7 See *La Opinión,* January 21, 2013, and February 12, 2013, at www.laopinion.com and www.impremedia.com, accessed February 12, 2013; and *Milenio,* February 20, 2013, at www.milenio.com/cdb/doc/noticias.
8 See Plan Nacional de Desarrollo 2013–2018, Gobierno de la República at http://pnd.gob.mx/, accessed June 22, 2013.
9 See www.votoextranjero.mx/c/document_library/get_file?uuid=fce8dbba-63e7–4e1e-946e-e09fd59de581&groupId=10157, accessed June 6, 2013.
10 See www.pewhispanic.org/2013/05/01/a-demographic-portrait-of-mexican-origin-hispanics-in-the-united-states/, accessed June 6, 2013.
11 Interviews with Javier Díaz de León, Mexico D.F., October 8, 2012, and Iván Sierra Medel, Mexico D.F., October 16, 2012.
12 Interview with Arnulfo Valdivia Machuca, coordinator, Migration Affairs, Transition Team, President-Elect Peña Nieto, appointed later as director of IME, Ministry of Foreign Affairs, Mexico D.F., October 4, 2012.
13 Cf. Informe Final del Voto de los Mexicanos Residentes en el Extranjero, Proceso Electoral Federal 2011–201, p. 403, 408, available at www.votoextranjero.mx/c/document_library/get_file?uuid=fce8dbba-63e7–4e1e-946e-e09fd59de581&groupId=10157, and Informe de los Resultados de la Votación Emitida por los Mexicanos Residentes en el Extranjero 2006, pp. 1–3, available at http://mxvote06.ife.org.mx/pdf/resultados_03_06.pdf.
14 See IFE statistics at http://siceef.ife.org.mx/pef2012/SICEEF2012.html#, accessed June 10, 2013.
15 See www.votoextranjero.mx/web/guest/reforma-electoral, accessed May 22, 2015.
16 Interview with Arnulfo Valdivia Machuca, Mexico D.F., October 4, 2012.
17 Interview with Javier Díaz de León, executive director, IME, Ministry of Foreign Affairs, Mexico D.F., October 8, 2012.
18 Interview with Iván Sierra Medel, general director, International Affairs, Office of the Presidency, Mexico D.F., October 16, 2012.
19 Personal communication with Fernando Urbina, Instituto Nacional de Migración, May 11, 2015.

20 See www.dof.gob.mx/nota_detalle.php?codigo=5343074&fecha=30/04/2014, accessed May 16, 2015.
21 See www.redglobalmx.org/about/, accessed May 22, 2015.
22 Personal communication with Rafael Fernández de Castro, director, International Studies Department, ITAM, Mexico D.F., October 19, 2012.
23 See Alexandra Délano: "¿Un año 'muy positivo' para la migración?" blog *Letras Libres* (December 23, 2013), available at www.letraslibres.com/blogs/frontera-adentro/un-ano-muy-positivo-para-la-migracion?page=full, accessed May 11, 2015.
24 Personal communication with Iván Sierra Medel, former advisor to the President, Mexican Ambassador to Guyana, May 15, 2015.
25 Online interview with Arnulfo Valdivia Machuca, former Director of IME, current Ambassador to Colombia, May 21, 2015.

Works Cited

Alba, Francisco. 2013, April. "Mexico: The New Migration Narrative." Washington, DC: Migration Policy Institute. Available at www.migrationinformation.org/Profiles/display.cfm?id=947.

Ayón, David R. 2006. "La Política Mexicana y Lamovilización de los Migrantes Mexicanos en Estados Unidos." In *Relaciones Estado-Diáspora: La Perspective de América Latina y el Caribe*, coord. by Carlos González Gutiérrez. Tomo II. México City: Secretaría de Relaciones Exteriores, Instituto de los Mexicanos en el Exterior, Universidad Autónoma de los Zacatecas, Asociación Nacional de Universidades e Instituciones de Educación Superior, Miguel Ángel Porrúa Librero-Editor. pp. 113–144.

Cano, Gustavo and Alexandra Délano. 2007, June. "The Mexican Government and Organised Mexican Immigrants in the United States: A Historical Analysis of Political Transnationalism, 1848–2005." Working Paper 148. San Diego, CA: The Center for Comparative Immigration Studies.

Délano, Alexandra. 2006. "De la 'no Intervención' a la Institucionalización: La Evolución de las Relaciones Estado-Diáspora en el Caso Mexicano." In *Relaciones Estado-Diáspora: La Perspective de América Latina y el Caribe,* coord. by Carlos González Gutiérrez. Tomo II. México City: Secretaría de Relaciones Exteriores, Instituto de los Mexicanos en el Exterior, Universidad Autónoma de los Zacatecas, Asociación Nacional de Universidades e Instituciones de Educación Superior, Miguel Ángel Porrúa Librero-Editor. pp. 145–189.

Délano, Alexandra. 2010. "Immigrant Integration vs. Transnational Ties? The Role of the Sending State." *Social Research.* 77(1), Spring: 237–268.

Délano, Alexandra. 2011. *Mexico and its Diaspora in the United States. Policies of Emigration since 1848.* New York: Cambridge University Press.

Durand, Jorge. 2004, March. "From Traitors to Heroes: 100 Years of Mexican Migration Policies." Washington, DC: Migration Policy Institute. Available at www.migrationinformation.org/feature/display.cfm?ID=203, accessed April 25, 2013.

Escobar, Cristina. 2007. "Extraterritorial Political Rights and Dual Citizenship in Latin America." *Latin American Research Review.* 42(3): 43–75.

Fitzgerald, David. 2006. "Inside the Sending State: The Politics of Mexican Emigration Control." *International Migration Review.* 40(2), Summer: 259–293.

Goldring, Luin. 2002. "The Mexican State and Transmigrant Organizations: Negotiating the Boundaries of Membership and Participation." *Latin American Research Review*. 37(3): 55–99.

González Gutiérrez, Carlos. 2006. "Del Acercamiento a la Inclusión Institucional: La Experiencia del Instituto de los Mexicanos en el Exterior." In *Relaciones Estado-Diáspora: Aproximaciones Desde Cuatro Continentes,* coord. by Carlos González Gutiérrez. Tomo I. México City: Secretaría de Relaciones Exteriores, Instituto de los Mexicanos en el Exterior, Universidad Autónoma de los Zacatecas, Asociación Nacional de Universidades e Instituciones de Educación Superior, Miguel Ángel Porrúa Librero-Editor. pp. 181–220.

Iskander, Natasha. 2010. *Creative State: Forty Years of Migration and Development Policy in Morocco and Mexico*. Ithaca, NY: Cornell University Press.

Kunz, Rachel. 2008, December. "Mobilising Diasporas: A Governmentality Analysis of the Case of Mexico." Working Paper Series "Glocal Governance and Democracy" 3. Institute of Political Science, University of Lucerne, Switzerland.

Kunz, Rachel. 2011. "Depoliticization Through Partnership in the Field of Migration: The Mexico-US Case." In *Multilayered Migration Governance: The Promise of Partnership*, ed. by Rahel Kunz, Sandra Lavenex, and Marion Panizzon. London: Routledge. pp. 283–310.

Lafleur, Jean-Michel. 2011. "Why Do States Enfranchise Citizens Abroad? Comparative Insights from Mexico, Italy, and Belgium." *Global Networks*. 11(4):481–501.

Rosenblum, Marc R. 2006. "US-Mexican Migration Cooperation: Obstacles and Opportunities." Federal Reserve Bank of Dallas, pp. 91–119. Available online at www.dallasfed.org/assets/documents/research/pubs/migration/rosenblum.pdf, accessed July 28, 2014.

Smith, Robert C. 2003b. "Migrant Membership as an Instituted Process: Transnationalization, the State and the Extra-Territorial Conduct of Mexican Politics." *International Migration Review*. 37(2), Summer: 297–343.

Soto Priante, Sergio. 2006. "Programa 3x1 para Migrantes." In *Relaciones Estado-Diáspora: Aproximaciones Desde Cuatro Continentes,* coord. by Carlos González Gutiérrez. Tomo I. México City: Secretaría de Relaciones Exteriores, Instituto de los Mexicanos en el Exterior, Universidad Autónoma de los Zacatecas, Asociación Nacional de Universidades e Instituciones de Educación Superior, Miguel Ángel Porrúa Librero-Editor. pp. 221–238.

Vila Freyer, Ana. 2007. "Las Políticas de Atención a Migrantes en los Estados de México: Acción, Reacción, Gestión. In *¿Invisibles? Migrantes Internacionales en la Escena Política,* coord. Imaz, Cecilia. Mexico City: Facultad de Ciencias Políticas y Sociales, UNAM/SITESA.

Waldinger, Roger D. 2009, December. "A Limited Engagement: Mexico and its Diaspora." Selected Works. Los Angeles: University of California. Available at http://works.bepress.com/roger_waldinger/38.

World Bank 2011. *Migration and Remittances Factbook 2011*. Second Edition. Washington, DC: World Bank.

10 Conclusions

Although the implementation of emigration policies in Latin America coincided with a worldwide trend of states' engagement with diasporas, the cases examined in this book constitute a small sample of the broad variations within that trend. This project has pursued the unveiling of specific factors that shaped national trajectories, addressed the similarities and differences between them, and looked at the implications for the multilateral management of migration flows in the Latin America–Southern Europe corridor.

This chapter summarizes the main findings and highlights how states have been redefining their governance techniques to reach out to citizens living abroad and in collaboration with other states, nonstate actors and migrants, too. South American states did so while moving toward a common (regional) view of how to best manage international migration and applying similar ideas that link human mobility to national development, state role in the regulation of socioeconomic processes, and human rights considerations. In other words, while the launching of new emigration policies has been a unilateral move, the process is embedded in an emerging regional ideational consensus on transnational governance techniques that includes, but it is not limited to, emigration.

This chapter is organized around the main research questions that guided this project: what has been done in South America, how has it been done, why has it been done and why now, and with what results. It closes with an elaboration of lessons to be learned from this study and a suggestion of further venues for investigation.

What Have South American States Done, and How?

South American states have lately embraced a new approach to population and migration issues. To begin with, they have brought those issues up in their agendas and opened some of them up for public debate and/or incipient dialogues with targeted segments of the population. In most cases, this implied ending with silence and/or neglect and acknowledging that human mobility cuts across several other areas of state interest and might be strategically linked to initiatives to regulate labor markets, reduce poverty and inequality, and, more broadly, improve socioeconomic conditions and democracy. Regarding citizens residing abroad, all countries studied here initiated and/or deepened outreach efforts to establish a relationship and cultivate links with the emigrant community and, to some extent, to mobilize it politically. In that sense, as overtures potentially leading to engagement, those efforts have been characterized here as *courting*.

For South American countries, the innovative nature of courting lies in the contrast with past policies that involved mostly neglect, silence, and underestimation or pejorative views of expats. The mechanisms of courting, though, do not differ much from what other countries around the world are doing. Policy tools have included a number of instruments, such as: (a) the creation or upgrade of specialized offices; (b) the creation of online channels of communication to transmit information to, and gather it from, emigrants, including their particular requests and demands and, in some cases, compiling databases and providing instructions about consular and other procedures; (c) the negotiation of a reduction in fees and paperwork for money transfers with banks and private agencies, including the acceptance of nontraditional forms of identification; (d) the launching of financial products and lines of credit to encourage and capture migrant transactions and support productive investments; (e) the update and/or passing of legislation regarding migrant rights, including norms on dual citizenship, voting rights, and parliamentary representation; (f) the coining of a specific label to name the diaspora and the extraterritorial jurisdiction they form, the use of friendly slogans, and discursive changes to signal, through rhetoric, the intention to include emigrants within the nation and request from them a commitment to collaborate in the nation's future; (g) the support of cultural events, national festivities, and migrant associational endeavors to symbolically reinforce ties with homeland and further reinforce the message of inclusion; (h) the structuring of dialogues and courting through schemes of migrant representation (e.g., consultation councils) and the organization of meetings, conferences, or workshops to discuss a common agenda and the future of the state–diaspora relationship, and (i) the creation of special programs to address particular demands or to cultivate links with particular migrant groups' interests (e.g., professionals, entrepreneurs, artists).

The modality of implementation has varied across the cases examined in this volume. Some countries invested heavily in institutional developments (e.g., Ecuador through SENAMI, Brazil through the adaptation of consular services). At different points in time, all of them considered centralizing migration policymaking in a single and more powerful agency; only Ecuador did it for a while. At present, most of them delegate in the Ministries of Foreign Affairs the management of issues concerning the population abroad, although there is increasing awareness of the need to coordinate consular activity with that of other migration-related offices within the state apparatus.

Regarding specific initiatives, some countries were keen on discursive innovation, such as Mexico, Ecuador, and Uruguay. A few focused on financial instruments due to the relevance of remittances for their economies, like Mexico and Ecuador. All of them facilitated citizenship retention or allowed dual citizenship. Only Ecuador awarded emigrants parliamentary representation. Only Uruguay has not reformed its legislation yet to allow extraterritorial voting. In all cases, voting from afar is relatively low, and states have done little to increase political participation of emigrants in homeland politics. In all cases, communication and other linkage mechanisms have been used as supports to other initiatives, mainly to reinforce those symbolic moves that keep courting alive, even at a low intensity rate, but are not the primary focus of state action.

Overall, efforts to organize the diaspora and structure the relationship have been controversial and often short-lived; the ones that show more continuity over time, like Brazil and Uruguay, have gone through adaptation and reforms. The same is true even for the country that exhibits the longest record of engagement with its diaspora next door: Mexico. From a political point of view, because meetings and other forms of formal dialogue provide the arena where key actors meet and relate to each other in a more or less institutionalized form, this may well be the most relevant area to monitor the evolution of courting and to look at to what extent state-led transnationalism meets society-led transnationalism and what kind of engagement is attained in each case. However, these general interactions capture only the sporadic interactions of public officials with a selected group of migrant leaders around a preset agenda, thus providing a partial view of whether emigration policies are actually making a difference in the daily lives of emigrants. In Chapter 8, a preliminary glance at this broader issue was presented in reference to Ecuadorians and Argentines in two destinations; its limited scope does not allow for generalizations, though.

Differences across cases allow for delineating national trajectories. The two smaller countries have innovated considerably inasmuch as their policy trajectories implied a departure from previous records. Ecuador launched an aggressive campaign to reach out to emigrants in various fronts, including several programs implemented in the destinations where the diaspora concentrates, as well as efforts to diffuse the model regionally and globally. This stands out as a very proactive and innovative case of courting in its initial phase. More recently, those initiatives have lost visibility and are being subsumed within the consular institutional structure. This suggests that the policy trajectory is adopting a more traditional consular approach that builds upon previous achievement but is not likely to lead to dramatic innovations. Uruguay has followed a slow, gradual, and relatively consistent path that ended with silence and denial of serious population and migration problems. It has included all instruments mentioned previously, as well as an attempt to increase the coordination of all areas of government involved in migration issues (not just the Ministry of Foreign Affairs), especially since migration return has created increasing and interconnected demands on the state apparatus. Yet, several factors have set limits to policy innovation. In particular, a strong attachment to territorial and traditional notions of citizenship precludes legislation update and stands in the way of full inclusion of emigrants in the country's political life.

The two larger countries also innovated considerably, although the visibility of the emigration problem was lower than in the smaller ones. On the one hand, Argentina targeted a particular destination (Spain) and some segments of the diaspora (e.g., former political exiles and human rights activists, scientists). It used very few tools and mainly followed an assistance-centered approach that faded in a few years. Today, emigration policy works in inertial mode and there is no evidence to anticipate further innovation or an attempt to generate substantive engagement. Brazil, on the other hand, adheres to a low-visibility and technical approach led by consular offices. I named this trajectory "courting without being noticed"; the state tackled the task of adapting and reforming the consular service to meet new demands and establish regular links with citizens abroad in all destinations, but it did so while maintaining a low profile. It is, nevertheless, a case of comprehensive and strategic state-led transnationalism, but it advances as demands arise through "surgical" steps and keeping migrant participation in policymaking within a relatively low level of politicization.

In sum, in general terms, the findings of this project document that courting has, indeed, contributed to delineating a new constituency and a new area of state intervention across borders. It has also encouraged some engagement of emigrants with home politics and, in some cases, further migrant political integration in the host society, too. But courting has not progressed in a linear fashion. It has not translated into intense engagement yet. It has remained at an incipient level that varies across cases and time. Some countries initiated courting and let it run on automatic pilot or inertial mode, as in Brazil and Argentina, respectively; others have initially made intense outreach efforts that have faded somewhat lately, like Ecuador and to some extent Mexico. In Uruguay, state-led initiatives keep progressing, but at a very slow pace, and they are generating uncertainty. Thus, it is evident that, as emigration waxes and wanes from government agendas, engagement with the diaspora is only sporadic and courting unfolds through cycles of intense linkages and partial withdrawals.

However, it is not so much the continuity of these policies that is at stake today. On the contrary, there are no signs of a possible policy reversal. It is rather the substance of it—whether or not emigration policies are enhancing emigrants' membership entitlements and practices in order to make their formal inclusion in the nation real and, perhaps, activate them politically in a more intense way. At most, some selected members of the diaspora are being invited to participate (more or less formally, depending on the case) in agenda-setting and policy discussions. The politics of emigration policymaking, which articulate domestic and international variables, provide the basis for the explanation of this outcome.

Why Have States Courted Their Diasporas, and Why Now?

States' motivations to engage with their diasporas were not uniform, although some common trends can be identified. There is no doubt that concerns with capturing migrants' resources was one of them. The relevance of remittances in Ecuador and human capital in Argentina and Uruguay underlined those concerns. But this study shows that it would be misleading to assume that this was the sole or main motivation. States went well beyond these instrumental goals to pursue the strategic objectives of some incumbents at critical junctures when political repositioning was taking place. In all cases, gathering political support was one of the goals for politicians coming to office: Lula in Brazil, Kirchner in Argentina, Correa in Ecuador, and Tabaré and Mujica in Uruguay. In other words, courting was prompted by the need to strength the role of leaders (especially those considered outsiders to traditional domestic politics) and/or to build up new governing coalitions. Differentiating themselves from past governments and redefining the national narrative was part of that coalition-building process. Hence, some of these left-wing leaders seized the opportunity to create an emotional link with some members of the diaspora; they all shared a record of activism against authoritarianism and human rights violations. The rhetorical shift toward migrant rights, pluralism, and democratization provided a common flag and encouraged dialogue, consultation, and incipient engagement. Electoral calculations were particularly salient in the case of Uruguay, where the diaspora played a critical role in the triumph of the Frente Amplio in 2004, and this made the launching of a new emigration policy unavoidable.

Moreover, in general terms, the timing of policy reform is linked to the increasing demands in consular offices that the last massive wave of emigration generated. The volume of those outflows and the emergence of new destinations, together with the more heterogeneous profile of the emigrant community and restrictive policies in receiving countries, generated an unusual number of requests for services and assistance in consulates and embassies abroad for all countries. Thus, all countries of origin had to provide some kind of response. For the two smaller countries with large diasporas, the visibility and urgency of the problem were more dramatic. In Ecuador and Uruguay, then, inaction was not an option.

Discrimination, barriers to entry, regularization processes, deportation threats, and precarious living and working conditions in which lives were at risk often called the attention of the international and domestic press, amplifying the call for state protection and assistance and creating incentives for the diaspora to mobilize.

This study also shows that domestic politics variables connected with regional ones. Policy innovations gained momentum as South American governments converged around neopopulist discourses and the agreement to move a sluggish regional integration process through a sociopolitical agenda that linked migration to national development, postneoliberal economics, and human rights considerations. This ideational consensus relied heavily on a critique of the legacies of neoliberalism in the region and, addressing generalized discontent, promised reparatory measures to the populations at home and abroad. At the same time, these ideas served to forge a distinctive identity for the bloc and give it a voice in international forums where its members advocated for an alternative model that supersedes the pitfalls of neoliberalism.

In sum, this study highlights the impact of domestic political processes on the creation of a window of opportunity for policy innovation. It also shows the interplay of levels of analysis and the need to go beyond instrumental explanations and existing typologies that assume a relatively uniform neoliberal rationale behind diaspora engagement processes. In the Latin American context, the timing and trajectory of emigration policies are to be contextualized in the synergies generated by processes of unfinished and unstable democratization, ideologically driven regional integration, and multilateral management of international migration.

Why Is Courting Not Leading to Engagement Yet?

Policy trajectories exhibit the difficulties of first coming to terms with the emigration problem, defining it as such so that it is incorporated in the governmental agenda, and later implementing outreach measures. In all countries studied here, we observe that state initiatives generate controversies and often face setbacks. While some changes have been institutionalized through legislation updates/passing and institutional reforms/upgrades, others have faded after a few years. Consistent and effective implementation over time faces diverse challenges. For different reasons, in Argentina and Brazil, the problem ceased to be considered an urgent matter and emigration policy is not the focus of governmental attention today. Apparently, Mexico is moving toward a similar situation. To some extent, the stabilization of migration outflows also moved emigration out of the spotlight in Ecuador and Uruguay. Therefore, the evolution of emigration policies thus far does not support the idea of a progressive path toward an outcome (i.e., engagement). Instead, it indicates the need to explore the cycles of intense state involvement and bureaucratic inertia. In the absence of emigration crises or a dramatic increase in migrant mobilization, it is plausible to expect continued fluid, selective interactions between states and diasporas with variable levels of both parties' engagement.

On the state side of the relationship, state engagement at the present seems to be anchored by an ideational regional consensus that makes the reversal of emigration policies unlikely. The harmonization of migration norms at the regional level and the commitment to manage human mobility multilaterally provide South American states with tools to adapt population governance techniques beyond borders and bring their post-neoliberal approach to negotiations with extrahemispheric receiving countries. However, states' commitment to deepen engagement with emigrants seems contingent on a policymaking dynamic plagued by tensions. On the one hand, the drivers of policy innovation (i.e., the actors that have been able to give critical impetus to changes, such as presidents and a few top officials) act in an intermittent fashion, and their leadership is not embedded in enough powerful or autonomous institutions that might take over the lead when necessary. In addition, lack of coordination, frequent turnabout of public officials and political appointees, and intrastate disputes are a constant and are certainly detrimental to policy consistency and sustainability over time. Three decades of partial and uneven reform of the state underlies these problems in all cases. As a result, in the area of migration policy a paradox emerges: states' attempts to adapt and redefine their government techniques in transnational spaces are constrained by their incapacity to transform their own internal structures and practices.

Therefore, state capacity to deepen engagement cannot be taken for granted. Even larger countries with presumably better-endowed resources, large budgets, and extended state apparatuses with a long record of intervention in socioeconomic development (e.g., Brazil, Mexico, or Argentina) face the challenge of addressing this paradox. Neopopulist governments sought to bring back the state to compensate for market-centered neoliberal policies and carry out a sociopolitical agenda that was sensitive to citizens' rights. This attempt found weak foundations in state apparatus and remains subject to the ambivalent nature of post-neoliberal projects. The latter is illustrated today by the contradictions and tensions between national popular discourses and the policies and the politics of dispossession (i.e., an emphasis on a social welfare agenda and inclusion rhetoric in parallel with increasing marginalization of some social sectors).

These contradictions might exacerbate another limit to state outreach efforts: migrants' distrust of politicians and state institutions. This generalized sentiment, rooted in a long-standing crisis of political representation, unmet social expectations, and memories of the political and economic crises that prompted emigration, discourages further engagement. As it was explained in Chapter 8, the call to contribute to the country of origin's reconstruction and development resonates with the feelings and aspirations of citizens abroad (including a vague, difficult-to-measure sense of patriotism and nostalgia), but it does not overcome the uneasiness caused by a traumatic record of state abuses and political disillusions. Individual leaders (e.g., Correa, Lula) may have helped re-create expectations and, indirectly, push courting to a new level, but their personal involvement in policymaking usually occurred at a high stage of decision making rather than in the details of daily implementation, and it tended to be sporadic. In fact, some state initiatives may not even require the continuous intervention of top leaders, as the case of Brazil suggests. Thus, individual leaders' involvement may be a necessary condition to signal political commitment and launch policy reform, but it is not a sufficient condition to deepen engagement.

In addition, sending states were also limited in terms of political partnerships at home. South American political parties had very little experience with constituencies residing outside of the territory, let alone in distant extrahemispheric destinations. In this respect, party leaders contrast with those in Mexico who are used to carrying out electoral campaigns across the border. More important, the crisis of political representation has seriously affected all political parties, making them unable to engage with both local and foreign constituencies. Thus, state partnerships in South America are likely to develop not with political parties within the governing coalition or in the opposition but with other actors who enjoy more credibility and rapport with emigrants, namely churches, religious organizations, and nongovernmental organizations working at destinations. These institutions have been crucial in offering general assistance; providing advice, space, and resources for migrant organization and claim-making; channeling demands; advocating for the defense of migrant rights; and supporting and facilitating courting.

Moreover, emigration has not resonated enough in domestic public debates. It has gathered attention temporarily (e.g., when rhetorical changes brought the issue to political campaigns) and in specific localities (e.g., town and cities of origin that in times of massive emigration lost most of their economically active population). Even in cases with large diasporas (e.g., Ecuador, Uruguay, Mexico), emigration has not been a constant, high priority concern. Specialized offices in charge of diaspora affairs do not tend to play a high profile role in political and public debates. Therefore, emigrants' needs, rights, and claims find limited echo in society. This is compounded by old criticisms and negative views toward those who left, thus raising limited support for their cause and for state investment in assisting them. This intermittent visibility supports the idea that emigration policies advance through cycles of variable courting intensity.

Finally, the evidence indicates that, when sending and receiving countries are geographically apart, transnational practices—either state- or migrant-led—are relatively weak. Long distance adds an extra cost to the mobilization of human and material resources that are necessary for sustained and substantive engagement. In spite of the advantages created by new technologies and more affordable transportation, physical encounters remain sporadic. Virtual encounters require less commitment and may soon fall into trivial exchanges. Thus, emigrants may take part in transnational networks and help reproduce them, but this does not necessarily translate into strong attachments and incentives to engage in home politics. In other words, long distances may create emotional distances. State-led transnationalism requires considerable investment when implemented over long distances. Hence, unless the situation of the diaspora is seen as dramatic enough to justify the investment, or the party in government has close political links with members of the emigrant community, states are reluctant to go much beyond the usual assistance and protection through consular offices.

What Are the Analytical and Policy Implications of Emigration Policies?

The previous sections suggest that a refinement of existing approaches to state-led transnationalism and migration governance can be attained by looking at the small sample of cases studied here. Four main insights may contribute to pushing the discussion further.

First, governmentality frameworks vary to accommodate changing balances between states and markets. The postneoliberal model departs from previous ones considerably (actually, it aspires to enact a partial, albeit consequential, reversal of its neoliberal predecessor). It brings the state back to center stage, but it pragmatically outsources the delivery of services to society by working through collaborations or partnerships (e.g., with receiving states, nongovernmental institutions, international organizations) within public–private policy networks. The emerging form of transnational governance makes several things possible: state intervention beyond borders, the management of populations that are geographically dispersed, and, to some extent, the molding of emigrants' dual political engagements.

Second, the impact of unfinished democratic transitions and dramatic crises has to be incorporated in the explanation. These processes have followed diverse paths across countries and regions, including politico-institutional crises, financial debacles, popular unrest, institutional breakdown, and various degrees of political and economic instability. Therefore, migration governance in these cases may involve simultaneous efforts to restore sociopolitical and economic order, recast national narratives, and reposition the country in the global economy, among other daunting tasks for ill-equipped states. The South American cases studied here illustrate how states coped with those processes and ably articulated domestic and international political projects (i.e., the formation of new governing coalitions at home and the elaboration of a distinctive regional bloc identity as a platform to gain leverage in international affairs). This is a multilevel dynamic that is totally neglected by existing studies in this field.

Third, the capacity of states to engage with diasporas consistently and sustainably over time cannot be taken for granted, let alone in cases where state rebuilding and reform during transitions or crisis aftermath are main tasks. Thus far, the literature on this topic has taken note of some intrastate politics, but it has been oblivious of the implications of state reform (or lack thereof). In this respect, the incorporation of South American cases may help revise existing typologies and illuminate cases in other regions of the global South.

Fourth, the detours and vicissitudes in the evolution of emigration policies suggest the need to revise celebratory accounts of outreach efforts. Engagement cannot be assumed either as a final outcome or as a cumulative, linear process. Courting is a more accurate figurative label for states' attempts to govern populations abroad. Courting, in the form of dialogues and regular rapprochements, better captures the possibilities and limits of state–diaspora relations than engagement. Also, all cases studied here suggest that courting usually unfolds through cycles of intense exchanges and partial withdrawals.

In this respect, the inclusion of Mexico in this study provided a long-term picture of state–emigrant relations that contrasts with the still-young emigration policies of South American countries. To some extent, and until recently, Mexico could have been taken as a model. Some of its features are specific to the case, such as the timespan, geographic proximity of home and destination sites, the size of the emigrant community, and extensive interdependencies (including formal economic integration) between sending and receiving states. As Rosenblum (2006:92) argues, Mexico has a unique ability to influence outcomes in this area of its relationship with the US. This is compounded by the socioeconomic diversity and relative mobilization capacities of different sectors within the emigrant community and the fact that there are several generations of Mexicans in the US—all factors that make generalizations about the Mexican diaspora inconclusive. This makes comparisons with other countries particularly difficult.

However, from the point of view of the main research questions of this book, the Mexican case supports the following arguments: (a) policy trajectories unfold through stages and cycles, but they do not necessarily and consistently progress toward more substantive engagement; (b) the interplay of domestic politics and foreign policy, in which processes of democratization, economic restructuring, and regional integration are closely intertwined, is analytically relevant in all Latin American cases; and (c) Mexico may have worked as a reference in the past in policymakers' learning, but policy innovation is almost null today, and this case is not seen as a model in the region. On this last point, while Delano (2014) finds evidence that the Mexican experience has encouraged policy learning and convergence in Central American and a few Latin American countries (especially in the expansion of consular and other services), I gather from interviewees that South American officials have a partial knowledge of the Mexican case and do not consider it a model to follow at all. On their part, public officials in charge of migration policy in Mexico were not familiar with what other Latin American countries have been doing. Instead, as I argue in Chapter 3, policy diffusion has happened in South America mainly through other mechanisms, which points out a key contrast with Mexico: the postneoliberal mindset that underpins the new normative regional consensus in South America has a more contestatory ideological content than what Mexico might afford in its relation with the US and aims at giving a distinctive collective identity to that subregion.

On the realm of practice, a comprehensive assessment of results and implications of emigration policies is a complex task. Sending states have used different instruments and have been selective in terms of the segments of the emigrant community or the destinations to target. Because the policy trajectories are closely linked to domestic politics processes, they involve country-specific features and time frames that do not allow for full comparison. Building on the evidence presented in previous chapters, I elaborate here on three areas in which emigration policy might encourage further state engagement in the future. These three areas also suggest potential venues for further academic investigation.

The first area of action concerns the nature of linkages. Assuming a long-term commitment with integrating citizens abroad in the nation and at least some continuity of the initiatives in place over several administrations, states might well attempt to strengthen linkages. This would imply going beyond regular consultation (e.g., consultation forums, annual meetings with representatives of the diaspora), joint declarations, and top-down assistance. The lessons indicate that the formation of consultation councils has been very controversial in all cases, casting doubts on questions of representation, accountability, and real incorporation in policymaking. The political dimension of extraterritorial citizenship (e.g., enfranchising, increasing voting turnout, broadening political rights) has not been a core priority for countries of origin. And migrant responses have been based on a variable combination of vague notions of patriotism, civic duty, homesickness, and individual responsibility. Therefore, the next level in terms of policy innovation lies in infusing linkages with meaning—that is, complementing symbolic moves with programs that may make a difference in migrants' daily lives, such as concrete projects to improve migrant living conditions that require active, frequent, and regular participation of all parties involved. References to formal membership and/or a remote realm of home politics would not lead to further engagement if they are not rooted in practices and lived experiences. This book shows that some states are better positioned than others to do so. Only some governments have sought that goal, and only in sporadic episodes; building up trust in state institutions and initiatives is a challenge, and private–public partnerships facilitate implementation. Hence, investigating under what conditions states might move consistently toward creating opportunities and fair conditions for meaningful and sustained engagement for all interested stakeholders is one possible venue for interdisciplinary investigation.

The second area of action speaks to the scope of linkages. Thus far, state-led transnationalism relates to special groups within diasporas, such as migrant association leaders, skilled workers, or professionals and entrepreneurs. This may make sense in the case of instrumental initiatives aimed at capturing migrants' human or economic resources. But when it comes to activating the diaspora politically, state outreach efforts require mobilizing both elites and ordinary emigrants. This also requires working consistently across destinations to address a generalized claim of South American diasporas: membership in the polity through both formal entitlements and democratic mechanisms. Appeals to political allegiances and cherished national sentiments usually raise different responses among groups and sites of residency, so they may have to be tailored to various audiences, but they will be ill-fated if they are not driven by an equalitarian and democratic notion of extraterritorial citizenship.

This study shows that state initiatives are plagued by tensions and contradictions in all cases, and it shows that the rhetoric of inclusion is not always matched with real commitment and engagement with all addressees. Capturing the votes of citizens abroad is one, but not the primary, motivation in most cases. Helping them to become more integrated and, eventually, a powerful lobby in the host society is an elusive goal for most sending countries, except perhaps for Mexico. Thus, further research is needed to identify cooperation opportunities between sending and receiving countries and to address how to change generalized perceptions in this respect. As we observe in the case of Mexico, too, this is a sensitive area for both elites and ordinary migrants that is usually kept aside from bilateral negotiations for fear of repercussions in other areas of the bilateral agenda. However, this may represent a missing opportunity to improve governance of human mobility if a broader range of interlocutors is not involved.

In close connection with the two points made above, there is a third area of action in which courting might be improved. In addition to attending to the types of measures and the target groups, sending states might improve relations with the diaspora by working on the fine tuning of political means and ends. This book shows that, as a particular subset of state–society relations, South American states often reproduce clientelistic and patrimonial political practices that are so common in domestic politics. Migrant empowerment has been part of the discourses and objectives but, as shown in Chapter 8, it has not materialized yet, and some policy developments cast doubts on this being a priority for states. Moreover, there is a fine line between politicizing and politicking the relationship. To some extent, politicization seems to be inevitable and needed to create incentives for both migrants and states to court each other; it also seems to be a healthy way to introduce changes. But the technical approach to migration management that international organizations promote has been charged with depoliticizing migration. In addition, there is the risk of politicization for electoral purposes only. When politicizing turns into politicking, credibility and trust are likely to be very low. In a muddy playing field, the potential for a mutually beneficial partnership may be lost. This risk seems to be more accentuated under governments of neopopulist orientation because their understanding of the political game has tended to underestimate representativeness and accountability in favor of plebiscitary and delegative democratic practices. Delegation tends to empower the leaders (who act on behalf of the vaguely defined "people") rather than ordinary citizens and to reproduce patronizing forms of relations. In sum, South American migration policies have been trapped in the same tensions as other social policies, oscillating between promises of inclusion and realities of exclusion. Exploring the possibilities of overcoming this paradox is a promising area for intra- and interdisciplinary dialogues.

Works Cited

Délano, Alexandra. 2014. "The Diffusion of Diaspora Engagement Policies: A Latin American Agenda." *Political Geography*. 41: 90–100.

Rosenblum, Marc R. 2006. "US-Mexican Migration Cooperation: Obstacles and Opportunities." Federal Reserve Bank of Dallas, pp. 91–119. Available online at www.dallasfed.org/assets/documents/research/pubs/migration/rosenblum.pdf, accessed July 28, 2014.

Index